The Roman House and Social Identity

This book examines a diverse range of house types in an effort to understand how people imagined and articulated their place in the Roman world, from Britain to Syria. Shelley Hales considers the nature and role of domestic decoration and its role in promoting social identities. From the Egyptian themes of imperial residences in Italy to the viticultural designs found in the rock-cut homes in Petra, this decoration consistently appeals to fantasies beyond the immediate realities of the inhabitants. Hales contends that fantasy served a key role in allowing individuals and communities to meet expectations and indulge aspirations, to conform and compete within the diverse empire. Employing a wide range of approaches to the study of the house and acculturation in the Roman empire, her book serves as a fresh synthesis of Roman domestic architecture and offers new insights into the complexities and contradictions of being Roman.

Shelley Hales is a scholar of Roman art and architecture. She is Lecturer in Art and Visual Culture in the Department of Classics and Ancient History at the University of Bristol.

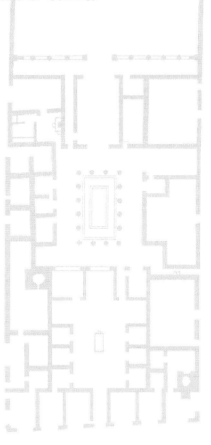

The Roman House and Social Identity

SHELLEY HALES
University of Bristol

CAMBRIDGE
UNIVERSITY PRESS

PUBLISHED BY THE PRESS SYNDICATE OF THE UNIVERSITY OF CAMBRIDGE
The Pitt Building, Trumpington Street, Cambridge, United Kingdom

CAMBRIDGE UNIVERSITY PRESS
The Edinburgh Building, Cambridge CB2 2RU, UK
40 West 20th Street, New York, NY 10011-4211, USA
477 Williamstown Road, Port Melbourne, VIC 3207, Australia
Ruiz de Alarcón 13, 28014 Madrid, Spain
Dock House, The Waterfront, Cape Town 8001, South Africa

http://www.cambridge.org

First published 2003

Printed in the United Kingdom at the University Press, Cambridge

Typefaces Sabon 10.5/14 pt. *and* Pompeijana Roman   *System* LATEX 2$_\varepsilon$ [TB]

A catalog record for this book is available from the British Library.

Library of Congress Cataloging in Publication Data

Hales, Shelley, 1971–
    The Roman house and social identity / Shelley Hales.
        p.   cm.
    Includes bibliographical references and index.
    ISBN 0-521-81433-2 (hb)
        1. Architecture, Domestic – Social aspects – Rome.   2. Architecture, Roman.
    3. Decoration and ornament – Social aspects – Rome.   4. Decoration and ornament,
    Roman.   I. Title.
    NA324 .H35   2003
    728'.0937 – dc21   2002073682

ISBN 0 521 81433 2 hardback
ISBN 0 521 735092

To Mabel & Arthur

Contents

List of Illustrations

Abbreviations

AAAH	*Acta ad archaeologiam et artium historiam pertinentia*
AJA	*American Journal of Archaeology*
AJPh	*American Journal of Philology*
ANRW	*Aufstieg und Niedergang der römischen Welt*
ARID	*Analecta Romanan Instituti Danici*
AUMLA	*Australasian Universities Modern Language Association*
AntJ	*Antiquities Journal*
BAR	*British Archaeological Reports*
Boll.Cent.Stor.Arch.	*Bollettino Centro di Studi per la Storia dell'Architettura*
Bull.Comm.	*Bullettino della Commissione archaeologica communale di Roma*
DOP	*Dumbarton Oaks Papers*
G&R	*Greece and Rome*
JDAI	*Jahrbuch des Deutschen Archäologischen Instituts*
JRA	*Journal of Roman Archaeology*
Herts.Arch.	*Hertfordshire Archaeology*
HThr	*Harvard Theological Review*
JRS	*Journal of Roman Studies*
JSAH	*Journal of the Society of Architectural Historians*
MAAR	*Memoires of the American Academy at Rome*
MEFRA	*Mélanges de l'Ecole Française de Rome*
Mem.Pont.Acc.Arch	*Atti della pontificia accademia Romana di Archeologia, Memoria*
PBSR	*Papers of the British School at Rome*
PCPhS	*Proceedings of the Cambridge Philological Society*
RA	*Revue Archéologique*

Rend.Pont.Acc.Arch.	*Atti della pontificia accademia Romana di Archeologia, Rendiconti*
RM	*Römische Mitteilungen des Deutschen Archäologischen Instituts*
TAPhA	*Transactions of the American Philological Association*
YCS	*Yale Classical Studies*

Acknowledgements

This book originated as my PhD thesis at the Courtauld Institute of Art and could never have happened without the ongoing support of Jaś Elsner as my supervisor. I have much more to thank him for than this piece of work. Without him and Valérie Huet, I might never have completed my first degree and certainly would not have seen the possibilities of ancient art. The British Academy made it possible for me to pursue my studies, and Roger Ling and Greg Woolf provided helpful and encouraging comments at the final examination of my PhD.

In the course of preparing the book for publication, I have passed through both Cardiff University and the University of Bristol and would like to thank all my colleagues, in particular Bill Manning, John Percival, and Kate Gilliver at Cardiff and Richard Buxton and Gillian Clark at Bristol. The students, both undergraduate and postgraduate, whom I have taught at these institutions have always asked searching, if not awkward, questions that made me look more deeply, and with fresh eyes, at my own work.

At Cambridge University Press, Beatrice Rehl has been incredibly supportive during the long process of preparing the book. The comments and suggestions of the anonymous reviewers have improved the manuscript immeasurably.

The Arts Faculty Research Board at the University of Bristol kindly helped with the production costs of this volume as did the Hugh Last and Donald Atkinson Funds Committee at the Society for the Promotion of Roman Studies. Roger Ling, Claudia Lang, Gudrun Wlach at ÖAI, Shari Kenfield at Princeton University, Alessandra Biagianti at Alinari, Katrin Stump at DAI, Jenny Golding at Verulamium Museum, and Allan Scollan at the British Museum all took a lot of time over my requests. Tim Bryant, Marie Bryant, Alf Crafer, Kate Gilliver, Ian Stewardson, and Margaret Stewardson helped with the collection and preparation of the illustrations.

Of course, thanks are also due to my friends and family, who have had to live with me throughout the process. In particular, Lloyd Llewellyn-Jones and

Shaun Tougher, without whom there is always the possibility that I might get more done but only at the expense of a lot of laughter. I couldn't do without Ian who was there from the very outset of this project, through drizzly field trips to Pompeii to final preparation. Finally, I would like to thank my family who have always patiently supported my academic career. I am very sorry that this book took me so long to write that some of them could not hang around any longer, and this book is dedicated to them.

Introduction

Most people would not dispute that a house plays a part in building identity. The majority of homeowners would probably like to think that their choice of house and its decoration reflected their own tastes and personalities. The house is the private, unobserved space of the family unit over which they have control. However, the average, modern house is unlikely to be able to tell you overmuch about the public life of the owner, that is the life spent under observation by the community subject to socially constructed codes of behaviour. Although the degree of opulence might indicate wealth or class, it is unlikely to afford much insight into the careers of those who live there. Above all, the modern house, in the West at any rate, is a retreat from life in public. Although new technology is making it more possible for people to work from home, those who do so remain very much in the minority. Similarly, although entertaining at home is hardly unusual, the leisure industry provides a wealth of public places for relaxing and socialising. Most of us work away from home, and a large part of our free time is spent in bars, cinemas, or leisure centres.

However, the role of the Roman house or *domus* in building identity is more acute. The Roman's house, it might be said, was his *forum*.[1] This takes account of the fact that no Roman ever stood alone; he was constantly judged in the wider context of his family, *familia*, and the functions of his *domus* could not be divorced from that of his public roles. In other words, there was no formalised segregation between public and private life that we observe in the West today. The *familia* itself, which should perhaps better be translated as household rather than family, was an institution encompassing birthright (sons and daughters), economics (slaves), and even politics (freedmen as clients), involving not only those bound to the *pater-familias* by birth or marriage but also by law.[2] Similarly, the Roman *domus* was simultaneously home, place of entertainment, business office, and lobbying platform.[3] The *paterfamilias* received his *clientes* here in the morning for the daily *salutatio* to distribute gifts, delegate errands and tasks, and demand political favours. In the evening, the *paterfamilias* did not frequent the *tabernae*, the haunt of the morally and economically bankrupt, but instead entertained his *amici* (friends and associates) in his own *triclinium*.[4]

Although the elite lived very public lives as either Roman senators or provincial decurions, serving as patrons, magistrates, and priests, these public roles were amplifications of domestic duties, from managing clients to performing due sacrifice to the household gods. The house provided a setting for both domestic life and a public career. Birth, marriage, and death and their associated rituals all occurred largely within the house, shaping a Roman's very existence.[5] If, in modern anthropological terms, the house is understood as an exoskeleton through which the inhabitants encounter society, then this is even more so the case of the Roman *domus*, which was a visual, architectural construct of the *familia*'s identity and proof of participation in Roman society.[6]

When a Roman was born, an altar to Lucina, goddess of childbirth, was set up in the *atrium*, the foremost room of the house, and the threshold of the front door was decorated with flowers to announce the joyous occasion.[7] A passer-by would have no need to see the inhabitants of the house in order to appreciate the occasion; the house itself announced the event. Similarly, a marriage between two young members of the elite was literally a marriage between houses. A procession between the bride's family home and her new, marital house showed the private connection to the public. Again, the threshold advertised the news to the outsider; the bride decorated the door posts of the home with wool before she was carried over the threshold.[8] But perhaps the funeral best demonstrates the interaction of public and private in the domestic rituals of Rome. The deceased was laid out in state in the *atrium*. On the day of the funeral, the funerary procession, including actors wearing the ancestor masks of the family, made its way to the *forum* for the funerary oration before moving out beyond the city boundaries, the *pomerium*, to the tomb. This procession neatly traced the man's life, uniting his home with his public arena, the *forum*, and placing him within the context of his ancestry. The final part of the procession linked his life in Rome to his death without the city walls, the family tomb the equivalent of the *domus* for the deceased branch of the *familia*.[9]

These rituals, which took place within and around the *domus*, demonstrated to the household and the outside world that the family were living according to the traditions of Rome.[10] The performance of domestic rituals are a manifestation of the *familia*'s Roman identity. Their repetition across Rome over generations lent them an air of deliberate timelessness. The apparent constancy of these traditions is crucial in legitimising the present social structure by rooting it in the distant past.[11] Ritualised domestic activities involved the playing out of *mores*, traditional customs and values, bringing such constructs of Roman behaviour to life in order to justify one's identity as Roman.[12]

The decoration of the house in the course of such rituals and even the permanent arrangement of rooms in the houseplan to accommodate the occurrence of these rituals can be seen as a constant confirmation of the householder's Roman identity. Decor is not simply a reflection of personal taste – though Romans were certainly not unaware of perceptions of taste and style and were quick to mock the bad taste of others – it is a way of asserting yourself and your family's right to be a part of Rome.[13] It is not just a question of personal identity but rather one of political and social persona. The men you meet in your *atrium* at the morning *salutatio*, you meet in the *forum* in the course of canvassing for electoral support or making financial arrangements. The modern politician might return home, slip into something more comfortable, and indulge in his own personal tastes and nobody need be any the wiser (as long as the tabloid press does not intrude). However, the ancient magistrate should appear never to discard his *toga*; his house should appear to be open at all times. Vitruvius, the author of a surviving Roman architectural treatise, recommends just this. His plans for the elite *domus* revolve around the need for openness and the public nature of the elite household.[14]

To find the physical incarnation of the words of Vitruvius, studies of the Roman house have traditionally turned to Pompeii and the extensive domestic remains there. This might not be surprising – after all, Pompeii offers the largest body of evidence available to the historian attempting to recover domestic patterns – but it is not without problems. The marriage of Roman text and Campanian visual evidence takes no account of the degrees of separation that come between the two media. Consequently, the domestic architecture of the houses of Campania is still today understood in terms of the Roman, literary evidence. The Pompeian House of Pansa (VI.vi.1) (Figure 1) is used to provide an apparently canonical example of the Roman, Vitruvian plan with its *atrium*, peristyle, and *hortus* opening progressively around a central axis of symmetry.[15] At the same time, the various functions

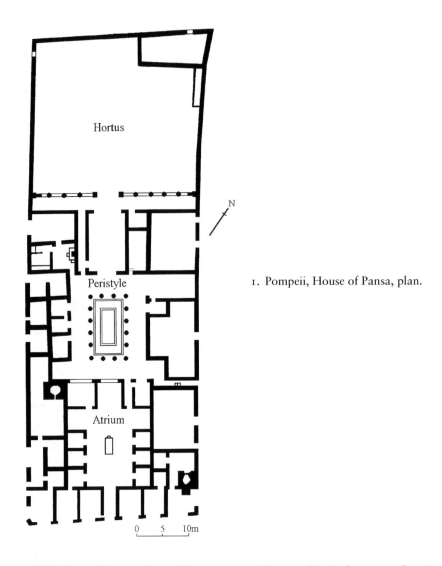

1. Pompeii, House of Pansa, plan.

of the house known from the texts are given a physical context by simply applying Latin terminologies to each room on the Campanian plan. This provides the viewer with a neatly labelled plan that categorises each area of activity within the house. The *tablinum* is the master's study, the *triclinium* is the dining room, and the many *cubicula* serve as bedrooms.[16]

More recently, increasing attempts have been made to escape this simplistic and inflexible model. New work on the distribution of artefacts around the *domus* have done the most to expose the rooms of the *domus* as multifunctional.[17] The *atrium* in particular was home not only to the *salutatio* but also to the household cult and even storage and production. These results hint at a lack of exclusivity between activity and setting. Whilst the architecture and decoration of the *atrium* might seem eminently suited to social activities, such as the *salutatio*, it was clearly the backdrop for more lacklustre domestic chores. It must be admitted, then, that the uses of the *atria* demonstrate the versatile nature of both the decoration and the role of the room. Although the grand appearance of the *atrium* might evoke its public role, that was not its only function.

This is not art as representation but art as impression, bolstering the patron family's desire to participate in Romanised public life and to impress their fitness to do so on those who visited them. The view shows an impression of *Romanitas* and not the reality of Pompeian daily life. The architecture has become indicative of the literary debate of what it is to be Roman. The house is a cultural symbol of *Romanitas*, a visual sign that, through the apparent embodiment of Roman culture in its art and architecture (made explicit through the practice of Roman ritual in the domestic sphere), would immediately spark recognition in the Roman viewer.[18] The house gives the impression that this Pompeian is a true Roman.

To our modern logic, this impression is surely contradictory. The Pompeian cannot be a Roman, and any impression given by art and architecture to that effect is easily refuted in reality. However, the Roman did not live in such a simple world of clear-cut definitions. The ancient world was a world where boundaries of centre and periphery, mortal and divine, real and mythical, even public and private were continually blurred. This was a world where Italians, as enfranchised citizens after the Social War, could become bona fide Romans. It was also a world where emperors became divine after death and where the entrance to the underworld had a precise geographical location near Cumae.[19] Town bled into country through the *suburbia*, and personal, bodily functions and care such as defecating and bathing were communal activities.[20]

The text of Vitruvius is an attempt to define boundaries – to brand houses as Roman and public when in fact these are not clear-cut distinctions. The text tries to overlook these difficulties, to impose individual, defined categories on what are actually ever-shifting sliding points along a scale. In other words, the text seeks to cover contradictions of existence that, in reality, cannot be resolved. The house can never be termed either precisely public or private, except in the artificial construction of literature. This rhetorical construction of the world is not confined to discussions of Roman houses; in fact, it applies to all discourse on what it is to be Roman. Such a discourse involves being seen to justify one's place within the complex, rhetorically constructed diversities between centre and periphery, town and country, public and private, and so on.[21]

Like the Vitruvian text, Pompeian houses themselves appear to set up clear distinctions between public and private space, which, in reality, simply cannot be disentangled. Like the text, the art and architecture attempt to build an impression of life within the house. This possibility has been largely overlooked in discussions of the Roman house. Indeed, in one of the most recent publications concerning domestic space, Laurence worries about the necessity to distinguish between "lived space" as it is found in the archaeological record and "perceived space," which survives in the textual descriptions.[22] The literature, he notes, tends to represent domestic situations in the terms of "the ideology of what it is to be Roman." Of course, we would retort that art and architecture do likewise. Although he does suggest that the spatial form of the Roman house is structured to construct and reinforce a dominant ideology, he does not apply his model to a discussion of the role of art and architecture within it.

The investigation of the houses of the empire, then, is an investigation also into the art of impression, the ability of art to produce an impression or fantasy at variance with, or beyond the possibility of, reality. As such, it deliberately flouts the ancient and modern conceptions of ancient art as a medium in pursuit of representation and naturalism. Instead it discusses the freedom of art to invent a reality for those for whom it was commissioned, to help them assume an identity and to create fantasies of status in order that they might participate successfully in the Roman world.

The investigation into impression has a further implication. The houses of Pompeii are not an imperial blueprint. Most of them were originally the homes of a local, Samnite elite. They can be used only to demonstrate one community's attempt at being Roman. However, the *domus* has never been studied as an imperial phenomenon. Although several works have reviewed the range of domestic architectural types found across the empire, no attempt has been made to discuss the function and nature of the house using empire-wide examples in the same way as the *villa* has been studied.[23] The most interpretative recent works of the function of the house have chosen very localised areas to mark their point. Of these, Thébert's work on the houses of North Africa has done the most to understand the Roman house in terms of an imperial rather than Italian phenomenon.[24] Most others, including Wallace-Hadrill's influential work on the social function of the *domus*, have stuck to Pompeii as their location.[25]

To some extent, the lack of a cohesive empire-wide survey of urban housing has been enforced by the varied nature of the evidence and traditional scholarly responses to it: the *domus* of Rome is known mostly to us through literary sources, the richly painted remains of Pompeii have been the preserve of art historians, whilst the ruins of the provinces have fallen to the archaeologists. In trying to combine these areas in one study, it is also necessary to struggle with all these disciplines. The result is that each section of this book must adopt a different approach to deal most effectively with the available material. Throughout, every effort has been made to synthesise the material and to apply a consistently interdisciplinary approach to the evidence but the reader should be aware that, at times, certain disciplines will loom larger than others.

To investigate the art of impression in the domestic context of the Roman empire, this book will begin with a consideration of the literary conception of the role of the house in promoting a *familia*'s *Romanitas* in Rome. It will demonstrate how these conceptions were tested to their limits by the palaces of Rome's first *familia*, the imperial household. Second, these findings will be related to the archaeological evidence of Campania, and a close examination of how individual identity is constructed within the decorational programmes of the house itself. The third part is concerned with building a picture of how the houses of the provinces created impressions in their domestic art and architecture to ensure the local elite's participation in empire. Only by setting local evidence for Roman housing into the wider imperial context of Rome and her provinces is it possible to appreciate the dynamics of Romanisation. In doing so, we can see how elites all over the empire must assume their position within the Roman, rhetorically constructed poles between centre and periphery, town and country in order either to aspire to or rebel against the cultural expectations of *Romanitas*. By viewing all these examples together, it is possible to begin to appreciate the complexities of building a Roman identity and the power of the art of impression to overcome them. The temporal scope of this study will, therefore, primarily be the first century B.C. and the first two centuries A.D. At this time, the expanding empire was forcing redefinitions of what it was to be Roman in the face of the inclusion of more and more alien territories, races, and cults within the Roman world. During the second century, this process of Romanisation reached its apex when Hadrian ended the tradition of imperial expansion and offered a new definition of empire, which culminated in Caracalla's extension of the citizenship in 212, endowing everyone with an official, Roman identity. The final chapter, however, takes us to the end of Antiquity as it was experienced in Ephesus to ascertain the long-term developments of imperial, domestic space.

The wide range of this book means that much remains unaccomplished. Geographically, an investigation into the houses of the provinces has had to be selective. Whilst having noted the numerous rhetorical contradictions of

Romanitas, many of those have had to be passed over in favour of the main theme of centre and periphery. The relationship between town and country, in domestic terms between *domus* and *villa*, has received less attention than the complexities that even cursory attention demonstrated the topic might have deserved. It must be stressed that this book is specifically concerned with urban housing. Although the text acknowledges the role of the *villa* throughout, it follows Roman rhetoric in treating the country house as secondary to the *domus*. Literature was insistent on differentiating the *domus* as seat of a family's *Romanitas* from the *villa*, haven for un-Roman behaviour and deviance.[26] Most importantly, this book remains above all the preserve of the elite. More work must be done to consider the worth of the art of impression to those lower down the social scale whose artistic efforts are often dismissed as merely imitative of their superiors.[27] However, I hope that these omissions are not indicative of the paucity of the scope of this book but of the breadth of its conception and intention. The aim of this book is twofold: first, to assess the role of domestic art and architecture in building an impression of those who lived within the house and, second, to examine how these houses and the identities that they projected reflect the process of acculturation across the Roman empire. By looking beyond Rome both geographically and chronologically, we will be able to appreciate how the dynamics between Rome and her provinces were altered as the inhabitants of the empire set to work building an identity for themselves.

PART ONE

THE HOUSES OF ROME IN ANCIENT LITERATURE

1

The Ideal Home

The biggest difficulty in studying the role of the *domus* in Roman society and the contribution that art and architecture made to that role is the almost complete lack of archaeological evidence in the city of Rome (Figure 2). Continuous occupation has meant that these houses are largely lost forever, except where they have been preserved, sheltered by more monumental building projects. The painted rooms from the republican House of the Griffins (Figure 3), for example, survive in part because they were filled with rubble when the slopes of the Palatine were levelled to create a terrace for Emperor Domitian's palace. As a result, we are left only with literary descriptions of the houses of Rome, moralistic discourses on the luxury within them, and incidental mentions of houses as backdrops to the lives of historical figures. However, all these combine to form a substantial body of evidence that is crucial to our understanding of how Romans regarded their houses and of the significance they held for their owners and those who visited and viewed them. An investigation of this literature must come before a discussion of the art and architecture of the houses of Italy and the provinces since it provides us with a social context with which to study those remains. In these first two chapters, we will assess the importance of the *domus* in Roman society and the close link between the appearance of the house and the elite owners who dwelt within it. How did the *domus* affect and promote its occupants' identities? As a preface to this investigation, however, we must consider the ways in which Romans constructed and interacted with the literature and art and architecture around them.

In one of Cicero's many letters, the republican orator is found writing to Lucceius, a contemporary historian, about his inclusion in a work in

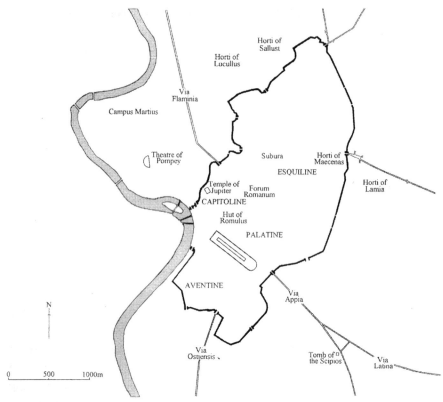

2. Rome, plan of the Republican period.

progress. He is very clear on how the project should take shape, not only as to the manner in which his achievements should be styled but even as to what exactly the extent of those achievements are.[1] As far as Cicero is concerned, the main thrust of the narrative will be to support his own claims to fame in as elegant prose as possible. The presentation, rather than the actual attainment, of his achievements is his most important goal. This presentation, of course, is not completely freeform. Rather, it involves the historian's application of a framework of Roman rhetoric to Cicero's life through the process of *inventio*.[2] In expecting his life to be presented as the cultivation of *virtus* in pursuit of *gloria*, Cicero is writing himself into the tradition of Roman historical heroes – men such as Marcus Furius Camillus who conquered Veii and freed Rome after the Gaulish sack.[3] Through the application of similar rhetoric, Cicero, a *novus homo* from Arpinum, can expect to be inserted into this tradition of *Romanitas*. Successful presentation by Lucceius will ensure Cicero's identity as Roman, regardless of his "true" origins.

3. Rome, House of the Griffins, wall painting. Photo: Koppermann, DAIR 66.208.

As Cicero was not from Rome, constructing himself as an archetypal Roman was crucial to his social and political success. As a result, he might be presumed to have been particularly sensitive to what exactly constituted *Romanitas*. Unfortunately, a concise definition of Romanness cannot be found in Latin literature. The closest a Roman author comes to defining Roman behaviour is Virgil in the *Aeneid*. In Book Six, the role of Rome was revealed to be to create empire. His prescription provided a neat definition of the ultimate difference between Roman and Greek, who would instead excel at the arts and sciences.[4] What is certain is that *Romanitas* was never based on a purely racial qualification in the same way as classical Greek identity was constructed. Whereas to be Greek, at least in the classical era, was an inalienable birthright and a community experience, being Roman seems to have depended much more on variable factors. Roman military legends are not based on group heroics like the three hundred Spartans who defended Greece at Thermopylae but on individual heroes, men like Horatius who single-handedly defended the Sublician Bridge against the Etruscans.[5] Such heroes proved themselves Roman by exhibiting recurring moral standards: *fides*, *honos*, and most of all *virtus*, a particularly Roman brand of courage.[6] All young Roman women were brought up in the shadow of Lucretia, who killed herself rather than live with the shame of having succumbed to rape.[7] A person could prove him- or herself worthy of Roman citizenship by adopting these *mores* just as an individual born in Rome could lose the right by straying from those values. Again, these *mores* were never explicitly spelled out but were legitimised by tradition. In the name of tradition, these *mores* could be constantly redefined as needed, always appealing to the authority of Rome's most distant ancestors.

The emphasis of Roman tradition on ancestral values reveals another layer of identity in Rome, that of the *familia*. The family was a central element of Roman society, ruled over by the *paterfamilias*, the senior male. The idea of continuation in family life was very strong; the presence of the dead in the form of ancestor masks in the *atrium* and family tombs on the edge of the city all reminded the present generation of the past. The family line was ensured in many symbolic ways – the final kiss passed on the last breath of a dying member to the next generation, sons bore the name of their father and forefather.[8] Leading families boasted of their long lines, tracing their ancestry back to the legendary heroes who had first displayed Roman *mores*. The Roman family was an all-embracing institution, in which all the household, even the slaves, belonged. To this extent, the family unit became an excellent medium through which to attain *Romanitas*. Individuals who might be personally excluded from becoming Roman by virtue of their low status or lesser gender might find themselves able to exploit their family name. Just as the males of the family shared their names, so women were given feminine versions – Claudia, Julia, and so on. Freed slaves also took the *praenomen* and *nomen* of their former masters. The recognition of the family name might well earn the bearer greater respect than might ordinarily be applied to their persons. Though it is possible to see examples of this happening in the republic, with the high public profile of women like Sempronia, mother of the Gracchi, it is not until the empire that these links are fully clear. As imperial Rome became centred around one family, anybody associated with that family and its *paterfamilias*, the emperor, also attracted attention. The early Principate was often understood as an era of empresses and freedmen because these formerly subservient members of the household learned to acquire prominence by exploiting their names and positions.

Of course, if Rome was to be a successful city, then *Romanitas* must also be demonstrable on a community level. The Roman populace was brought together through participation in public rituals and activities, which implied adherence to the traditional *mores*. This entailed both isolated events, such as sacrifice, or ongoing lifestyles, such as the pursuit of a military or political career. However, most important in the bid to ensure a reputation as the embodiment of *Romanitas* was to be commemorated as a Roman, either in literature or art – hence, Cicero's interest in his historical representation.

Cicero's attitude towards image-making is confirmed by Pliny the Younger, writing over a century later. In composing a eulogy for a dead

youth, Pliny's method of investigating the boy's life was not to research
the character or events of that life from objective sources but to ask the
parents exactly what they wanted written. Clearly he expected his clients
to dictate the content of the commission. Both sides were open about their
relationship and dependence on each other and the text, seeing themselves
engaged in a perfectly legitimate transaction of presentation.[9] It is crucial
to our understanding of Roman self-presentation, that the identity of Rome
and the character of *Romanitas* was continually being rewritten by the elite,
who tailored definitions of what it was to be Roman to suit their own
position.

Both Pliny and Cicero attest to this method of representation extending
beyond literature. Pliny explained his request to his subject's parents by
employing this comparison:

> [A]s you would advise a sculptor or painter who was making a por-
> trait of your son, what he ought to portray and what to improve, so
> also guide and direct me.
>
> Pliny *Eps.* 3.10.6

Art is also a mode of presentation, working to the advantage of the elite
with commissions designed to flatter and empower its patrons. Selective
presentation might entail the manipulation of the most basic physical traits
of a portrait to provide a more imposing characterisation.[10] The tradition
of the veristic portraiture of the Republic (Figure 4) offers an indication of
how rhetoric dominates art. The features of each senator are tailored to
fit the rubric of *Romanitas*; they wear the care-worn, austere expressions
of experienced and dedicated men who have surrendered their lives to the
service of the state.[11] Again this rhetorically motivated portraiture was very
flexible. Anyone could "look" Roman, it was just a question of correct
application.

That this very mannered portraiture is known today as veristic reflects
the nature of Roman attitudes to these literary and artistic images, which
may seem to us to be entirely artificial creations. Romans insisted art
was a process of *mimesis* and were determined that the results of artistic effort conveyed *veritas*, in much the same way as Tacitus purported to
write his histories *sine ira et studio*.[12] In other words, whilst Cicero and
Pliny both acknowledged the versatility of rhetoric and the process of
inventio in creating literature or art, the finished product was nevertheless
perceived as "true." It would seem that the elite, as controllers of the production of art and literature, preferred identity in Rome to be built on these
constructs.

4. Veristic portrait. Photo: Copyright © The British Museum.

To understand why rhetoric played such a dominant role in Roman public life, it is necessary to consider the nature of Roman politics. Both Cicero and Pliny understand the manipulation of literature and art as affording a chance to compete within the system and to aim at becoming the very embodiment of *Romanitas*. In effect, this entailed endeavouring to emulate the heroes of the past. The competitive nature of the senatorial elite, particularly during the Republic, is well attested as the leading families co-operated with each other to preserve their collective control over the state and yet competed amongst themselves to gain positions of authority within the Senate. Political stability depended on the ability of the elite to compete but also to remain equal. This may account for the heightened awareness of representation and its increasing standardisation – the rows of veristic portraits reveal an elite all in pursuit of the same goal and tailoring their own identities in order to compete effectively.[13] As an artificial construct, rhetoric allowed the widest possible participation; it gave all the elite an equal chance in the race to "out-Roman" each other. In Cicero's time, as the republican system was beginning to disintegrate in the face of the manifestly unequal super-generals, rhetoric became increasingly important in affording equal access to media of self-presentation and promotion. This impression of authority, which was thus afforded to those aristocrats who were becoming less and less integral to the practical governing of Rome, allowed the guise of republican government to be upheld.

At the same time, the application of this rhetoric was, to a large extent, self-regulatory. Each of the major rhetorical *topoi* played with preoccupations of *Romanitas* in an attempt to overcome the dichotomies on which Roman culture rested. Rhetoric makes *Romanitas* seem simple. In reality, to define what it was to be Roman is extremely complicated. In the absence of any precise definition, all aspects of Roman life, even those that were contradictory, could be legitimately held up as proving Romanness. So, for example, the perfect Roman might be pictured equally as an illiterate peasant farmer or as an urbane man of letters. Rome was an empire of urban centres but, in a pre-industrial society, was ever dependent on the produce of the land. Rhetoric responds to this apparent dichotomy by inventing *topoi*, some that support the country and others that support the city.[14] By breaking down some of the conflicts of *Romanitas* into standard *topoi*, they were simplified and brought safely into everyday circulation. There they could be mediated within a controlled environment of regulated principles of presentation. This clearly allows the patron a choice in how to present himself at any one moment, as prosperous landowner or cultured urbanite; the adoption of either stance will validate his *Romanitas*. However, in opting for one, he must temporarily pass over the other and thus open himself to attack for scorning that overlooked aspect of *Romanitas*.

The widespread application of rhetoric was essential to the existence of a highly competitive senatorial elite; it enabled individual members to compete without wiping each other out. A culture built on rhetoric allowed the elite to regulate itself, the versatility of its *topoi* enabling any senator to prosecute an enemy or to defend himself.[15] A senator became innocent or guilty, depending on the rhetoric used against him; he could vindicate himself or exact revenge by similarly manipulating the world around him. The great emphasis on oratory in education was therefore of central importance to the success or failure of the pupil in his future life.[16]

As competition increased, however, these dichotomies, which gave rhetoric its versatility, began to gape ever wider. Members of the elite were forced to go to further extremes in the pursuit of fulfilling the requirements of one particular *topos*, leaving other aspects of their *Romanitas* increasingly exposed. As such competition escalated, it was inevitable that increasingly lavish presentation would be accompanied by ever more fervent attack until, finally, all notion of co-operation and equality was squashed to the extent that the political system could no longer be sustained.

All of this has a considerable impact on the study of art and architecture. The visual arts were understood as important media for conveying rhetoric. Ancient texts often interpret art and architectural developments as expressing wider rhetorical themes. The moral breakdown and increased ambition of the late Republic, for instance, was often understood in terms of increased competition in lavish housing.[17] Consequently, it might be expected that the architecture of the Roman house had a role to play in conveying an impression of the inhabitants' Romanness. Because Rome was conceived of as a group of like-minded individuals as much as it was one civic, communal unit (like a Greek *polis*), that Romanness must be architecturally expressed in individual domestic units as well as on a public level. The Roman *domus* becomes the medium through which the Roman family communicated with the wider community and expressed and justified their place in that society. Just as we recognise a Roman town by its amphitheatre and basilicas, buildings that seem to exude *Romanitas*, so a *domus* conveyed the identity of the family who inhabited it.

Second, the *domus* was not simply a medium that could be used to reflect rhetorical *topoi*. It played an active role in promoting an impression of *Romanitas* by delineating the space within which the chief domestic rituals of Roman life could be enacted. The development of Rome was understood to have entailed a process by which individual family units gradually expanded to the size of neighbourhoods and from there went on to form a whole city of extended families.[18] As a result, the ritual life of Rome originated from and referred back to the *domus*. The house was at the very centre of Roman behaviour. Consider religion: if the *pax deorum*, the religious basis that protected Rome, could be seen to be safeguarded publicly in the sacrifices at the temple of Jupiter on the Capitol, it was daily tended by the worship of the household deities in family *lararia*. The temple of Vesta, at the heart of the Forum, which contained the eternal flame of the city, was nothing but a magnification of the hearth fire that kept every Roman *domus* alive.

Socio-political order, too, was oriented around the *domus* of the Roman elite. Every morning the great *atria* of the elite were open for the *salutatio*. This ritual was an essential element of the patron–client network that stimulated both the economics and politics of Rome. As every Roman citizen was a client or patron, this network purported to work as a way of bonding society, providing connections between the wealthiest and poorest, in a city that was otherwise dominated by strong status divisions. The *salutatio* provided the means to realise this connection on a daily basis. At the first hour, every client presented himself at the house of his patron. The large *atrium* space of the *domus* was perfect for accommodating these early morning visitors. The client would pay his respects, acknowledging his ongoing obedience to his patron, whilst the patron would reciprocate by the donation of *sportula*, either a gift of food or nominal amount of money. The system was much reviled by patron and client alike, but it had its advantages. The poor client might receive some protection by the scheme, and the patron, an electoral base and social prestige.[19] Every time the *salutatio* took place, the relationship between patron and client was affirmed, and the patron's power was acknowledged. By establishing such rituals and normalising them over the years, the elite created real power for themselves through the portrayal of that power in everyday ritual.

Most importantly, these domestic rituals conveyed the Roman identity of its participants. Observation or avoidance of appropriate rituals conveyed assent to or dissent from Roman society. One of Cicero's most potent attacks on his arch-enemy Clodius involved his infiltration of a secret, female ritual dressed in drag.[20] Such blatant disregard for ritual and tradition was enough to present him as an enemy of all things Roman. Rhetorical and ritualistic denials are the fundamental means by which people fashioned their responses to the Roman political system.

The institutions of rhetoric and ritual promoted an ordered Roman society where the community acted as Romans by obeying these cultural guidelines. Architecture offered a whole cultural package, affecting both communication and action. Its visible construction offered the opportunity for rhetorical presentation, while its space provided the context for ritualistic practices. For Cicero, this was the link between *locus* and *ethos*, providing an environment that would promote a particular mode of behaviour.[21] The belief that place could influence behaviour further increases the importance attached to the *domus*. A recognisably Roman house, that is a house whose appearance seemed to conform to rhetorical ideals of *Romanitas* and whose space made room for familiar ritual activity, was enough to guarantee the homeowner's acceptance as a Roman.

Rome depended on this link between place and character in perpetuating her authority as centre of the world, instilling order in her citizenry by her very cityscape,[22] but there remained a fear that individuals could break free of cultural constraints. These are the attacks that Cicero reserves for his worst enemies. In the *Philippics*, he constructs criticism of

Mark Antony around his confiscation and subsequent inhabitation of the house of Pompey:

> In his house there are brothels in the place of bedrooms and inns in the place of dining rooms.[23]
>
> Cicero *Phil.* 2.28.69

Similarly, Clodius is accused of turning his own home into a brothel.[24] In the course of the *Verrine Orations*, a prosecution of the former governor of Sicily delivered in 70 B.C., the *topos* becomes further twisted. This time, Verres is accused not of degrading his own house but of inappropriately elevating the boudoir of his mistress to the status of praetorian court.[25] In all these cases, the subjects are unable to tailor their activities to their surroundings, plunging *Romanitas* into an ever-widening abyss.

Through the rhetoric of architecture and space, the house created an impression of *Romanitas*. At the same time, we must be aware that the rhetorical construct of the literature is in itself framing a reaction to the rhetoric of the house. In other words, the author shaped his approval or condemnation of the homeowner by bringing rhetoric into play either for or against the house. Both literary description and architectural arrangement are equally loaded constructions of identity and not mere reflectors of "reality." If we want to investigate these identities further by finding out how a homeowner could construct a succesful home for himself and his family, we must do what the Romans themselves were trying so hard to avoid: to look behind the rhetorical constructs and to examine those conflicts that enforced their invention. We must be continually aware that every literary presentation of domestic architecture was attempting to resolve these difficulties either through approbation or condemnation.

LUCULLUS AND SENATORIAL HOUSING

It is very difficult, however, to understand how a republican Roman might construct an ideal *domus*. The heightened, negative competition of the late Republic severely affected the sources which contain vehement attacks on personal property. As the political framework of senatorial co-operation fell apart in the face of increased competition, building was presented as becoming more and more lavish. Reaction was couched in the terms of moral outrage, a rhetorical chorus of disapproval. During this period, then, we can only construct a successful house with reference to the presentations of unsuccessful homes that were subjected to literary attacks. Rather than discovering the moral, urban *domus*, we are forced to explore its greatest antithesis, the luxurious, country *villa*.

L. Licinius Lucullus was considered the epitome of the ambitious, republican builder, his luxurious villas even appearing in the work of the Christian apologist Tertullian and in the fourth-century history of Ammianus Marcellinus.[26] His villas became shorthand for the spiralling competition that was symptomatic of the breakdown of the late Republic. The Lucullus who is presented to us in the second-century biography written by the Greek Plutarch was consul in 74 B.C., an *optimate* and one-time ally of Sulla and hero of the First Mithridatic War.[27] However, having been recalled to Rome, he was refused a triumph for three years until his ally, Cicero, reached the consulship in 63 B.C. Lucullus's problems largely seem to have stemmed from his close association with Sulla at a time when the *optimate/popularis* divide was causing increasing division within the Senate. He began to take a back seat in politics, and his retirement gained him far more attention in the sources than his military exploits, as the infamy of his string of villas spread.

Faced with a wealth of rhetorically incompatible material concerning his subject's life, Plutarch resorted to *inventio*, reconstructing the biography as sensibly, to a Graeco-Roman audience, as he could. The life of Lucullus was split into two parts: the first the *locus* of favourable rhetoric concerning his rigorous political activities and the second the depository for the attacks on his private life and the lavish villas in which he passed it.[28] Lucullus starts out as the man of *virtus* as he pushes back the boundaries of the Roman empire and searches for public *gloria* in the service of the state. On return, however, Lucullus turns his back on the city of Rome and retreats to his country villas, immersing himself in his private life and investing all his resources into greater and greater displays of *luxuria*. In an attempt to impress upon his contemporary audience the excessive scale of the Lucullan building projects, Plutarch writes that

> [e]ven now, when there has been such an increase in luxury, the *horti* of Lucullus are counted among the most lavish of the imperial *horti*.
>
> Plut. *Luc.* 39.2

Plutarch is very clear that the work was funded by the great wealth that Lucullus amassed on his eastern campaigns. In other words, this apparent corruption of Roman *austeritas* was portrayed as a direct result of the general's stay in the East. Rome herself was absolved of the guilt of fostering such behaviour, and blame was heaped on the East, even though, whilst there, Lucullus is presented as having been a model Roman general.[29]

The luxurious extent to which the villas of Lucullus consumed this wealth is recalled in a number of texts. At his Tusculan *villa*, his contemporary Varro "described" an aviary filled with birds adjoining the dining room. The very air, the most free of all the elements, became part of the decor and entertainment.[30] Such projects were so nefarious that Lucullus is largely remembered as

> suspending hills on great tunnels, winding circles of sea and streams for the rearing of fish around his homes and building houses in the sea. Tubero the Stoic, on observation, called him Xerxes in a *toga*.
>
> Plut. *Luc.* 39.3

The theme of luxury is represented throughout these texts as control over the elements; air, land, and sea are all tamed for the entertainment of Lucullus. Such displays of megalomania were a well-attested character trait of the eastern potentates like the Persian king Xerxes. Again, by including Tubero's remark, the Greek Plutarch draws accusations of luxury away from Rome.[31] There is no room in the rhetoric of *Romanitas* for such behaviour. Battlefields and basilicas are shown as the public arenas of *Romanitas*; the private, luxurious *villa* represents the *locus* of eastern moral laxity.

As we have noted, these accusations survived, with great tenacity, even into the literature of the later Roman empire, ensuring the preservation of the memory of Lucullus as virtually the paradigm of a gluttonous wastrel. His un-Roman behaviour affected the reputation of his villas, which had to become the *locus* for deviancy. The established relation between *ethos* and *locus* allowed no other interpretation. However, Plutarch had recorded an alternative view of Lucullus that embodied the *ethos* of *Romanitas*, and this other Lucullus clearly needed somewhere to live. Cicero invented the *locus* for this characterisation, creating a new concept of the Lucullan villas.

As a friend of Lucullus, Cicero's instinct must have been to rehabilitate his subject into the tradition of *Romanitas*. He could not hope to deny that Lucullus was an extensive builder, but he could attempt to divert the blame. In his defence, Lucullus became the victim of his imitators, those who passed over *mimesis* of his *virtus* in favour of copying his villas.[32] This is the negative side of a society based on presentation. Usurpers can claim a place in society that is not "rightfully" theirs through judicious acquisition of goods. As his knight and freedman neighbours eagerly imitated his own display, Lucullus was forced to invest more into his home to maintain the appearance of his higher status and thus preserve appropriate social order.[33] In effect, Cicero's Lucullus becomes the protector of Roman order and not its betrayer; the display of luxury is inflicted on him by the Roman social system itself.

When Cicero invents a visit to one of the offending villas, he finds not Xerxes, surrounded by improbable earthworks, but Cato the Younger, descendent of the most Roman of Romans ever to have lived. Living up to his family's reputation for *austeritas*, Cato is sitting in a library pouring over the Lucullan collection of Stoic texts! The only extravagance here comes from one who

> at the utmost leisure and with the greatest amount of books seemed as though he was gorging himself with books, if we can use this term for such a distinguished occupation.
>
> <div align="right">Cicero <i>De Fin.</i> 3.27</div>

Our conception of the *villa* has now been totally reversed as Cato and Cicero settle down to philosophical discussion. The *villa* is shown to be an appropriate *locus* for *Romanitas*, and Lucullus is fully reintegrated into senatorial tradition. Cicero's efforts show just how powerful rhetoric could be in rehabilitating reputations. His success was only temporary, however. Later sources reverted to the negative image of Lucullus that had been widely accepted by republican readers.

THE IDEAL HOME

The villas of Lucullus became canonical models for the excessive building craze of the late Republic. When Augustus founded the Principate, following his victory at Actium in 31 B.C., which ended the conflict that had arisen from the effects of this competition, Roman authors would have to fit him and (more importantly for our purposes) his house within the rhetorical tradition of domestic architecture. Suetonius provides us with a particularly loaded "description" of the House of Augustus on the Palatine hill.

> It was remarkable neither in size nor elegance; it had short colonnades with columns of Alban stone and the rooms were bereft of any marble or remarkable floors.
>
> <div align="right">Suet. <i>Aug.</i> 72.1</div>

The passage is remarkable in its complete aversion to luxury, a theme that occurs again and again as the account progresses: Augustus's furniture was barely fit for a private citizen, and his soft furnishings were very ordinary.[34] Most tellingly, whilst Lucullus attempts to tame nature, Augustus tolerates the forces of the elements, sleeping in the same bedroom all year round despite his constitution's aversion to Roman winters.[35]

In a second rebuttal of the presentation of Lucullan domestic architecture, the House of Augustus is specifically located on the Palatine at the heart of Rome. Since it was previously the home of Hortensius, a leading republican orator, the house was able to assume its place within Roman tradition. Dedicated to serving the state,

> Augustus, having built his house, made it all over to the public, either because of the contribution which the people donated or because he was *pontifex maximus* and so wanted to live in rooms that were both private and public at the same time.
>
> Dio 55.12.

Suetonius also places emphasis on the urban-orientated life of the *princeps* who, in order to escape the town, must rely on the hospitality of his freedmen in the suburbs. Augustus does own villas, but they are modest affairs – his contempt of luxurious country piles is demonstrated by his destruction of one belonging to his granddaughter, Julia.[36]

This account of Augustus's domestic arrangements can only be understood as a reversal of republican building *mores*. For the first time, the Roman elite were confronted with the model of the perfect *domus*. The emperor came to be seen as the keeper of public morals, endeavouring to regulate social competition.

The rhetoric surrounding the House of Augustus shows an attempt to redefine the proper limits of domestic presentation. The account of Suetonius stresses a new emphasis on simplicity and publicness that stands in direct opposition to the luxurious private retreats of the villas of Lucullus. This opposition can be understood as a concentration of effort specifically aimed at implying that such disastrous self-display was now over. After the chaos caused by the hyper-competition of the late Republic, peace had to be accompanied by the impression of a new sense of order and restriction in domestic display.

In essence (and much more broadly than just in the realm of architecture), the invention of a new tradition of *Romanitas* was a process of mediation between Augustus and the rest of Rome. Augustus had to rearrange Rome as the *locus* of imperial rule, to restore a new sense of order that would support his position. At the same time, the rest of Rome strove to make sense of Augustus by working his position into their traditional view of Rome. Architecture played a crucial role in this reorganisation, as the face of Rome was renovated in order to place the *princeps* within the city's visual tradition.[37] Suetonius wrote that Augustus had rebuilt Rome, fashioning in marble what once was brick.[38] Augustus himself, in the *Res Gestae*, which decorated the walls of his Mausoleum as well as temples in the provinces, compiled a list of buildings he had either built or restored.[39] Rome was now a Principate, and the *Res Gestae* provided the impression that architecture was displaying allegiance to the new regime.

VITRUVIUS: BUILDING UNDER THE PRINCIPATE OR BUILDING THE PRINCIPATE?

In seeking a contemporary discussion of architectural practices of Augustan Rome, we are rewarded with the *De Architectura* of Vitruvius. Published towards the end of the first century B.C., the book consists of ten volumes covering not only the ins and outs of public and domestic building from the materials to the design but also sections on machinery and even astronomy. Even now, Vitruvius is raided as a font of knowledge on the technicalities of Roman architecture.[40]

In fact, a close reading of Vitruvius reveals a lack of detailed technical advice behind the apparent barrage of information: the architectural knowledge of the *De Architectura*, like, say, the farming advice contained within the *Georgics* of Virgil, is primarily aimed at the enthusiastic amateur.[41] Whilst didactic treatises imparted a range of information about their topic, they were aimed at providing the elite with entertaining literature as much as with practical manuals. Just as any other ancient literary work, didactic poetry shaped its content to demonstrate a predetermined rhetorical "moral." This can be demonstrated through the republican didactic texts concerning agriculture, composed by Cato the Elder in mid-second century B.C. and, a century later, by Varro. Both of these use a discussion of *villa* estates to employ the familiar rhetorical topos of *luxuria*. Varro, in particular, seems preoccupied with the decor of villas; even his section concerning fish farming and fishponds includes a sideswipe at Lucullus's extravagance.[42] The dominance of the *villa* in the work, however, reveals Varro's intended audience. His didactic poetry was ultimately written not for the farmer but for an elite urban audience, who read (or rather listened) at their leisure and whose experience of the country was shaped by the view from the *villa* and not from the fields. Didactic should perhaps be understood as a lesson of how the elite gentleman might disport himself in certain situations rather than instruction in the intimate details of a particular trade or discipline.

The authoritative tone of didactic made it a perfect vehicle for rhetorical constructs of morality, very useful, we might suppose, for conveying an Augustan message. But its sombre authority might also work to the advantage of the elite who wrote it, using the credibility associated with the genre to write themselves a commanding role in the Principate and normalise their high social position. The use of didactic to assert the author's rather than the *princeps'* view of Rome is most obvious in its subversion by Ovid. He uses this genre to challenge Augustan rhetoric in the *Ars Amatoria*, offering his own moral alternative to the prudish order of the new society.[43] That Augustus was equally aware (or at least could be presented as being so) is demonstrated by his reputed expulsion of Ovid to the Black Sea.[44]

It is highly unlikely that Vitruvius would be unaware of this discourse of negotiation. At the outset of the work, Vitruvius makes some fuss of professing his affiliation to the Augustan cause, dedicating the *De Architectura* to the *princeps*.[45]

> Since I was obligated to you by such kindness that I need not fear poverty until the end of my days, I began to write this for you; because I noticed that you have in the past and are still now constructing many buildings, and also because, for the rest of time, the greatness of both your public and private buildings will stand for the greatness of your achievements so that your memory can be handed down through coming generations, I have written precise rules so that, considering them, you can have notes both for works you have done before and for whatever works will be done in the future by you; for in these volumes I have revealed all the theories of the discipline.
>
> Vitr. *De Arch.* Praef. 3

Straightaway, the reader must be aware that Vitruvius's manual is inspired by Augustan building projects. The redefinition of society under the Principate was encouraging a widespread reexamination of established practices. In fact, Book Six has been identified as an attempt to justify the social system through architecture.[46] Section Five advises fellow architects how to build homes for clients of different professions and status, a discussion very carefully divided into rank: those *qui commmuni sunt fortuna* (those of a common fortune) for whom

> splendid entrance ways, dining rooms and reception halls are not necessary;
>
> Vitr. *De Arch.* 6.5.1

and those who *fructibus rusticis serviunt* (depend upon the fruits of the land) through to the *feneratoribus* (bankers) and *publicanis* (tax collectors) and eventually the *forensibus* (lawyers) and *disertis* (orators) who require something

> more elegant and more roomy for the reception of audiences.
>
> Vitr. *De Arch.* 6.5.2

Vitruvius is now free to discuss the homes of the *nobilibus*.

Such careful distinction of rank and the privileges or material wealth appropriate to each station can be understood as a direct reaction to Cicero's defence of the magnificent villas of Lucullus. By laying out the type of house appropriate to each rank, Vitruvius can hope to prevent such super-competition spiralling out of control again. In fact, the reassertion of order and the delineation of the privileges of rank is a recurring theme of the rhetoric of the Principate in every aspect of life. Only by enforcing a strict emphasis on the reordering of the rest of society could Augustus hope to safeguard and normalise his own position at the apex of the Principate. However, Augustus did not compose the *De Architectura* and was not responsible for the building of elite homes. The advice on the construction of these homes was written by a man of education and must have been meant for an educated, elite audience. As much as the work coincides with the idea of creating order, this is essentially an ideal republican order that safeguards the senatorial position. The rest of the *De Architectura* attempts to legitimate that order, not least by including a lengthy discourse on astronomy. The undisputed order of the universe and the place and function of the cosmic elements lends credibility and an air of tradition to the artificial order of society.[47]

Vitruvius devotes most attention to the homes of the senatorial elite, implying that these are the houses that matter. We must remind ourselves that throughout the late Republic, political chaos was increasingly intimated through lavish buildings as ambition drew the elite to make ever more luxurious attempts to compete with their rivals. Pliny the Elder, with hindsight, traces such display back as far as 78 B.C. when

> [t]here was not a house in Rome more beautiful than that of Lepidus but, by Hercules, within thirty five years it did not hold a place amongst the first hundred.
>
> Pliny *N.H.* 36.110

The rules of elite architecture need to be redrawn to show a peaceful and co-operative Senate body, both compliant to but a match for Augustus. Vitruvius caters for their living requirements in the following, often quoted way:

> But for the nobility, who must carry out business for the state by holding office and magistracies, high regal entrance rooms (*vestibula regalia alta*), great halls and spacious peristyles (*atria et peristylia amplimissa*), woods and wide walkways finished in a majestic manner must be built; besides this libraries and basilicas on a scale

> comparable with public buildings, because in their homes are often
> held both public consultations and public trials and disputes.
>
> Vitr. *De Arch.* 6.5.2

This passage has provided the starting point for many discussions on the
public function of the aristocratic *domus*. It is read in conjunction with the
opening of the chapter where the author compares the private rooms of
the *domus*, which he recognises as the *cubicula*, *triclinia*, and *balnea*, with
the public areas of the *vestibula*, *cava aedium* and *peristylia*, access to which
is unrestricted:

> to which, although uninvited, anyone of the people can come by
> right.
>
> Vitr. *De Arch.* 6.5.1

This distinction has been particularly applied to the houses of Pompeii. The
large *atrium* and tiny *cubicula* of houses such as the House of Pansa (Figure 1)
can be produced as evidence to support the text.[48] Nor were such lavish
houses lacking in Rome herself. The third-century Marble Plan – a map of
the entire city, which now only survives in fragments – clearly pictures the
ground plans of *atrium* houses amongst the *insulae* and public buildings of
the crowded city.[49] However, the senatorial *domus* Vitruvius describes is
not simply a construction of brick and mortar. It is also a construction of
rhetoric, a presentation of elite housing that shares clear affinities with the
later, Suetonian "description" of the House of Augustus.

The elite house is open because the owner is engaged in civic business,
not locked away in private retirement like Lucullus. Splendorous decoration is located in the public area of the house, enhancing the proceedings
and providing a setting for the interaction of householder and visitor. Any
luxury (and, of course, this word and its moralistic overtones are strictly
avoided) is shared with outsiders – another stark contrast with the hidden
extravagances of Lucullus. The house Vitruvius describes is an *exemplum* of
the ideal *domus*, an *exemplum* that Augustus might be expected to sanction,
although not a home that a senator might actually choose to live in. On the
other hand, it might be proposed that Vitruvius has preempted Augustus in
arguing the case for elite housing. These houses are *magnificentia*, certainly
not simple. The author's confident assertion that this is how the nobility
should live normalises and pleads the case for the continuance of senatorial display. The idea that such *magnificentia* is needed for public service
rather than private gain removes any blame from those very houses that

were the aim of such opprobium in other sources. From either point of view, Vitruvius is revealed as the architect of political order as much as of domestic space. He creates for us the ideal *domus*, which appears to overcome conflicts in Roman culture – conflicts between *luxuria* and *austeritas*, public and private, town and country – which left Lucullus so open to attack. However, if we are to understand the Vitruvian *domus* fully, then we must explore these tensions further. We must investigate exactly how they might be accommodated.

THE PLACE OF LUXURY IN THE LIVES OF THE ELITE

The theme of luxury in the rhetoric of domestic architecture has already been made familiar to us through the contrasting descriptions of the villas of Lucullus and the House of Augustus. Lucullus was attacked for his part in the competition of increasingly lavish elite housing, encouraging the escalated growth of luxury – a process that was generally understood as inevitably increasing through time. Hence Pliny, whilst appraising the republican home of the senator Lepidus as the most splendid house of its age, must admit that it had been left way behind by the extravagance of successive years.[50] That the *horti* of Lucullus were seen to still defy competition well into imperial times further justified moralistic disapproval. By anticipating and competing with this future extravagance, Lucullus's homes defied the natural process of degeneration and thus proved their own luxurious excess.

Pliny's insistence on the ongoing degeneration of Rome was a commonplace. It was a primarily moralistic *topos* where the distant past became a model for a traditional *Romanitas*, which had been subject to gradual erosion, especially by the influx of luxury from the East, until the enervated and profligate present was reached. As such degeneration was understood to find its physical expression in the increasingly lavish houses of the elite, it was inevitable that Vitruvius would both have to justify domestic display and imply that it was now under control.[51]

Augustus's attempts to offer an alternative to the Republic necessitated a halt to the degenerative conception of time and the creation of a cyclical rhetoric, with the Principate representing the start of a new era, after the nadir of the late Republic and Civil War. A Golden Age was reborn, celebrated by the Saecular Games and heralding a new era of peace and prosperity.[52] Necessarily, the beginning of a new cycle entailed comparison with past beginnings and the Augustan theme included many alliances with

the past and the myths of early Rome; the Hut of Romulus becoming the central *locus* of these legends:

> Their life was that of herdsmen and they lived, fending for them-
> selves, on the mountains in huts built with wood and reed. One of
> these, still around in my day, on the Palatine facing towards the Cir-
> cus, was called the Hut of Romulus, which those who care for these
> things guard as holy.
>
> Dion. Hal. 1.79.11[53]

Here was the model of *Romanitas*, which clearly influenced the accounts of the *austeritas* of the House of Augustus. After all, Augustus was the new Romulus. The public, physical expression of this link included the building of his own house on the Palatine in direct visible proximity to the preserved Hut of Romulus, making them neighbours in morality, time, and space.[54]

In effect, Augustus was seen as shifting the development of domestic display back to its roots, before it had had the chance to escalate into *luxuria*. But Augustus could not rid Rome of *luxuria* altogether. Cicero had highlighted the need of Lucullus to maintain his superiority over his social inferiors, and Vitruvius appears to have condoned that practice in prescrib-ing *magnificentia* for the homes of the senatorial elite. A member of this rank simply could not afford to withdraw from competitive display if he was to maintain his standing in society and its accompanying privilege of power.

But why should fear of luxury dominate accounts of housing rather than other aspects of excessive building, such as size? Here, the definition of luxury itself, as expostulated upon by Pliny the Elder in his *Natural History* of the mid first century A.D., provides an answer. Nature was the harbour of all things decent, providing everything needed for survival. The impulse to create man-made things demonstrated a hubristic desire to overcome and subvert the limits of nature in the search for unnecessary luxuries.[55]

Lucullan building schemes invited criticism precisely for their attempts to invert the elements, hollowing the land and filling the sea.[56] Much later, Seneca became the prime exponent of this *topos* as a means of attacking senatorial housing.[57] The Domus Aurea, which belonged to Seneca's pupil, the emperor Nero, was attacked on precisely the principles Seneca attacked in others, including building a sea in the midst of Rome.[58] Perhaps the best surviving example of such projects is the *villa* at Sperlonga, often attributed to Tiberius. There, a *triclinium* was built out into the sea, in the mouth of a natural grotto decorated with grand sculpture (Figure 5).[59] Seneca's stance is perhaps most clearly expressed here.

5. Sperlonga, "Grotto of Tiberius." Photo: SJH.

> Don't they live against nature who sow orchards on their ut-
> most turrets, whose woods sway on the roofs and gables of their
> houses...don't they live against nature who throw the foundations
> of bath houses in the sea and who do not consider they swim in
> luxury unless the hot pool is struck with wave and storm?
>
> Seneca *Eps.* 122.8

The thrust of the rhetoric employed by both Pliny and Seneca is that artifice and luxury are contrary to nature, the universal truth. This idea is in
marked contrast to the continual literary emphasis on *veritas* in representation. The most complete defence of *veritas* in art comes from Vitruvius
himself who, in discussing wall painting, is driven to attack the fantastic
monstra of contemporary decoration.[60] His criticism is reinforced by his
contemporary, the poet Horace.[61] Elsner understands their insistence on
"realism" as a "rejection of subversion," of the "unreal and anti-realistic."[62]
In this model, luxury is subversive because it flaunts, rather than hides,
its presentation as artifice. But it also goes further. In following the laws
of nature, the display of the elite would be circumscribed by the limits
of the possibilities of nature.[63] However, in breaking those laws, the elite
potentially multiplied their options to infinity. Free from the constrictions
of what was real or natural, anything was possible. Competition would

spiral out of control. The insistence of the Augustan authors in attacking luxury and artifice can be understood as a rhetoric aimed at restricting excessive competition and giving the impression of unity and dignity among the elite. The discussion of luxury was forced into a framework dictated by moralistic assessments, avoiding the more dangerous issue of the pivotal role of luxury in maintaining and restricting the power of the elite.

VILLA AND *DOMUS*

Vitruvius built up a rhetoric of the *domus* as an elegantly decorated, open townhouse that served the interests of the state. As part of the process, rhetorical themes such as nature, now saved from its inversion at the hands of *luxuria*, and privacy were ejected from the city. They needed to be relocated and found themselves transported out to the country. The countryside *locus* in which they were deposited, of course, was the *villa*. We have already met the *villa* as it was presented in the polemic literature of the Republic. The *villa* was the antithesis of the *domus*, a rhetorical opposite to the urban family home, dominated by Roman *mores*.

Just as Rome was reinvented during the Principate, so too was the country. Virgil's *Georgics* and *Eclogues* had already begun this process during the Civil War, creating an idyllic world where nature was respected as both provider and tormentor.[64] "Unnatural" luxury and competition were a world away as the countryman knew only allegiance to the rural deities, to whom he offered due reverence.[65] This world of the pastoral idyll became the retreat of the townsman, a place where he could lay aside his burdens safe from the pressures of political competition and enjoy what nature had to offer.[66] Even in Rome itself, the houseowner could find temporary release in his man made countryside. The famous garden wall paintings that decorate a subterranean room in Livia's Villa at Prima Porta create a "natural" setting in the suburbs (Figure 6).[67]

The desire to enjoy such a retreat appears frequently among the litterati; Horace sings the praises of his "little farm," which had been a gift from the literary patron Maecenas. The estate is always presented as modest but satisfying and is set squarely against the grand estates that so profited their senatorial owners.[68]

The enthusiasm for such country retreats gained momentum in imperial times. Pliny the Younger suggests that for the urban(e) scholar, a country property is desirable but it need not have more than a nominal amount of land.

6. Prima Porta, Livia's Villa, garden painting, south wall. Photo: Photo Alinari (Anderson).

> Moreover, for scholarly masters, as he is, a small amount of land is
> more than enough; so that they can clear their heads, refresh their
> eyes, steal through their grounds, tread every path, know all the vines
> and count all the trees.
>
> Pliny *Ep.* 1.24.4

Suetonius, the biographer and the subject of this letter, requires a country
retreat, not for financial gain, but for the sake of fulfilling his notion of the
rhetorical ideal of the country. Pliny himself was an enthusiastic exponent
of the rural idyll he experienced from his *villa* at Laurentum:

> I hear and say nothing which I regret to have heard or spoken, no-
> body around me slanders anyone with malicious talk, I censure no-
> body unless I myself write with too little ability; I am distressed by
> no hope or fear, disturbed by no rumours; I speak only with myself
> and my books.
>
> Pliny *Ep.* 1.9.5

Lucullus could have well cited similar reasons for his retreat into the country
away from the dangers facing him in the turbulent politics of Rome.

This idyllic portrayal of country life had its drawbacks, particularly in
the hands of subversive love poets and satirists who were able to turn
the *topos* on its head and present Rome, by contrast, as the *locus* for
luxury and unnatural vices.[69] The poet Tibullus was particularly clear in

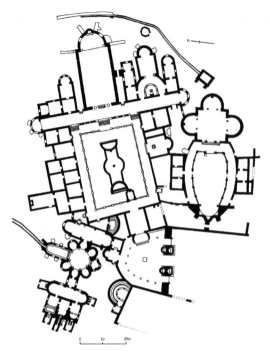

7. Piazza Armerina, *villa*, plan.

presenting this dichotomy, setting the furtive, and none too successful, love affairs with which he struggled in Rome, against an ideal pastoral world where he lived in simplicity with his devout and devoted mistress, now his wife.[70]

This rhetoric of the countryside provided an atmosphere in which *villa* life was not necessarily a luxurious disgrace as it had been for Lucullus. Instead, as the empire progressed, the championing of country life offered a positive rhetoric to an increasingly disempowered elite whose political role was taken over by the imperial household and eventually by paid bureaucrats. In imperial discourse, country pursuits come to the fore – hunting, for instance, became a popular elite sport only in the early Principate.[71] The physical evidence points to much higher investment in the *villa*, which becomes larger with respect to both land and buildings. The eventual result of this trend can be seen in the fourth-century Piazza Armerina *villa* in Sicily (Figure 7), where elaborate and extensive architectural arrangements are married with the evidence of two famous hunt scene mosaics.[72]

Between the country and the city a clean division was drawn, both *loci* becoming the setting for distinct types of behaviour – Rome was the place for public, socio-political duty, and the countryside was the seat of private leisure and repose. The connection of each *locus* with the appropriate *ethos* was already such a commonplace in the Republic that Cicero employed it in his defence of Publius Sulla. Protesting his client's innocence against a charge of electoral malpractice, Cicero maintains that Sulla was in Naples at the time and thus certainly devoid of blame. Naples is seen here as the country, a place of relaxation and not of conspiracy, the *locus* of which is the city of Rome.[73] Such defence would seem appropriate enough in a society that framed itself within these rhetorical *topoi*. The *villa* is the *locus* of precisely opposite activities, *otium* as opposed to the *negotium* of city life. The *villa* was free from the onus of having to define *Romanitas* – it was not used to create pasts or ensure futures but to facilitate an indulgent present. A man's *villa* might be the one place where he could temporarily escape the binds of his Romanness and be himself. Being less encumbered by convention, *villa*s seem to have been perceived as places that afforded the freedom to indulge in individual whims, whether artistic, sexual, or whatever. Vitruvius himself applied these distinctions of place to his assessment of domestic architecture through his definition of the *domus* and the *villa*, their opposing roles most succinctly expressed in the reversal of *atrium* and peristyle in the *villa*.[74]

With such tidy definitions, Vitruvius neatly encapsulated the pastoral view of the countryside promoted in other Augustan authors. However, such idyllic accounts avoided the extent to which the elite's presence in the countryside affected their city life. At the most fundamental level, the senator maintained his monetary eligibility for his rank with the proceeds from his country estates.[75] As much as the elite hid their dependence on nature by consuming their wealth in inverting it, their social success could be ruined by agricultural disaster. The division between *domus* and *villa* was, at this most basic level, artificial – *domus* depended on *villa*. It is, presumably, as insurance against this potential disorder that Vitruvius lays down his precise definitions of *villa* and *domus*, insisting on a division that supports the *ethos* and *locus* connection and maintaining a safe distance between the rural and the urban. In doing so, such rhetoric tried to put a stop to the elite's attempts to transfer both nature to the city and social life to the country, endeavours to reconcile conflicting tensions in their political existence.

During the late Republic, as these activities brought them under increasing attack, the elite began to look for a solution whereby they could safely combine both urban and rural elements. The suburban *horti* that grew up to ring ancient Rome were that solution. The *suburbium* was a liminal place subject to neither city, country or the restraints applicable to either and, as such, afforded an opportunity to escape censure.[76] The Scipio family owned *horti* as early as the mid second century. However, the spiralling trend for extensive pleasure parks was, unsurprisingly, said to have been started by Lucullus. Eventually the *horti* attracted the interest of the emperors who were equally sensitive to social attitudes towards display. As the Principate wore on, more and more senators left their *horti* to their emperors, Maecenas signing his over to Augustus, until the city became ringed by imperial gardens, a formidable presence that nevertheless defied categorisation.[77] It would seem that the collection of *horti* by successive emperors represents a concerted effort on their part to control this dangerously free architectural type. The extent of the luxury of such sites is made clear by the excavations of the Horti Lamiani, which yielded a vast selection of gold leaf and gems, once studded in the furniture and walls.[78]

PUBLIC AND PRIVATE

In attempting to find an appropriate place for display in the town house, Vitruvius located it in the public parts of the house in direct opposition to the private *villa locus* of the luxuries of Lucullus. His emphasis on the open, public nature of the house reflected the publicness of both the House of Augustus and the *domus* of Caesar before him.[79] In all these cases, the open nature of the house reflected the owner's participation in public life and the fulfilment of his socio-political obligations. The good senator would inevitably keep an open house.

Or would he? It is telling to compare the Vitruvian attitude with that of the later senator Fronto, as expressed in a letter dated between 157 and 161 A.D.

> For each of us private men, if the door keeper did not guard the doors and was not wholly alert, excluding from entrance those not invited, but allowing the inhabitants to walk outside freely whenever they want, then he would not be guarding the house properly. And whereas public colonnades, groves, altars, *gymnasia* and baths are open freely to all, private ones are barred with iron and doorkeepers.
>
> Fronto *Ep. Graec.* 5.1

This passage demonstrates a radically different approach to the *domus*. Is it at all possible to reconcile the resulting dichotomy? Is it perhaps merely the result of the cultural changes that overtook Rome as the empire wore on? By Fronto's time, the Senate was largely absolved of its political responsibilities, whilst the realities of imperial power were all too apparent. However, Pliny the Younger gives us evidence that the rhetoric of the open house did survive into the second century A.D. Delivering a panegyric to the emperor Trajan in 100 A.D., he praises the emperor for fostering a social climate in which people are free to

> frequent safe and open homes.
>   Pliny *Pan.* 62.7

So how can these attitudes be reconciled? Certainly ancient sources speak of a custom of keeping *domus* doors open, but nowhere is there mention of indiscriminate admission[80]: at the most, the conception of the openness of the house applies to social rituals, such as the *salutatio*, and these are always constrained by their adherence to a certain time of the day, to a certain predetermined and regular audience, and to the circumscribed customary ritual. The practise of unrestricted access only ever appears to apply to the grounds of *horti*, and these parks are very rarely equated with an official, residential *domus*. Similarly, Plutarch uses the rhetoric of open, public living to demonstrate Cicero's dedication to the state, assuring us that

> [h]is house did not have a doorkeeper.
>   Plut. *Cicero.* 36.3

The element of praise implicit in the text must imply that this was not the usual state of affairs in the homes of the elite (any more, of course, than we should believe it was true in the case of Cicero).

In direct opposition to these accounts of the open and inviting houses of Rome, other texts attest the employment of slave doorkeepers and heavy locks. This theme was particularly popular amongst the love elegists who often found themselves separated from their mistresses by such unresponsive devices. The plea of the forlorn lover to the stubborn door or even the lament of the door itself, bemoaning its unrelenting task, are regularly found in this genre; several of the examples of which date precisely to the Augustan Principate.[81]

To try to find a resolution to these apparently incompatible presentations of the public and private nature of the Roman house, we might turn again to the panegyric delivered to Trajan by Pliny. The author deliberately contrasts the ease of access encountered in a visit to Trajan in the imperial palace with the obstacles put up by his adoptive father's predecessor Domitian to ensure his own privacy.[82] Here, the rhetoric becomes overtly moralistic, equating openness with the good emperor and secrecy with the deposed tyrant.

To be private is here interpreted as an unwillingness to participate and even a secret desire to destroy the norms of participation and the very fabric of society. The inability to see behind closed doors caused fear and suspicion, an implication that the houseowner had something to hide. Hence the concealed became the *locus* of revolution and dissent, with both the traitor Manlius in 385 B.C. and the conspirator Catiline in 63 B.C. presented as nurturing rebellion in secret meetings behind closed doors.[83] Unbeknown to the public, Catiline's house has become a military camp headquarters.[84] This tradition of paranoia survived unperturbed through to the Principate. Tacitus portrays the original assassination plot against Nero by Piso and accomplices in the failed revolt of 65 A.D. as aiming to do the deed at Piso's *villa* at Baiae. Piso however refused, insisting that the killing take place in a public space in Rome to reflect the public feeling towards the emperor. In this plan, the assassination becomes a deed for the public good and on the public's behalf instead of a private act of rebellion that would bring guilt on Piso and his *villa*.[85]

In the face of this tradition, it is easy to see why Vitruvius would have emphasised a rhetoric that condoned the openness of senatorial housing in order to demystify the homes and their owners and lay both open to scrutiny. To be public was to participate fully in political and social life, implying a willingness to serve the state. But even here a caveat would apply – to be too public, in the context of building to encroach too much on the public sphere, could be construed as arrogance and a deliberate attempt to tip the equilibrium of senatorial or imperial power in one's own favour. We might recall the activities of Pompey who

> [a]fter that, it is true, when he was erecting the famous and beautiful theatre that bears his name, he built close by it, like a small boat tugged behind a ship, a more splendid house than the one he had had before.
>
> Plut. *Pomp.* 4

In inventing a new rhetorical tradition of order in domestic architecture, Vitruvius had to wrestle with conflicts at the heart of the house: between *luxuria* and *austeritas*, public and private, city and country. His architectural prescriptions aimed to bury these conflicts. The *atrium* houses, which appear to reflect Vitruvian descriptions, had found a way to deal with these tensions. The tensions are still there, and we should expect to find them played out in the archaeological evidence. A successful house would explore them within carefully circumscribed limits.

The literary texts of the late Republic and early Principate were preoccupied by the turmoil of socio-political life. That houses figure prominently in that literature is a sure sign, in itself, of their important role in Roman society. The practical role of the house as a centre for all aspects of domestic and public life ensured its importance. However, it also played an ideological role. The house was a crucial medium through which the family could define their *Romanitas*. The Roman houseowner showed who he was through the rhetorical conventions he obeyed in the construction of his house and by the ritual demands that determined his use of space. The *domus*, as the very centre of Roman life and thought, had to deal with and resolve all the tensions of being Roman on a daily basis. In Chapter 2, we will investigate how the ideologies of Romanness explored in *domus* might affect the daily lives and careers of the elite families who lived in them.

2

The House and the Construction of Memory

W e have seen how the perceived link between an individual's environment (*locus*) and behaviour (*ethos*) led to the possibility that a *domus* could help shape the *Romanitas* of those who lived in it. The house was carefully constructed to give the impression of conforming to ideas about what constituted Romanness. In this chapter, we must widen the discussion to see how the house aided interaction between an individual and the outside world. Vitruvius demonstrates that the elite house was seen as a powerful tool in building an impression of political authority through conspicuous display. Even before the *De Architectura* was published, a whole barrage of moralistic rhetoric already existed to counteract the excessive embellishment and exploitation of domestic architecture. Our next task is to consider why the texts place such emphasis on the house and react to it with such suspicion. Exactly how great was the impact of the *domus* on the public socio-political life of Rome? Why was domestic luxury so dangerous?

To answer these questions, we must investigate the connection, in the Roman imagination, between the house, its owners, and their public personae. We must also consider the position of domestic architecture within the cityscape of Rome. In doing so, we are fortunate to have literary access to an ancient case study of this phenomenon – the saga of Cicero's house on the Palatine.

The biography of Cicero, as it has been reconstructed in modern times, tells us that he was born in Arpinum in 106 B.C. but was educated in Rome.[1] As a result of this education, he was then able to take his place in Roman society by virtue of his legal and rhetorical abilities, gaining a quaestorship in 75 B.C. His subsequent political success was no mean achievement; the

Republic is not noted as a political system especially conducive to social mobility, particularly so at the time of Cicero's ascension when the senatorial tensions that would eventually explode into the civil wars were already mounting.

If Cicero was to be accepted, then it was of paramount importance that he was seen as integrating perfectly with the senatorial elite both in his politics and his behaviour. In the Senate, he acted in total opposition to the populist reformism espoused by another outsider, Marius (coincidentally also from Arpinum), his career strategy being strictly in accordance with the constitution. He both presented himself and was presented as a staunch *optimate* who defended the oligarchic Republic with a stubbornness that would eventually lead to his proscription and his subsequent execution. After his exposure of the Catilinarian conspiracy in 63 B.C. he even became *pater patriae*, affirming his acceptance at the heart of Roman society, where not even birth could have delivered him.[2]

THE POLITICAL HOUSE

Cicero's activities in the housing market are so illuminating because, as a *novus homo*, Cicero is self-conscious about every move he makes as he follows the suit of Roman society. In doing so, he makes explicit the motives of house building that other senators keep implicit. Politically advantageous house building appears to have entailed the acquisition of a plot in a highly conspicuous area through which a man could present himself conforming to the rhetoric of *Romanitas*. Cicero, according to Plutarch, first lived in an unspecified house in Rome that belonged to his father. After his eventful consulship in 63 B.C. and in keeping with his elevated political profile, he indebted himself to Publius Sulla in order to buy a prestigious house on the Palatine, an elite stronghold at the heart of Rome.[3] The house had once belonged to M. Livius Drusus, a Senate reformer who had brought his political career right into the *domus* when he was stabbed there by an unknown assassin who concealed himself in the crowd of Drusus's supporters.[4] The move was also an important tactic in assuring a successful future. Fortunately, Cicero passed on his reasonings on the political advantages of home owning to his son in the *De Officiis*. This treatise is concerned with the correct way to seek and hold office and hence to establish a place in Roman society and a significant part is dedicated to the nuances of domestic architecture.[5]

> For a man's dignity can be augmented by his house but can not be sought totally from the house.
>
> Cicero. *De Off.* 39.139

Unfortunately, Cicero's dignity was not to be augmented for very long. The tale of the orator's downfall in 58 B.C. is well documented both by himself and historians and biographers, ancient and modern.[6] We are told that it was brought about by Clodius, a *tribunus plebis* and ally of Julius Caesar who, along with his fellow triumvirs, Pompey and Crassus, was making a concerted effort to exceed the bonds of republican office. Political history finds many reasons why Clodius instantly turned his might against Cicero, who was both a political nuisance for Caesar and a personal enemy of Clodius himself. He forced Cicero into exile on the grounds that he had illegally executed the Catilinarian conspirators five years earlier, ingeniously turning the *pater patriae*'s height of glory into the depths of disgrace.

As Cicero fled to Macedonia, his political career seemed over. In Rome the physical trophy of his previous success, his *domus*, was pulled down by Clodius who built over the razed site a shrine pointedly dedicated to Libertas and an extension of his own home. This move was perceived as an act of utter elimination of Cicero and all he stood for. Cicero himself recognised the humiliation involved. After all, he perceived that his house was

> in sight of almost the whole city.
> Cicero *De Dom.* 37.100

Everyone would look to the Palatine and immediately realise that Cicero had been erased from the conceptual and political map of Rome.

Cicero's distress over the matter supersedes the economic or sentimental loss of his *domus*. On return from exile in August 57 B.C., his priority was to win back the site and rebuild his house because only then

> I will clearly see and perceive that I am reinstated.
> Cicero *De Dom.* 37.100[7]

Unfortunately for Cicero, this was not an easily accomplished goal, involving long negotiation with both the Senate and the *pontifices*. In modern times, we would expect the return of the property to be a mere formality; after all, Cicero had been officially recalled by unanimous vote. The deliberation over the restitution of the site demonstrates just how powerful a role architecture played in republican Rome. For Cicero, his own presence in contemporary Rome was worthless compared with the lasting defeat and humiliation that would ensue if the site of his home remained beneath Clodius's temple. He eventually won back his home, but it was ever after susceptible to attack, not only by Clodius but later, allegedly, Mark Antony.[8]

Cicero's personal situation and his shortcomings as a successful Roman builder have been dealt with elsewhere.[9] Here it is enough to use the saga of his house as an *exemplum* of how the Roman *domus* acted as an intermediary between the politician and his public. The Roman population clearly organised their responses to the orator with reference to his house, whether malicious or flattering. Not only do we find that the use of the house reflects the owner but that the very presence of the house affirms its occupant's existence on the political scene. The *domus* was where the senator should be, where both his roles as private *paterfamilias* and public magistrate were reconciled. It created his *locus* in both society and the empire. In his account of the sack of Rome by the Gauls in 390 B.C., Livy has the Senate return to their family *atria* to await death with their homes and city, each in the centre of his world.[10] This story is significant in showing us just how closely intertwined the public and personal lives of Roman senators were. Although these old men, who demonstrate their communal solidarity by fleeing en masse to the Capitol, have made a conscious effort to separate themselves from the rest of the community, they have not forsaken their public roles. Each senator awaits his fate dressed in his robes of civic office, serving Rome to the end.

Another example of the close link perceived between house and self in ancient Rome might be found in the assassination of Julius Caesar. Caesar's wife interpreted a warning of her husband's impending murder from a dream in which the honorific gable fell off the façade of their home.[11] Caesar's house was not just a passive medium through which responses to him were framed; it was an active tool in promoting himself and his family to the outside world. Its physical collapse was the forerunner of the obliteration of Caesar himself.

One of Cicero's concerns as a homeowner was that, if the house was to be the mediator between the individual and the community, then it had better be as visible as possible. Velleius Paterculus describes Drusus commanding his architect to maximise the visibility of his home and hence his own public profile.[12] The more exposed the house, the more visible and, therefore, the more dignified the occupants might become. The immediate context of the *domus* must also convey the right impression. The Palatine was an area renowned for its *Romanitas* and political tradition, home to contemporary high-ranking magistrates and popular heroes of the past. Amongst Cicero's contemporaries, Mark Antony, Caecilius Metellus Celer (consul in 60 B.C.), Lutatius Catulus (consul in 78. B.C.), the *triumvir* Crassus, and the orator Hortensius all had Palatine addresses. Recent archaeological investigations have confirmed its dense occupation of substantial homes.[13] Plutarch credits both Gaius Marius and Gaius Gracchus with having lived around the Forum, a reflection of their *popularis* politics.[14] Suetonius takes this further by locating the young Julius Caesar in the Subura, the slum district of Rome.[15] The homeowner might have expected the associations of a place to affect the popular perception of his own *ethos*. He himself became linked with the *memoria* of the prestigious *locus*, which he had made his home.

Such ambitious interest in self promotion through the acquisition of real estate, however, had its limits. Public opinion forced Poplicola, a man who earned great fame for his defence of the Republic, to demolish his own home in 509 B.C.[16] Although he was well respected for his achievements, the construction of his house on the highest part of the Velian Hill was seen as overambition, a move towards tyranny. Publius was careful to rebuild his *domus* on a more equalising level.

It is telling to note that writers were often disingenuous on the motivation of public display. Plutarch talks of Gaius Gracchus buying a house on the edge of the Forum so as to be more democratic, overlooking the fact that the Forum afforded the most visible locations in the whole of the city. The same biographer blithely understates Cicero's move to the Palatine as merely a generous gesture to spare his supporters a walk.[17] Careful reading is needed here to understand the implications of the site that Cicero himself does not shy from stating. Such refusals to acknowledge ulterior motives in house buying throughout ancient literature are both signs of awareness of the uncertainty of political life and the extensive effect that rhetoric was perceived as playing upon political success.

Cicero himself is also sensitive to these difficulties and the potential danger of the *domus*. In defending the young Caelius from an assortment of political and moral charges, Cicero explains the youth's relocation to the Palatine as a move made simply to be nearer the esteemed company of Crassus and himself – a fairly pallid defence but one obviously deemed necessary in order to allay any accusations that may arise from such a politically suggestive move.[18]

THE VIEW: AN APPEARANCE OF PUBLICITY

The house, then, served a double role as a medium through which the family constructed its place in Rome and the Roman populace experienced the family within. Elite homeowners wanted their house to be as visually accessible as possible. The biggest house was a waste of investment if it was tucked away where the vast majority of the populace would never clap eyes on it. The view was one of the most important aspect of the *domus*. It is clear from legal arguments that the view was seen as part of the house, a crucial medium through which insider and outsider could communicate.[19] The view was a dual carriageway of sightlines along which the viewer's eye could travel in either direction to or from the house. The view into the house implied the openness of the *domus* to the public. It implied the euergetic outlook of a patron who had nothing to hide. The viewer could look straight through the building, enjoying a visual access that he might not hope to gain in physical terms.

The view was hardly a coincidental feature in elite houses; it was considered a necessity because it carried great opportunities in enhancing visibility and hence presence for little cost and achieved aspirations without the need to materialise them. The owner of a typical Vitruvian *domus*, standing in his *atrium* was presented with the view of his domain – the *tablinum*, the peristyle, and often the landscape beyond. The owner saw his realm extending as far as his vision across the Forum Romanum. The view thus provided an aspirative fantasy of power.

According to Cicero, a Lucius Fufius, having bought a house with a guarantee as to its light,

> immediately negotiated with Bucculeius because, if any little part of his view was blocked, even though it might be far away, he considered his light was changed.
>
> Cicero De Or. 1.39.179

The restriction of his view meant for Lucius the shrinking of his fantasy of authority, which was clearly as important to defend as the physical elements of his *domus*. In a city where power largely rested on appearances and visibility, there was a fine line between the real and the illusory, and both were equally worth fostering.

Elsewhere Cicero presents us with a friend who has been more ambitious, creating a direct view from his house to the theatre, a very deliberate projection of a private place onto a public building.[20] The owner extends not only his phantom authority over the public monument but also the fantasy world enacted on the stage, further confusing reality and illusion. The viewer looks from the real status symbol of the *domus* through the real view (implying an illusory extension of the house) into the imaginary world of the theatre played out on the real public stage. Reality and illusion become inextricably mixed.[21] The viewer can no longer absolutely separate the different degrees of truth in his experience and is left with an overall impression of the *domus* and its owner, which transcends these categories.

The importance of the view to the senatorial homeowner is demonstrated by a *controversia* of Seneca. A rich man has burnt down his neighbour's tree because it blocked his view, accidentally gutting the poorer man's house in the process. The victim retorts:

> A view is opened up with fire. 'It blocked the view'. What? Do not bands of slaves block our way as we walk along? Do not walls built up to immense height impede our light?
>
> Seneca Cont. 5.5

The view here is just another natural thing to be abused by the rich in pursuit of maximizing the impact of their lavish homes. Seneca can only disapprove as the elite assume yet another tool with which to create fantastic impressions of their own authority.[22]

MEMORIA AND IDENTITY

Of course, the question has to be asked: if there was such a struggle for a Roman both to make visible his own *domus* and to regulate the visibility of those of others, what was there actually to see? The *domus* of ancient literature does appear to have put on a good show. The *atria* with their collections of portrait busts and spoils were museums of the family's history and current status. Pompey displayed ship-prows, captured in the campaigns against the pirates, in his *atrium*.[23] Plutarch's account of the murder of Gaius Gracchus has him struck down by spoils taken from the *atrium* of Fulvius.[24] Overlooking everything were the ancestor busts themselves, a visible link to the family's past.[25] Taken together, these displays, both permanent and impermanent, acted as a lesson to both the inhabitants and the visiting public. The achievements of his ancestors fired the current *paterfamilias* to sustain the family's reputation. They reminded the visitors of the pedigree of their host. The ability to place an individual within a wider family group went a long way towards establishing his identity.

Each new generation was supposed to benefit from and add to the collection of souvenirs in the *atrium*. Cicero frames attacks on Sallust and then Brutus, by accusing them of abandoning and selling their ancestral homes.[26] Brutus now has no place to display the busts of his distinguished ancestors. Such actions translate as reckless arrogance and a deliberate refusal to operate within the usual elite norms of behaviour. The *domus* was constantly under pressure to measure up to public life, and insofar as it reflected the families' public achievements, it instantly occasioned the rhetorical defences and assaults that attempted to resolve the ensuing tension between public and private.

The outward display of this compulsion was the material or symbolic embellishment of the façade to promote the family's fortune in the public arena; the outward opening doors of Poplicola, the gable on Caesar's home, and the crown and laurels on the doorposts of the House of Augustus were all special honours accorded by the people for special distinction.[27] Such gestures had to be carefully regulated; the receptors of such honours are by far the exception rather than the rule. Again, the entrance was the place to record not only political success but also family events. All these decorations, both inside and outside the house, allowed it to become an advertisement for its past achievements, its current status, and its future potential. They mediated between an individual and the city by providing the individual with a family identity demonstrably grounded in tradition. Most importantly for the Roman psyche, it provided the individual with a visible past.

MEMORIA AND DAMNATIO MEMORIAE

In a literate world, it is difficult to appreciate how, in a generally nonliterate society, the visual is employed to create communications and present ideas. In the ancient world, the visual carried many of the burdens that we are more accustomed to ascribing to words, and Cicero himself confessed that people reacted far better to what they saw than what they heard.[28] It seems that the visual was a significant basis of thought, a hypothesis reinforced by the standard technique of memory, which advocated a memory based on images, not words. This memory technique, advocated explicitly by Quintilian, implies that the Romans were accustomed to receiving messages from the art and architecture around them.[29] They expected to see images as depositories for *memoriae*, and they were aware that the architecture around them could induce certain feelings or recollections.[30]

A Roman's house provided a permanent visibility in the Roman political landscape, a mnemonic for his public significance – his house allowed him a base from which both to see and to be seen. It provided him with a presence in Rome that allowed him to participate in the rhetoric of *Romanitas* and so to compete within Roman society. Even when away from Rome, the house maintained his profile and the memory of his achievements.

The mechanics by which the visual media managed to combine both presence and *memoria* is perhaps best explained by reference to sculpture. Belting's description of how saint images worked in the early church show surprisingly close connections with the funerary busts of republican senators in their ability to combine presence and *memoria*.[31] The busts were the presence of the deceased, standing in the *atrium*, that provided the narrative *memoria* of the past through its decoration with symbols of familial achievement.[32] These two strands of recognition were brought together in the particular ritual of the funeral procession where these busts were paraded through the streets.

The potency of images in preserving an individual's presence and creating a *memoria* of that individual was a valuable tool in the competition to promote one's *Romanitas* and so to invite social and political success. As patrons, the elite were able to take advantage of these properties of the visual by commissioning art to specific instructions. The right elements had to be included because the creation of the work involved building a *memoria* for future generations. The huge numbers of veristic republican portraits, all apparently conforming to the same rubric within their own types, are evidence of how an elite, always competing with itself within the correct limits of display, attempted to mould its own remembrance for posterity.

The *domus* offered every family an opportunity to create an individual *memoria* that would outshine those of their rivals. This would account for the prolific building of *domus*, which Strabo, as a Greek outsider, found so peculiar to Rome. Writing under Augustus, Strabo composed a *Geography*, which visited key cities of the empire and made brief comment on their distinguishing features. His account of Rome places a great deal of emphasis on domestic building that

> go[es] on unceasingly in consequence of the collapses, fires and repeated sales (these last, too, go on unceasingly): and, indeed, the sales are intentional collapses, as it were, since the purchasers keep tearing down the houses and building new ones, one after another, to suit their wishes.
>
> Strabo *Geog.* 5.3.7

Strabo's observation reminds us again of the Roman preference for presentation over reality. Roman rhetoric insisted on the old family home, kept within the same family for generations. However, it would seem that families were constantly on the move, looking for bigger and better property discarding old *memoriae* for new. At the same time, newcomers did not have ancestors and *memoriae* to accommodate. Cicero simply took over the *domus* and memories of Drusus, adopting his reputation as his own. New homeowners might inherit physical relics of the glory of past inhabitants along with the house shell itself. So, as much as we are led to believe that Romans were slaves to tradition, it is important to note that it is often invented tradition, manipulated in order to serve the needs of the present generation.

DAMNATIO MEMORIAE

It was inevitable, given the competitive climate of Rome, that as the members of the elite were working to secure their own *memoria*, they were all too aware of their rivals' efforts in the same direction. The close association between a man and his house meant that attacking an enemy through his *domus* was an effective weapon. It therefore became a frequent and effective procedure and certainly one with which Cicero was familiar. In 62 B.C., Q. Metellus Celer, a *praetor* during Cicero's consulate in the previous year, wrote to him complaining that he would have hoped that Cicero could have prevented an attack on his brother's property caused by some offence his office as tribune had entailed.[33]

As senators lost favour, they faced losing their houses. Writing to his brother, Cicero remarks that one such senator, Appius, is in such a bad political position that his house is under immediate threat of attack.[34] Nor is Cicero himself above such practices; he even demonstrates how to set up a simple verbal attack on a house as part of his treatise on oratory.[35] In the *De Haruspicem Responsis*, he goes as far as to accuse Clodius of precisely that which he himself is accused of, namely having within his home a consecrated site.[36] The devices of rhetoric are free to all, and there is no reason why a man should be exempt from attack with a particular *topos* just because he is employing the same line against another.

The reason why such attacks were so frequent and, often, so extreme must be connected with the role of the house as a memory bank. The destruction of the house entailed the obliteration of the victim's physical presence but also eliminated the means by which he might be remembered. The point of reference that confirmed his existence and identity was destroyed. The ashes and rubble of the site would always link him with destruction and deviance since it only preserved the *memoria* of the penalty; this device, the *damnatio memoriae*, was particularly effective in ensuring eternal disgrace.

Damnatio, as effected through architecture, had been prevalent for many years before the empire and in equally effective measure, if not to such a lavish extent. Cicero lists a number of ancient criminals whose memory had been punished in such a way. In many of his examples, the site was deliberately never rebuilt but left barren as a permanent reminder of the culprit's disgrace. A barren site triggered memories of a name, but the framework for constructing memories of the man behind the name were missing. The only worth of the name became its association with an empty plot. Maelius was accused of treason in 438 B.C., his house was razed, and the ground was left empty, known as the Plain of Maelius.[37] The punishment was particularly severe – whereas other great names of the past had their houses recycled for the glory of new names, Maelius's name would survive into future generations in association with an empty plot and the accompanying notions of deviance. On the Carinae, the house of Spurius Cassius who was condemned for treason in 485 B.C. had a temple of Tellus built over it – the city reclaimed its land from the individual.[38]

The threat of *damnatio* was a strong deterrent in a society obsessed with the opinions of future generations. To Roman logic, the complete obliteration of statues and buildings would be the less objectionable since the disgrace would exist only amongst the contemporary generation. To be subsequently forgotten might seem more appealing than lingering in perpetuity as an enemy of the state. The Roman instinct was to look backwards, not forwards, for inspiration. Contemporary Romans were in the constant shadow of their ancestors, from whom they took *exempla* and learned mistakes. As Cato the Elder had been constructed as the archetypal Roman in the days of Cicero, so the Younger Cato might hope to be similarly remembered by his descendants as they tried to fit the immediate past into the distant mythical constructs.[39] Nor would their houses be left behind. In Cicero's own corpus of letters, a correspondent named Patro appears anxious to purchase the home of Epicurus, his hero, in order to preserve the philosopher's memory. Cicero comments that to make light of Patro's plea for the house would be to mock his Epicurean principles, presumably by making light of the need for each culture to nurture its own *memoriae*. Cicero clearly understands the motive for preserving the house if not the value of the *memoria* attached to it.[40]

SPREADING PRESENCE

A *domus* in the centre of Rome, then, earned a crucial presence for the ambitious Roman elite. However, it is only an effective presence when it is being viewed. The biggest drawback of the house was that it was a static monument, it could not travel around Rome, much less beyond, with its owner. One solution to this problem might be found in the multiple acquisition of property, in the city, in the area *sub urbe*, and in the countryside of Italy.

Martial talks of an acquaintance of his who is green with envy of the epigrammist because he has been able to purchase a house *sub urbe*.[41] To

Charinus the visible sign of Martial's success is more enviable than his literary acclaim. Martial can be construed as successful because he is no longer invisible, the condition of the weakest. By establishing a dual visibility, both in the heart of and on the edge of the city, looking over the country, he is on his way to the ultimate goal of visual omnipresence, signifier of universal power. The importance of the *horti* in signifying presence both to those inside and approaching Rome is demonstrated by the high tower in the Horti of Maecenas from which Nero watched the Great Fire of 64 A.D.[42] Unfortunately, only the so-called auditorium of Maecenas survives on the site today. However, its remains testify to the extent of the park. The structure is a *nymphaeum* in the form of a hemicycle with floor mosaic and painted walls. The walls were also interspersed with regular niches decorated with landscape paintings, recalling the allure of the countryside.[43] Of the families whose *domus* we met earlier, most are also presented as having *horti*. Cicero himself tried to buy the *horti* of Drusus just as he had taken over the Drusus site on the Palatine.[44] Caesar had two *horti*, one at the Colline Gate and one at the first milestone, so he might be present at every stage of the journey to and from Rome.[45] These residences are sometimes referred to simply as pleasure gardens, but their social importance is intimated by Pompey's *horti*. His house on the Carinae had *horti* as did the *domus* he built on the Campus Martius to accompany his theatre. This practise implies the interchangeability of the function of *domus* and *horti*, the one being a *horti* where there should be a *domus*, the second a *domus* where there should be *horti*.[46] Both were of equal political importance.

This apparent intertwining of *domus* and *horti* might help to further understand the relationship between *domus* and *villa*. Cicero seems to have constructed a map of Italy from his own *villas* and those of his friends. His letters are headed with addresses that range from Arpinum, his home town, as far as Brundisium. Historically, this common practice of widespread modest investment is economically explicable.[47] Land holdings were scattered around the country to minimise the danger of localised adversities and to get around the intense competition for land that inevitably arose among the elite in a pre-industrial state.

An economic solution to land-ownership, however, does not satisfy the emphasis on widespread *villa* building on that land. The extent to which comfort and luxury were considered essential on such sites can be demonstrated by the Villa of Fannius Synistor at Boscoreale, not far from Pompeii (Figure 8). This *villa* is predominantly a working farm; its forepart, including room 24, is dedicated to agricultural production. The living area of the *villa* is rather small; nevertheless, it is lavishly painted with some of the most

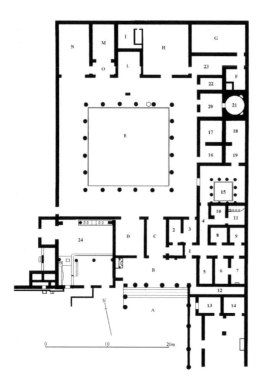

8. Boscoreale, Villa of Fannius Synistor, plan.

famous wall paintings excavated in Campania (Figure 9). A *villa* can be justifiable only if it is understood that it implies the presence of the master; a presence that, of course, is perpetuated by the building even if the master never visits.

Absence from Rome necessarily implies presence elsewhere. Holidaying Romans built up valuable client bases in the areas surrounding their villas, thus politicising and making public an architecture associated with private *otium*. Sulla allegedly decorated his *villa* at Tusculum with pictures of his martial exploits.[48] The decoration of several Campanian *villa*s make reference to the public lives of their owners. The *atrium* of the Villa at Oplontis is painted to resemble a *domus atrium*, complete with *clipeatae imagines* (Figure 10). The *atrium* of the Villa of the Mysteries was once decorated with a frieze showing weapons, giving an impression of the martial prowess exhibited by spoils and weapons in the homes of the Roman aristocracy. The potential political advantage that might be gained in exploiting the *villa* in this way might explain why Vitruvius tried so hard to distinguish between *villa* and *domus*.

On a social level, too, the *villa* was not practically so removed from city life as Vitruvius made out. It is ironic, though indicative of the versatility of rhetoric, that the man who protested the innocence of Publius Sulla on

9. Boscoreale, Villa of Fannius Synistor, bedroom m. Photo: Metropolitan Museum of Art, Rogers Fund, 1903 (03.14.13).

10. Oplontis, *villa*, *atrium*, wall painting. Photo: SJH.

the grounds of his presence in Naples should reveal this most clearly. In the senatorial recess, so many senators visited their *villa*s that Cicero was able to write

> [W]e occupy Cumae as if it were a little Rome.
> Cicero *Ad Att.* 5.2.2

The *villa* itself could be affected by the intrusion of socio-political obligations as Cicero's presentation of his *villa* at Formiae as a public hotspot in the spring of 59 B.C. demonstrates:

> I own a *basilica*, not a *villa*, crowded with the people of Formiae.
> Cicero *Ad Att.* 2.14

During the Civil War in particular, as chaos reigned in Rome, Cicero's involvement is played out in a string of *villa*s across Italy, including a meeting with Caesar in a *villa* at Arpinum.[49] Conversely, at a time of political inactivity, his *domus* becomes a private retreat:

> My house, which is inferior to none of my *villa*s, is more restful than the most deserted place in the world. And so not even my work in which I am engaged without interruption, is disturbed.
> Cicero *Ad Fam.* 6.18.5

These comments would seem to suggest that all Cicero's properties, both *domus* and *villa*, fulfil a joint, politicised function of which Vitruvian rhetoric allows no expression.

Cicero's letters show the importance of widespread *villa* owning for other than economic reasons. His conception of Italy seems to come almost entirely from the safety of his own or his friends' *villa*s. Every part of the country is viewed and interpreted through reference to the ruling elite of Rome. No part of Italy can be strange or disorienting to Cicero since he is always in sight of a point of reference with which to make sense of his surroundings.[50] As the *domus* works in the city, so the *villa* fulfils a similar role in the country, framing the outsider's impression of the owner and the owner's experience of the outside world.

Other domestic properties around Rome, in the suburbs and even further abroad, might all be part of promoting family presence. It is worth noting that Cicero's expulsion by Clodius entailed the confiscation of his *villa*s as well as the destruction of his *domus*. However, the harsher treatment of the *domus* demonstrates the perception of its higher political importance. Although extra properties could help advertise presence, they were not perceived to be the seat of the family. This was the job of the *domus*. Even if a man owned a hundred other homes, a central *domus* was required to act as the *locus* of power and the focus of all the other dwellings. As Martial suggests,

> whoever lives everywhere, Maximus, lives nowhere.
>
> Mart. *Epig.* 7.73.6

The family *domus* established the identity of its occupants and linked them with their past and with the city and its own history. Without that link, even the most prolific *villa* owner remained invisible or, worse, highly visible as an *exemplum* of un-Romanness, as Lucullus had become.

THE INTERACTION BETWEEN ROME AND HOME

The interest of Romans in the view from their houses stresses the dependence of the *domus* on its immediate urban context. But what precisely was the relationship between town and home? At its most basic, Rome could be understood as growing from the house. In many respects, the city was an overgrown house and the house, a microcosmic city. So, for instance, they are both built around a hearth and contained within divinely protected boundaries. Just as the *domus* represented the family's past and present, so the cityscape of Rome preserved the presence and *memoria* of the entire citizen body. Different buildings represented different moments in Rome's history, either specifically, as with triumphal arches that recalled particular campaigns or, more generally, as the Curia represented the Republic.[51] Through ritual, acted out within these buildings and the spaces around them, each structure was linked with its neighbours to create a *memoria* of Rome.[52] The public architecture of Rome implies the presence of a collective *memoria* of the long history of Rome's glory, appealing to and constructing the rhetoric of *Romanitas* through architectural type.

Despite these similarities, however, it was commonplace in Rome to see the house and the city as two separate, contrastable entities. Rhetoricians used the phrase *domus forisque* as a matter of course.[53] Their efforts to carefully categorise and separate the two glossed over the complex interaction between them. Despite the temptation to dismiss houses simply as microcosmic recreations of the city, it would be wrong to approach the city as an amplified, communal house. This supposition is overtly simplistic and does not allow for the complex interactions between the communal and the personal.[54] As much as the public crossed the boundary into the domestic, so too did domestic life seep into the city. Of course, on a basic level, this is inevitable, everybody has to leave their house. However, Romans went to some lengths to maintain their familial identity even in public. Wedding, funeral, and coming-of-age processions foistered the family onto civic space. Even slaves, the lowest members of the household, might be used to promote family presence through the wearing of a livery that proclaimed the house for which they worked.[55] The city was not simply the place for collective identity to be expressed, it was also a public stage for individual family competition. As Vitruvius himself states, like the *domus* the *forum* is venue for both public and private business.[56] The idea that the monuments and the landscape of the city recreated a collective history of Rome's past is countered by the fact that it was also a history of certain individuals' rise to greatness.

The use of public monuments as family donations and memorials is clear from the names of aqueducts, theatres, and basilicas, which all bear the name of their donors; the Circus Flaminius and Porticus Metelli preserve the names and *memoriae* of two of the Republic's greatest military heroes; the first was built by Gaius Flaminius when he was censor in 220 B.C. and the second, by Q. Caecilius Metellus Macedonius, victor of the Battle of Pydna in 168 B.C.[57] Such memorials were effective because they survived as landmarks for generations; monuments that had been built by one great member of the family lasted in perpetuity to reflect on succeeding generations. The result of these privately commissioned building programmes was that an elite individual was surrounded by his household even when he left his own *domus*. His family presence was there to help him along as he built his own political career, adding to the *memoria* his family enjoyed in the city.

The very richest families of republican Rome had not just commissioned one great monument and been content with that. Instead they spread their presence around the city with public buildings as much as they did with domestic structures. Leading families could trace their political presence in Rome through the topography of their dedications. The Scipios perhaps offer the fullest example of a family who stamped their presence in every part of Roman life. The house of P. Scipio Africanus, the hero who defeated Hannibal at Zama in 202 B.C., is located by Livy behind the Tabernae Veteres next to the Roman Forum on the Vicus Tuscus.[58] His family members were also intimately connected with the temple of Jupiter Optimus Maximus to the extent that, according to Valerius Maximus, the bust of Scipio Africanus was kept in the temple *cella*.[59] This temple had quite literally become their *atrium*, and the ancestors of the Scipios were placed in the public sphere. The ancestral tomb, too, was an important public commemoration of the Roman family. The tomb of the Scipios marked the spot of their final resting place, linking back to their home at the very heart of the city.[60] The tomb overlooked the crossroads of the Via Appia and Via Latina, two of the major roads leaving/entering Rome. The tomb façade apparently contained statues of Scipio Africanus, his brother Lucius, and the poet Ennius, all looking over and greeting visitors to the city. To the west, also beyond the *pomerium*, the Horti Scipionis overlooked the Campus Martius.[61]

Families like the Scipios made the city theirs during the Republic, but their efforts were eclipsed by Augustus's huge civic building programme. As he set about redefining the monuments of Rome, Augustus built himself into the city's landscape and so into the tradition of *Romanitas*. A double *memoria* came to resonate in the buildings of Rome – the first was a collective *memoria* of *Romanitas* and the second served to insert the founder or restorer of each building into that landscape of Roman tradition.

It was in serving as the focus for this *memoria*, stored in various monuments across the city, that the *domus* became so important. We have been continually drawn back to the public nature of the house and its prime role in socio-political life. It is perhaps not surprising that those rooms associated with public functions were described in civic terms. Pliny writes that the creation of public monuments directly necessitated a similar practice at home:

> Soon a *forum* was created in private houses and in the *atria*: clients thus began to honour their patrons.
>
> Pliny *N.H.* 34.9.17

Cicero had already demonstrated that the first task of the homeowner was to maximise the possibilities of the house becoming a "public" place:

> But my house, as you say, is a *forum*.
>
> Cicero *Ad Att.* 12.23

As the façade of the house shared personal achievements with the world outside, the interior of the house afforded an opportunity to bring back to a personal level that which the family shared with the rest of Rome. Within the *domus*, free from public censure, the elite could revel in their achievements and preempt achievements yet to come. Earlier in the chapter, we met with the practice of displaying spoils in the *atrium*. This tradition directly reflects the decoration of spoils that are reported to have graced the Rostra or the dedication of other spoils in the temples of Rome. The comparison is illuminating. It demonstrates how the house aped both the religious and political sphere.

The lack of division between the political and religious in ancient Rome is well attested. In architectural terms, we find that the Senate house was a *templum* – a consecrated area – and that the senators were equally happy to meet in temples themselves if the occasion demanded.[62] The house made acute these similarities of function by concentrating the form and effect of public display, placing itself at the centre of debates about the use of buildings. It becomes impossible and irrelevant to decide whether the *atria* mentioned earlier were predominantly *rostra* or temples because they capture the essence of both.

Cicero's own particular interest was in recreating elements of Greek city life. The most illuminating mentions of this are found in the ongoing saga that is Cicero's passion for art collecting as conveyed in the early letters to Atticus. In these he seems to be determined to recreate a Greek *gymnasium*. As well as insisting on the appropriate statues, he mentions all the associated architectural elements including a *xystus* and even a *palaestra*.[63] This insistence on recreating city architecture on a domestic scale reminds us of Vitruvian talk of the necessity of peristyles, libraries, and basilicas in elite homes to serve as the set for public interaction. The example of Cicero, however, demonstrates the corollary effect of such architecture in serving the homeowner's ego and aspirative fantasies.

For many, confining display to the home might well have seemed a safer option than airing familial aspirations and arrogance in public. However, the desire to privatise the public world was a delicate proposition. The increased focus on housing at the expense of public spending in the late Republic shows how there was a reorientation of interest amongst the elite in concentrating on individuals and their own increasingly large client bases.[64] At this point, there are clear attempts to undermine distinctions between public monuments and private house.[65] The story of M. Aemilius Scaurus conveys an initial moral resistance to the increased merger. He decided to transfer the imported marble columns and Greek sculpture with which he had decorated his theatre to one of his *villa*s. He received his comeuppance when, his enraged slaves burnt the house down.[66] By the end of the Republic, however, the situation had changed dramatically as the increased political emphasis on the individual allowed Pompey to make the link more explicit – building himself a new *domus* right under the shadow of his theatre, which held his image along with that of Venus.[67]

Vitruvius's own efforts to re-publicise such appropriated structures make this clear. To be under suspicion of coveting the public invited not only *invidia* since it excluded the majority from a share in the experience but also speculation on one's fidelity to the state. Perhaps because of this, authors make a clear distinction between public and private spending and display in an attempt to avoid incriminating themselves. Cicero himself, only too eager to discuss his own and his brother's home improvements in his private correspondence, is careful to subscribe to the standard ideology in public;

[t]he Roman people hate private luxury but prize public magnificence.

Cicero *Pro Mur.* 76[68]

Similarly, in prosecuting Verres, Cicero feigns ignorance of the art market in order to magnify his quarry's transgression.[69] Such a move may seem ludicrous to anyone familiar with Cicero's early letters, which talk of little else besides his own acquisition of sculpture, but modern ideas of consistency are irrelevant here. What is more pertinent is that, again, the ability to employ the appropriate rhetoric in the situation at hand has enabled Cicero both to further his own career and to cover his own back. The audience is assured that Cicero is wholly innocent of such crimes.

Private luxury was rhetorically explained as stemming from public magnificence. The elite, trying to balance their public and private splendour, inverted the public/private *topos*. Pliny the Elder parades a list of names of those who were the first to succumb to such vices in the past, the very organisation of the material conveying the driving competitive forces behind these acts. The use of marble in a domestic context, as demonstrated by Scaurus, was particularly associated with excessive luxury.

Republican and Vitruvian fear of the private and hidden was born out of the peculiar habit of forcing the private into the public and vice versa. If the *domus* had been an entirely private entity, there would have been little interest in how the elite deployed their wealth there. In Athens, where a clear distinction was made between political and familial life, there is little literary interest in the houses of public figures. Similarly, the archaeological remains show that the absence of political pressure on the house resulted in simple, uniform homes.[70]

It was inevitable in Rome, then, that political competition on such a personal level would be translated into domestic art and architecture and that considerable interest would be invested in the houses of others. There was always the fear that the impression conveyed by a neighbour's house might gain him an advantageous political position. In the intense competition of the late Republic, the house and the "luxury" therein became more and more prominent in literature as the elite resorted to any form of attack in the scramble for power.

In Rome, civic space was not easily distinguishable from domestic space. Just as the distinction between public and private space was blurred, so was the threshold between house and city. It is not simply a question of the *domus* being, to some extent, public, but of Rome also becoming private. A successful Roman identity rested on a similarly complex interplay of individual, familial, and communal qualities. In helping to construct those identities, the house brought together within it the public achievements of the entire *gens* but scattered out aspects of the family's life into Rome. The truly successful families of Rome were those who had this balance and whose houses were simply the centre of a nexus of communications that linked house to outside. Public and private were played out equally within and without the house.

The evidence presented in these first two chapters demonstrates just how important house and family were in mediating the life experiences of the individual with the Roman, urban environment. The house offered each individual a *locus*, a presence not only in space but also in time, recalling the achievements of his family through *memoria*. Within the complex layers of public and private we can begin to appreciate the complexity of Roman identities, which rested on this interplay and the powerful role that domestic architecture could play in articulating that identity. The *domus* was crucial in providing its owners with a past, present, and future, which, in turn, was elemental in ensuring their acceptance by the city. It was a window through which the inhabitants might experience Rome and through which Rome could view them. However, we can, at the same time, witness the means by which individuals could manipulate architecture so as to present a Roman appearance and artificially create a *memoria* that wrote them into Roman history. The *domus* had become one of the main instruments through which an elite family could proclaim themselves to be at the very heart of Rome. However, the creation of the Principate eclipsed this senatorial competition with the person of the emperor. The emperor surpassed the power of the Senate, and likewise his home, quite literally, cast elite *domus* into the shadow. In Rome today, the remains of the imperial palaces form the only extensive domestic sites in the whole city. They show us how the most powerful Roman might live at the centre of his empire.

3

The Imperial Palace

In the first two chapters we saw how the elite families of Rome used their *domus* to establish a *locus* for themselves and their *memoria* in Rome and to make a link between their private and public profiles. However, under the emperors, these *memoriae* and the houses that propagated them soon found themselves threatened by the imperial presence on the Palatine. The eclipse of a whole community of elite homes for one super-*domus* reflected the process whereby the collective rule of the Senate was replaced by one leader, an emperor, who passed on his rule, in dynastic fashion, to another member of his *familia*. Rome now had just one family, the Julio-Claudians. They dominated both private and public space with family monuments: the Forum Augustum, Curia Julia, Porticus Octavia, Theatrum Marcellum. We might compare this family's attempts at making themselves at home in the city with that of the Scipios. Augustus had a house in the heart of the city and a huge mausoleum on the Campus Martius. Rather than dedicate a new building in the Forum Romanum, he built an entirely new *forum* for himself. Whereas the Scipios honoured their great ancestor in the Temple of Jupiter, Augustus built a temple for his father.

The writers of the imperial age, however, were slow to react to change. They insisted on thinking of the palace as simply a superior *domus*. Pliny the Younger and Suetonius treated the palaces of the emperors with the same rhetorical devices that had once been applied to republican senatorial housing.[1] The political and moral intentions of Augustus and Nero were portrayed as being as clearly demonstrable through their domestic arrangements as had been those of Cicero and Lucullus.

But this was not the extent of imperial power. From the Principate of Augustus onwards, the emperor came to be a living centre of empire rather than simply a player in Rome. The imperial house, therefore, must stretch itself further, establishing a connection not only between itself and the city but also with the rest of the empire. It was the centre from which must radiate its owners' presence over the entire Roman world. As much as Augustus built a new Rome, he also constructed a new empire, defining the boundaries of his world and linking centre and peripheries. Agrippa's map in the Porticus Vipsania demonstrated to the Roman public the defined *forma* of the empire.[2] Meanwhile, the personifications of the provinces on the precinct wall of the Ara Pacis were reflected, across the Mediterranean, in the Sebasteion at Aphrodisias.[3] These images helped the inhabitants of the Roman world to visualise the empire, their place in it, and the role of the imperial family at its very heart.

The successful presentation of the emperor relied on this co-operation between centre and periphery. Images of emperors at arms or offering libation, dressed as gods or naked like heroes appeared throughout the empire. They were there to demonstrate the emperor's wide-reaching authority. However, they also reflect the attempts of local populations to create a positive impression of their own participation in the Roman empire. They basked in the reflection of the powerful images of the ultimate leader, the emperor. The imperial image was both an expression of central power and an impression of that power as it was conceived on the peripheries, as local populations made him the centre of their own worlds.

The Prima Porta Augustus, standing in the pose of the Classical Greek *Doryphorus*, is often regarded as the ultimate expression of Augustan ideology (Figure 11). On the breast plate, Roman victory is set at the centre of the cosmos. Augustus's personal divine connection is made explicit by the Cupid at his feet, related through a common ancestry from Venus. This one image provides the impression of the emperor's pivotal position at the centre of the universe. More than in any other surviving monument in Rome, all the links of imperial ideology were made manifest and coherent. What is usually implicit through analogy is here made explicit on and around the body of the *princeps* himself. But this image does not come from a public context. Although it is generally assumed to be based on a civic bronze prototype, it was found in the Villa of Livia at Prima Porta, to the north of the city.[4] Augustus is as much *princeps* of his own home as he is of Rome itself.[5] Could it be that emperors, like their senatorial predecessors, saw their homes not as a retreat from the public world but as the principal *locus* for the reiteration and confirmation of their authority? And what did an emperor require to feel truly at home? This was one of the many

11. Prima Porta Augustus,
Musei Vaticani, Rome.
Photo: Photo Alinari.

questions that Augustus would have to ask himself when he established the Principate.

THE HOUSE OF AUGUSTUS

The domestic residence of the *princeps* was an important *locus* for the *memoria* of the emperor. Consequently, it was inevitable that it would play an important role in defining the impression of power. In trying to build that impression, Augustus had to use methods that were immediately recognisable to the senatorial elite. That elite instinctively looked towards his house on the Palatine, as they had looked towards their competitors' houses during the Republic.

We have already seen how literary descriptions of the House of Augustus applied old republican rhetoric to the new *domus* of the Principate, viewed as if it were the culmination of traditional practices, an ideal *domus*. The House of Augustus was, and is, regularly judged by its publicness and simplicity. Suetonius, writing for the entertainment of the emperor Hadrian and his court in the second century A.D., insisted that its only adornments were textiles spun by Livia and Julia, two most unlikely craftswomen.[6] This literary presentation of the house served as a brief moment of simplicity between the Plinian tales of the great republican houses and the later extravagant palaces of ensuing emperors.[7]

If Augustus was to be housed successfully, his *domus* would have to satisfy the most critical rhetorician. It was precisely under Augustus that the republican tradition of the open house was validated by Vitruvius. But Vitruvius makes no mention of how a man of such novel rank as *princeps* should be housed. On one hand, the work can be understood to strike a blow for republican values. Book Six promised the nobility that there was no higher station of homeowner than their own. As the work was specifically dedicated to Augustus, it served the *princeps* with an invitation to behave within those same status limits. On the other hand, the failure to provide advice specifically for the *princeps* might allow Augustus carte blanche to house himself as he saw fit.

The form of the first imperial home has been used to exemplify the careful ambiguity that Augustus, or at least his craftsmen, had used in other monuments of the Principate. The actual house may have been small by late republican standards, but it was set in a large complex that, in character, far exceeded any previous extravagances. The area to the side of the original house was filled by the Temple of Apollo and the relocation of the fire of Vesta here from the Forum.[8] Pompey may have built his home in the shadow of his theatre, projecting his house as far as possible into public space, but here the public institution was physically transposed to the private sphere.[9] The Temple of Vesta was not simply a place of worship, it was the heart of Rome, home to the sacred flame that kept the city alive. In moving the hearth to his house, Augustus further elided the identity of his family with that of Rome. Suetonius's rhetoric avoids having to address the implications of such a move by detaching these temples from the house proper. In addition, it was reported that eventually Senate meetings were held in the house itself.[10] A whole set of Roman civic rituals were relocated in a private house. Inevitably, this transferal caused growing confusion between the public, Roman and private, Augustan spheres. Dio declares the entire property public, just as Caesar's pontifical home had been.[11] As he was writing in the third century, his attitude would imply that the ambiguities of the House of Augustus were still deliberately overlooked three centuries after they were first conceived.

The situation of the *princeps's* house on the Palatine also helped the authors create a rhetoric of an austere, noble house. The hill was the site of the Hut of Romulus, the founder of Rome and *Romanitas*.[12] It was also the long-established stamping ground of the elite, and the nucleus of the Augustan complex had once been a republican *domus*. The reputation of

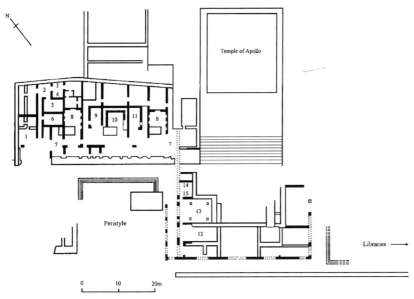

12. Rome, House of Augustus, plan. After Carettoni.

the previous owner, from whose family the site was confiscated, helped to maintain links with republican tradition.[13] Again whether intentions were positive or negative remained unclear; would Augustus quash that voice or personally carry the tradition? It could only be postulated with hindsight that the Palatine would become the preserve of the Caesars, that they would steal all previous connotations of the hill. When *palatium* became the name for imperial residences regardless of location, the process set in motion by Augustus became clear.[14] A whole district of Rome had been reserved for personal use.

However, whilst Augustan authors were eager to confine the *princeps* within republican housing traditions, the layout of his *domus* reveals that Augustus had far exceeded those traditions. The imperial residence was swallowing Rome long before the Domus Aurea was built over the singed remains of the city in 64 A.D. Perhaps this is what we should expect from the domestic architecture at the very centre of the empire. The emperor's house could appropriate civic Rome itself quite literally. The House of Augustus was in a position to provide an ultimate expression of *Romanitas*. As such, the imperial *domus* could escape the bounds that governed the domestic display of the republican elite.

We have the advantage, in discussing the House of Augustus, that we have what are generally supposed to be its remains on the Palatine (Figure 12).[15] The proximity of this building to other Augustan projects on the hill certainly implicates it in the Augustan ambience, whether or not we literally believe Augustus slept here. The core of the house, at least as it survives, seems to consist of several individual suites with their own internal symmetry that open around a peristyle. Unfortunately the relationship of the interior complex to an entrance, mentioned in the texts as a grand portal flanked with laurel trees and a civic crown, remains uncertain.[16] In its absence it is only possible to say that, whilst not necessarily a Vitruvian paradigm, the house itself does not seem very remarkable.

According to Suetonius, this private House of Augustus was an austere affair, bereft of decoration. In fact, the house on the Palatine retains a wealth of wall decoration with complete painted schemes surviving from several rooms. The reason for this omission, other than exaggeration of Augustus's *simplicitas*, might be postulated by looking back to the Republic. In referring to excessive self-promotion during the late Republic, authors such as Pliny or Seneca pay particular attention to architectural and sculptural display but never pass comment on wall painting.[17] Wall painting, despite the voice of Vitruvius, would seem to have been the acceptable medium for creating impressions within the private sphere.[18] Suetonius did not mention the paintings of the House of Augustus because wall painting was not on the list of dangerous luxuries. As a result, its inclusion would serve no rhetorical purpose.

But is wall painting really of so little interest? The painting that survives in Rome shows that it was frequently used to create an impression of freeing the viewer from the financial or spatial constraints of the house. The Villa at Prima Porta (Figure 6) and the Horti of Maecenas both featured paintings that transported the viewer to country gardens. In the House of the Griffins on the Palatine, a neighbour to the Caesars and later to be destroyed by them, wall paintings featured colonnades and halls sheathed in marbles (Figure 3), a fantasy which elevated the status of the owners. Being the one element of decoration that Augustus and the elite could use with impunity, its iconography afforded the opportunity to display the most blatant aspirative and powerful impressions. However, the new, public monuments of Rome more than adequately conveyed Augustan aspirations. What then did his family require of their wall paintings?

ROOM OF THE MASKS; PALACE AS THEATRE

In room 5, the Room of the Masks, the painting is well preserved on the west and south walls (Figure 13). The painted dadoes give the impression of projecting podia on which the architecture of the main part of the walls rests.

13. Rome, House of Augustus, Room 5, wall painting. Photo: Koppermann,
DAIR 66.23.

This light architecture consists of broken walls flanking a central *aedicula.*
Through the central *aediculae* are views of rustic shrines – pillars surrounded
by votives and sacred enclosure walls. The walls of the flanking architecture
appear open at about two thirds of their height and on the resulting shelves
sit theatrical masks, which give the room its modern name. Along the top of
this architecture runs a frieze of *bucrania* on the south and strange winged
creatures on the west. Astride the whole lot are painted fantastical, ghostly
animals.

   The compositions shun reality; the whole wall is set against a white
ground, negating the realism that the architecture in the foreground appears
to set up. The fantastical creatures on the gables and friezes very definitely
remove us from the world of solid realities that Augustus was attempting
to create in Rome itself. Vitruvius criticises such fantastical art in his description of wall painting designs, condemning the depiction of fabulous
creatures and designs that could not exist in nature. The architect's definition of fantasy is rather restrictive here; in its wider sense, it is possible
to see that fantasy extends beyond the monstrous to the themes of the
panels themselves. Here we see fantasy breaking free of the restrictions of
the city of Rome and the new regime's professed dependency on its institutions. The rural landscapes reflect not the epic outlook of the *Aeneid* but the

semimythical pastoral life of the *Georgics* and *Eclogues*.[19] The rustic shrines bear simple offerings and demonstrate a close association with nature by the intertwining of shrine and tree. The scenes provoke reminders of the *topos* of the simplicity and piety of the earlier generations of Rome and also serve to naturalise the message of the scenes and, by extension, the impression sought by their owners.

A close inspection of the shrine on the west wall reveals the gifts of pipes and a *pedum*, which clearly recall the sacro-idyllic world and the shepherds and satyrs who inhabit it. This is not the realm of the city gods but of the country and its ancient deities. Augustus had learnt that his power must be consolidated with reference to the civic world of Rome, and not to the foreign or the rustic. He built civic monuments, based himself in the city, not even owning a *villa*, and allied himself with gods from the official Roman pantheon. The wall painting in this house, however, explores a different world. The main panels of the Room of the Masks transported the viewer from the order of the city to the unpredictable wilds of nature, apparently collapsing the boundary between town and country. The shrine painted on the south wall has been identified as a shrine of Apollo. Here is another side to the god so publicly venerated in the temple incorporated into the Palatine complex. The image reminds us that the world and the power of the gods stretch further than the boundaries of Rome. This homeowner is *princeps* not simply of Rome but also of the semimythic ideal world of the countryside.

Carettoni saw the most important overall theme of the room to be the world of theatre, likening the architecture to stage scenery and drawing particular attention to the four masks. In doing so, he inserted the paintings of the House of Augustus into the wider historiography of ancient wall painting, which has continually debated the theatricality of the medium and has tried to assess the function of the recurring theatrical motifs.[20] The allusion to the theatre has a direct result on our understanding of the main panels of the room. By framing those panels, the stage architecture appears to distance the reality of the viewer's position in the room from the fantasy world of the wall painting.

The popularity of the modern idea of the theatricality of Italian wall painting might be explained by its use in flagging up a clear division between reality and fantasy. Theatrical motifs might help Augustus precisely because they appeared to profess the whole composition as fantasy. They assured the viewer that the chaos of the countryside was being kept at bay. Simultaneously, though, they blur the boundary between fantasy and reality. At what point does the painting stop and the room start? The *princeps* was able to give the impression that the scope of his authority extended to the mythological haven of the pastoral world. Whilst, in public, Augustus had to assert his control over civic Rome, here he was able to concentrate on other realms.

The potential of this room's iconography reveals why Vitruvius, albeit unsuccessfully, may have discouraged fantastical iconography among the lesser ranks. The painted impressions of the Room of the Masks can be paralleled all over Campania where the vast majority of Italian wall painting survives. The red room in the *villa* at Boscotrecase features shepherds and travellers visiting very similar simple shrines in idyllic country settings.[21] There is an impression of commonality here, not only between the aspirations and fantasies of the Augustan family and the Italian elite but also in the medium though which they express themselves.

However, the shared experience implied in the paintings is largely a smokescreen. The fantasies of these paintings were matched in reality by the Temple of Apollo in the house grounds. Augustus was only pretending that his wall paintings were fantasy. His power was not demonstrated by the size of his house. It was not simply an amplification of republican practices, rather its difference lay in the changing relationship of domestic fantasy to political realities.

ROOM 15; ANTONY OR AUGUSTUS?

Room 15, on the upper level, was situated in the southeast wing which joined the "domestic" part of the house to the libraries and the Temple of Apollo.[22] The painting is conceived as a schematic architectural framework (Figure 14). Each wall is divided into three by a painted projected podium on which stood a slender columnar architecture. Behind this was a series of large panels and central *aediculae* framing sacro-idyllic landscape paintings. The painted architecture was decorated with many friezes that featured lotus blossoms and branches and stylised obelisks, once flanked by heraldic griffins and then by blossom cups. Cult objects such as ritual ewers and peculiar spherical buckets stand on the sills, adding to an elusive but cumulative Egyptianising iconography.

As with the images of the Room of the Masks, the painting of this room impinged a different world onto the Roman. It evoked the sinister and fascinating world of Egypt, geographically so distant but always threatening to overturn Roman *mores*. The existence of this theme in the home attributed to Augustus seems obtrusive. This is not just the official residence of the *pater* of Rome, the very centre of *Romanitas*, but the personal home of the man who had only recently fought off the threat from Egypt. Following the Battle of Actium, one of the victor's most pressing tasks was presented

14. Rome, House of Augustus, Room 15, wall painting. Photo: Koppermann, DAIR 82.2152.

as being to re-Romanise the elite at the expense of Antony's reputation as a Roman who failed because his head was turned by a foreign queen.

The use of Egyptian motifs in domestic wall painting is echoed in the neighbouring House of Livia, which features a frieze of an Egyptian landscape. Imagery featuring worlds beyond Rome was already popular in the Republic, as is demonstrated by the famous Nilotic mosaic from Praeneste.[23] The interest in exotic, foreign worlds offered a further medium through which Romans could negotiate their identities, setting their Romanness against the temptations of indulging in or exerting control over other worlds. For Augustus, as *princeps* of the entire empire, such negotiation was a necessity. There would have been little to be gained in not assuming Egypt into Augustus's private, painted world when the elites around him felt free to adopt Egyptian imagery in various media; just outside Rome itself, every citizen could view the pyramid tomb of Gaius Cestius, a typical republican fantasy run wild and realised in travertine.[24] If Augustus wanted to claim that he had beaten the perpetrators of such excesses, he must appear to be master of their fantasies as much as he seemed to shun them.

Whilst public, literary rhetoric served to distance Egypt; at home, Augustus could challenge Egypt head on. The private Augustus was as free to indulge in Egyptian fantasy as the next man, proud to be pharaoh of his own home. In his house, the *princeps* appeared to indulge in private display like any other aristocrat with scenes of rural landscapes and restrained motifs from exotic cultures. Only these fantasies could be validated by the reality of Augustus's position: Augustus really was pharaoh of Egypt.[25] Although traditional rhetoric might ignore it, the House of Augustus posed a serious challenge to conventional divisions within rhetorical *topoi* – public and private, reality and fantasy. Republican custom was stretched to its limits.

The imperial family, and particularly the person of the emperor, was becoming inextricably linked with the city of Rome itself. Augustus could not be contained within the limits previous conventions had put on the private individual – the whole of Rome was his platform and his home. As much as Augustus was himself becoming a symbol of Rome, a living representation of Rome's authority and focus of others' aspirative fantasies, he was also the signified. Augustus was the power of Rome, a new living centre.

Here began the creation of the emperor as public icon, an image created by imperial art and ceremonial ritual. By late Antiquity, the emperors of Rome had learnt that the only way to preserve their position as public icon was to retreat into privacy. Public appearances were only undertaken where carefully orchestrated rituals avoided any insight into the emperor's human condition.[26] Although this was not to happen until the late empire, the early emperors were already aware of the need for separateness. Practitioners of traditional rhetoric pretended not to understand this aspect of the imperial condition. Pliny the Younger's panegyric to Trajan, delivered in 100 A.D., portrays the emperor as ordinary citizen engaged in everyday, social ritual. Such a presentation only works if everyone is agreed that he is not normal (as the very mode of panegyric would suggest).[27] Whilst it was pretended that the emperor was a private individual, accountable in public, he was a public icon whose impression of authority was best maintained by a certain privacy and aloofness, at least enough to preserve the enigma of authority. Privacy became not a matter of restriction, confining republican fantasies to the house, but a provider of exclusivity.

The creation of the Principate saw the concept of *Romanitas* devolve onto one man. Augustus and his house became symbols of that *Romanitas*, a focus for Rome, Italy, and empire. His individual, familial, and communal identitites were all brought together, one and the same. Augustus was Rome. However, as much as it is possible to cite evidence for the House of Augustus becoming a concentrated Rome, so it is possible to see the house dodging the focus trained on it and instead looking beyond Rome to Egypt, to semimythical landscapes and the gods themselves. These interests are dismissed as fantasies by virtue of their medium as wall painting – fantasies familiar to any member of the elite. But for the emperor, the distance between reality and fantasy was very different than it was for the elite of Rome and Italy. It would remain to be seen how long subsequent emperors would be similarly content before they decided to make public realisation of their greater, empire-wide authority, which for now was confined to paint.

BAD EMPERORS AND THEIR MAD HOUSES

Of course, Suetonius's treatment of the House of Augustus must view the house not only as the culmination of republican traditions but also, with hindsight, as the first of the imperial palaces. By the time of Suetonius, a history of palaces could be written, observing the development of the Palatine from the Domus Tiberiana to Domitian's Domus Flavia.[28] The House of Augustus had to be constructed, in retrospect, as a paradigm for these later *domus* (as literary tradition insisted on calling the imperial residence).[29] Most explicitly, it had to be presented as the direct opposite of the "bad" palaces of Gaius and Nero.

Having set up Augustus as a paradigm of leadership, it was not surprising that imperial authors contrasted his example with its antithesis: the mad, bad emperors, Gaius and Nero. The pair are depicted as deluded megalomaniacs, eager to deviate from the norms of *Romanitas* in any way possible, not least in their domestic arrangements. Did their domestic lives depart so much from traditional standards that they were bound to be seen in terms of deviancy, or rather was their perceived deviancy demonstrated by such a presentation?

When Gaius came to the throne, he had a faultless family background; he was the son of the great general Germanicus nicknamed Caligula by his father's doting troops. When Gaius took his place as *paterfamilias*, however, he is presented as failing either to respect or to capitalise on his family's *memoria*. He refused to attend the funeral of his grandmother, Antonia, and slept with his sisters.[30] He preferred to ally himself with the Olympian family, declaring himself a god and demanding appropriate veneration.

Pliny the Elder's criticism of the Palatine complex of Gaius places it in the same league as the later Domus Aurea.[31] The palace was accused of encircling and swallowing the city. From the Palatine, the complex had reached so far into the Forum that it was said that Gaius, determined to prove his ranking among the gods, had made the Temple of Castor and Pollux his

vestibule, enrolling them as his bodyguards.[32] Other rumours concerned
plans to build a bridge connecting Palatine to Capitoline, so that he could
share Jupiter's home.[33] To make matters worse, Gaius was also the owner of
several of the major *horti* that ringed Rome, holding the city captive.[34] The
archaeological evidence suggests that the Caligulan extensions had reached
the bottom of the Palatine where what appears to have been a huge peristyle
lay between hill and Forum. Perhaps this encroachment onto public space
was conceived as justification for the rumours.

If we wanted to rationalise the domestic arrangements of Gaius, it would
be possible to put them very much in the new Augustan "tradition." The
extension of the palace towards the Forum might reflect a practise, which
Royo attributes to Augustus, of creating a kind of ceremonial entranceway
to the Palatine complex in the Forum, achieved by Augustus through the
erection of the Temple of Divus Iulius and several arches.[35] The palace was
as capable of moving around its quarry, the public rituals of Rome, as it
was of transposing them up to its heart. Most importantly, following Augustus, these schemes all reflected a sole interest in the alliance of Gaius
himself and the city of Rome – a process that was completed towards the
end of the century when all three gates of the Palatine became those of the
palace under Domitian.[36] These extensions show to what extent the emperors were merging Rome and home. They finally collapsed the distance
between public monuments and private *domus*, which had been increasingly combined during the late Republic. Gaius's Palatine projects might
be understood as furthering the link between imperial and Roman identity, presence, and *memoria*. This architectural development can be equated
with the changes in bureaucracy. By this point, a considerable amount of
administration was beginning to devolve on the imperial household, particularly its freedmen. For an emperor, for whom the empire was home, these
categories were finally eclipsed.

Whilst the Palatine works of Caligula might seem decidedly sane in their
conception, it would appear that the mad emperor was equally sentient in
locating his more megalomanic projects outside the city. Elsewhere there
were rumours of extravagances worthy of eastern potentates – such as a
bridge of ships across the Bay of Naples.[37] These stories are careful to show
Caligula observing at least one *topos*, the imposed distinction between town
and country, not because he did, or indeed should, but because their creators
needed some transgressions in reserve with which to model the ultimate
imperial monster and his lair.

If Caligula's home had been considered threatening, that of Nero invited
unprecedented polemic. Nero far exceeded the transgressions of Gaius on

every count. He was presented as having even less concern for the norms of the *familia*, being singlehandedly to blame for the demise of the Julio-Claudian line, and killing not only extended family members but also his mother, wife, and unborn child.[38] Rather than ingratiate himself on Rome, he wanted to destroy it. Nero's first domestic project was the construction of the Domus Transitoria, which extended the plans of Gaius to link various parts of the city, this time the Palatine and the Esquiline.[39] However, a much more ambitious project was in planning. Romans were advised to flee to Veii as, after the purging fire of 64, work started on Nero's extensive new palace. The Domus Aurea was presented as decimating the city faster than the most determined B-movie monster. For the first time, it was made clear that incorporation of civic Rome into the palace was not the only possibility – demolition and replacement now became an enticing option. Nero's power as Roman emperor eclipsed the city. In fact, as before, these rumours seem to have been largely exaggerated. Although the palace certainly did encroach on once public territory, the threat to Rome was principally rhetorical rather than physical.[40]

On the other hand, the Domus Aurea would have seemed a hugely innovative project, transgressing many of the boundaries of Roman life and realising the most extreme fantasies of power. The Via Sacra was realigned to lead to the vestibule of the palace, dominated by the *colossus* of the emperor.[41] In keeping with the grand scale of his home, Nero's image towered over the colonnades around his vestibule in full sight of the Forum Romanum and, presumably, most of central Rome. The *colossus* reinforced the notion that the whole city had become Nero's residence. The vestibule acted as a gateway to a fantasy world of woodland and farmland, packed with exotic flora and fauna and dotted with buildings "like towns," colonnades, temples, and the Domus itself.[42]

The descriptions of the complex have caused some to see a close affiliation developing between Roman Caesars and eastern god-kings. However, Nero need not have been taking direct inspiration from Persia. Strabo's account of Alexander's palace at Alexandria, which boasted sanctuaries, theatres, and porticoes, implies close parallels with the Domus Aurea.[43] Many elements of Hellenistic palaces had already reached Italy. The *horti* of Rome were mini pleasure parks. In Pompeii, palatial elements can be found in peristyle gardens and, more extensively, in wall painting. *Cubiculum* m from the villa at Boscoreale near Pompeii, now restored in the Metropolitan Museum of New York (Figure 9), demonstrates the kind of painted landscape that links Alexander's palace to that of Nero.[44]

As for an emperor indulging in fantasies of un-Roman, exotic authority, Augustus has already revealed himself as Egyptian pharaoh in his frescoes. Now Nero had made such fantasies come true. The joke was that Nero, extravagant in this medium as in all others, had not abandoned paint, and Pliny tells us that his painter, Famulus, became a prisoner of the Domus Aurea.[45] Known mostly from engravings, his paintings featured heavily ornate architectures populated by posed "actors" or sculptures. Essentially these schemes are elaborations of the *aediculae* and masks from the paintings in the House of Augustus (Figure 13). They appeared to confess Nero's world as fantasy even when it was being physically realised over the ruins of Rome.[46]

In many ways, such an escalation of the show of imperial power should not come as a surprise. The competitiveness of Roman society and the consequent pressure on each emperor to outdo his predecessors almost become validation enough for the Domus Aurea.[47] Many accusations have been levelled against the Domus Aurea as a means of explaining its bad press: that it was a *rus in urbe*, country in town, that it shattered the delicately preserved image of *princeps*, that it was a ploy to destroy Rome and create Neropolis.[48] This very act has been understood as symptomatic of Nero's power – his ability to foist his own fiction on the world and force his subjects to become his actors.[49] Arguably, Nero had turned Rome into his stage set. Such a move could hardly be read as anything other than a disregard for Rome's traditions and an open disassociation of imperial authority from that of Rome. The emperor now lived according to rituals that had little relation to those of the Republic. New rituals require new space in which to be enacted; new space calls for new architecture with which to define it.

In the Domus Aurea, it was as if Rome had disappeared. The complex was not simply a *rus in urbe*. The distinction between *domus forisque*, *villa*, *domus*, and *horti* had all been collapsed to create the *palatium*. The palace took elements of all these types and threw them together, creating a liminal space, which only an emperor could be seen to control. Nero's house is only transgressive when it is shoehorned into the category of *domus*. As a *palatium aureum*, it is perfect. Such a small part of the Domus Area remains today that it is difficult to imagine the splendid entirety that the texts imply. In an effort to imagine the extent of the complex and to reconcile our own fantasies of the palace with the rather disappointing remains, the ruins of what might have been the core of the palace are now often imagined as only one half of a large, symmetrical wing (Figure 15). However, there are other, less-glamorous hints as to the palace's innovations, principally the

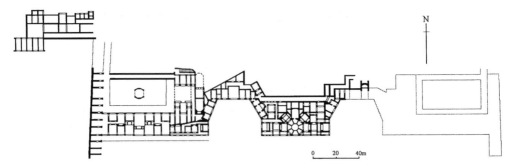

15. Rome, Domus Aurea, plan. The broken lines suggest the symmetrical wing, which some scholars have chosen to attribute to the complex.

predominance of vaulted, concrete architecture. Such techniques had been applied to utility structures for almost two hundred years, but before the building of the Domus Aurea, urban, domestic architects seem to have been little concerned with the advances in concrete architecture.[50] It was more important for homeowners to be seen to conform than to go out on a limb. Equally, the Domus Aurea failed to become a model for the townhouse after its construction. If it was anticipated or imitated at all, it was in the safety of the countryside where *villa*s provided more room for experimentation for an elite still expected to conform to a rhetoric that the emperor was increasingly overcoming. A *villa* on the coast at Planasia, perhaps of Flavian date, boasts an array of curvilinear features from apsed *oeci* to circular fishtanks.[51] It is symptomatic of the investment and innovation that the wealthy elite of Rome were prepared to sink into country estates. The shapes afforded by concrete architecture did not sit well with the open symmetry of the Roman house prescribed by Vitruvius. Columnar architecture is permeable; concrete architecture shuts the viewer within. A second effect is of disorientation. Imagine standing in the octagonal room of the Domus Aurea. The five sides of the octagon to the front and sides are each punctured by doorways to outer chambers. To add to the confusion, light reaches the suite in different directions from windows high above, one being the *oculus* directly overhead, the rest being openings down the outside of the dome into the outer chambers. Such architecture is demonstrably inappropriate for a senator who is supposed to be open and accountable at all times. For an emperor who needs to maintain his charisma and aloofness, it is perfect. In the city, concrete architecture was the preserve of public monuments and palaces – the most public of architectural practices proving perfect for the private world of the emperor. It would take a while for the townhouses of the elite to catch up, demonstrating again that the palace was an anti-type, rather than an *exemplum*, of the *domus* tradition.

The Domus Aurea was conceived by Nero's enemies and later polemic as a deliberate and acute attack on Rome, an attempt to sever Nero's personal authority and identity from that of the city. The emperor, supposedly the embodiment of *Romanitas*, was presented as its enemy. He was branded a *Graeculus*, a slave to the non-Roman, incapable of restricting and mastering his fantasies but instead imposing them on the urban landscape around him.[52] He treated his family as his enemies and his capital as an *urbs capta*, which he destroyed and rebuilt for his own ends. In doing so, he rejected the very group identities that rhetoricians could have used to disguise his perceived, personal shortcomings. Instead, he left his un-Roman characteristics completely exposed, and Rome found justification for fighting back – Nero and then the short-lived emperors Otho and Vitellius, who also lived in the Domus Aurea as successors to the Neronian tradition, were killed as traitors.[53]

The Flavian dynasty benefitted from acting on anti-Neronian rhetoric. Vespasian moved to the Horti Sallustiani where he might live, very publicly, as a private citizen.[54] The Domus Aurea was slowly dismantled and returned to the public domain; the Colosseum, the Baths of Titus and later the Baths of Trajan, the Temple of Venus and Rome all rose over the site.[55] At the same time, the Flavians built the Domus Flavia, the acceptable face of the *palatium*, never to be superceded within Rome. It is ironic that this success story should have been instigated by another "bad" emperor, Domitian. The Domus Flavia (Figure 16) saw the *palatium* return to the Palatine. Although it encroached as closely as possible on the public domain, dominating civic life in the Forum Romanum on one side and the city at leisure in the Circus Maximus on the other (Figure 17), it respected its limits.[56] Even today, in an attempt, presumably, to side with ancient acceptance of the complex, the ceremonial wing of the Domitianic palace has been seen as respecting the traditions of the *domus*. Its major reception rooms are often regarded as a magnification of the traditional *atrium, tablinum*, peristyle arrangement.[57] Nevertheless, Nero's innovations remained prevalent. The "house" dominated the city and seems to have been seen much further afield, as it was circulated as an image on coins.[58] The reception rooms ended in an apse where the emperor could be viewed, aloof from the main rectilinear space of the room. Statius likened an evening spent in such surroundings to an evening with Jupiter himself.[59] Elsewhere in the palace, more elaborate vaulted confections demonstrated that the new imperial architecture had truly taken hold. Even where emperors conceded to the Roman, it was no longer possible for them to do so as ordinary citizen. Whilst the adoption of civic, concrete techniques assured the populace of the emperors' role

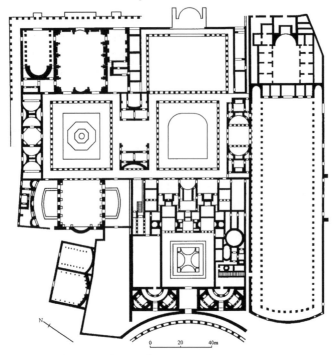

16. Rome, Domus Flavia, plan.

17. Rome, Domus Flavia, view from Circus Maximus. Photo: SJH.

as public icons of *Romanitas*, they also served to widen the gulf between emperor and citizen and to remove the *princeps* to an unattainable, private world. Of course, such seclusion can spell danger as much as safety. A paranoid Domitian is said to have installed opaque walls. They did not work – he was cut down in his own bedroom.[60]

So why, after Domitian's murder, didn't rhetoricians go to work on his house? Perhaps because they were prepared to see it as a *domus*. Indeed, appearing to observe the distinctions between traditional house types, Domitian had built a *villa* at Castel Gandolfo with baths, a theatre and a circus.[61] A veritable Domitianopolis, the presence of the *villa*, a location for "bad" behaviour outside the city, reinforced the notion that the palace back in Rome was, indeed, a *domus*, safe and accountable.

HADRIAN AND HIS *VILLA* AT TIVOLI

The Suetonian accounts of the early palaces are further contextualised by recalling that Suetonius is writing under an emperor, Hadrian, whose contribution to the tradition might be seen as the exact counterpoint to the Domus Aurea, a true *urbs in rure*. Only thirty years after Domitian, the *villa* built by Hadrian at Tivoli, not far to the east of Rome (Figure 18), invited literary comment by becoming the emperor's official residence.[62] Although Hadrian is credited with making the Palatine complex more hospitable, he never lived there nor did he inhabit the Horti Sallustiani, although alterations were also carried out there.[63] It was enough for Hadrian to establish a *memoria* of his own authority on these buildings whilst living at Tivoli, maintaining a subtle difference and beginning to test the relationship between the geographical centre of empire, Rome, and its living centre, the emperor.

In fact, developments in the emperorship since the demise of the Julio-Claudians could not fail to test this relationship. By the time of Hadrian, the dynamic between emperor, *familia*, and Rome had changed drastically. Hadrian was adopted by Trajan as his successor. Although this formality attempted to create for Hadrian an appropriate familial identity, he had no bloodlinks with his predecessors. Some even went so far as to locate Hadrian's birthplace in Spain. As a result, the different layers of identity that intersected so readily for the early emperors were much less easily reconciled with Hadrian.

Hadrian was generally constructed, by himself and by others, not just as another Augustus in a long line of Augusti but as a second Augustus, the bearer of a new imperial era.[64] He was the first emperor chronicled by the *Scriptores Historiae Augustae*, the heirs to the Suetonian tradition.

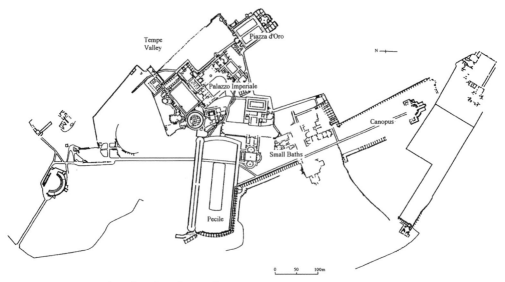

18. Tivoli, Villa of Hadrian, plan.

Like the first Augustus, Hadrian was seen to accompany his new concept of imperialism with an extensive architectural programme, including
the Pantheon.[65] But Hadrian did not confine himself to the city, spending
approximately half of his twenty-one-year reign touring the provinces, particularly in the East. Only Nero before him had thought to travel for pleasure, and that emperor's cultural tour of Greece only served to demonstrate
his madness, revealing his enslavement to Greekness and his inability to
govern Rome. The acceptance of Hadrian's tours mark a significant departure from this early model of empire, which depended on an imperial presence in Rome. Instead, Hadrian literally shared his presence throughout the
provinces by virtue of personal appearances and the building programmes
that made permanent these epiphanies.

Like Augustus, Hadrian called an end to expansionist policy. The empire
could again be understood as a defined whole, with a definite edge as
well as a centre. The empire's constituent parts could again be personi-
fied and displayed: on reliefs inside the Temple of the Deified Hadrian, set
up on the Campus Martius by Antoninus Pius in 145 and on coin issues
circulated around the provinces.[66] There was, however, a new aspect to
Hadrian's personifications. The personification of Roma had been worshipped together with Augustus across the empire, creating a world inhabited by worshipped centre and worshipping peripheries. Under Hadrian,
the Temple of Venus and Rome, an enormous Greek-style temple imposed
on the end of the Forum Romanum, brought a provincial cult and its

19. Hadrian, portrait bust, British Museum. Photo: Copyright © The British Museum.

architecture to the centre. In this way, Hadrian acknowledged the increasing separation between the physical city of Rome and the concept of Roma as centre of imperial power. This innovation began the process of lessening Rome's unique privileges, bringing her in line with the provinces.[67] She was just another city in the service of the living centre, the emperor.

These changes in the nature of imperial identity were matched by innovation in Hadrian's personal image. In Livia's Villa at Prima Porta, Augustus was seen at his most powerful as master of his private space (Figure 11). Conversely, out of literally thousands of pieces of sculpture found throughout the *villa* at Tivoli, a full catalogue of those pieces lists only eight portraits of Hadrian and none of them appear to make the extreme authoritative or divine claims expressed by the Prima Porta Augustus (Figure 19).[68]

The Augustan model had constricted the features of the early emperors within an idealised, ageless calm, a deliberate retort to the veristic portraiture of the republican elite (Figure 4). The Flavian emperors had found some recourse to the traditions of verism in order to free themselves from association to all things Neronian.[69] Hadrian, however, rejected both the imperial and the traditional portraiture of Rome, instead adapting the template of the philosopher portrait.[70] The bearded image of the Greek thinker had always been regarded by the republican, Roman aristocrat as his visual antithesis. Yet, whereas rhetoric had presented Nero's enmity towards Rome by cataloguing his Greek affectations, Hadrian's Graeco-ising identity escaped condemnation. Although accounts of his life are by no means devoid of criticism, Hadrian was crucially vindicated by a natural death and the reign of his appointed successor, Antoninus Pius, in 138 A.D.[71] The validity of his visual image was similarly indicated by a succession of bearded imperial portraits. Hadrian's private interest in Greek culture is not, then, enough in itself to explain the introduction of this bearded image. He was not simply a *Graeculus* trying to hide under the Roman mantle of his position. A change in the symbolism of what it was to look like an emperor must imply nothing less than a change in the concept of what it meant to be emperor, both a symbol and generator of *Romanitas*. Hadrian literally changed the face of Romanness. We might expect the *villa* at Tivoli to reflect a new understanding of the emperor and his empire.

Although Hadrian's choice of *villa* at Tivoli was legitimised, as had been the House of Augustus, by the incorporation of the remains of a republican *villa*, its emergence as official *palatium* was unprecedented. Augustus had attached great importance to a domestic presence in Rome. The absence of his successor, Tiberius, who secluded himself in his *villa* at Capri, had been presented as a disaster for the city and a sign of his own perversity. It is remarkable, then, that Hadrian's biographers present their subject as taking a full role in civic duties and do not find any discrepancy in the emperor's domestic withdrawal until the end of his life.[72] The same biographers apparently had no qualms as to the extent of the *villa* at Tivoli. In compiling a new generation of imperial biographies, the *Scriptores Historiae Augustae* followed the Suetonian formulae to new extremes. The scope of the project, in their words, far exceeded Nero's infamous *rus in urbe* – within the walls of Tivoli were recreated not only the monuments of the empire but even an Underworld through which Hadrian could race in his chariot.[73] The *villa* at Tivoli extended the usual Roman fantasies of domestic space to their ultimate expression. Whereas Domitian had adopted the *basilica* form within his Domus Flavia, the *villa* built entire, independent, civic structures. Where Augustus had a room he called his Syracuse, Hadrian apparently had the whole Tempe Valley in his garden.

THE BUILDINGS AND PLAN

The inclusion of independent structures recalling various civic monuments of the empire renders the plan of the *villa* initially confusing. A disarray of spatially unrelated structures on different axes proves an absolute antidote to the tradition of republican *villa*s, another reminder of the inadequacy of the terminology of elite housing for dealing with imperial homes. In understanding this plan, any study of Tivoli owes a debt to the work of Ricotti, which cannot be underestimated for its importance in divining the flow around the complex.

One of the most important aspects of Ricotti's work has been to prove the cohesiveness of the *villa*'s design from the planning of the *cryptoporticus* and covered walkways that criss-cross the site.[74] Despite the apparent openness of the plan, movement was actually fairly restricted, with most buildings reached from these passages that effectively control the circulation around the *villa*. This has important consequences for the understanding of the complex as a whole. The *villa* architects seem to have gone out of their way to disorientate and isolate. Visitors are denied an overall view of the plan of the *villa* since they travel between complexes in corridors and tunnels. Even open areas, such as the Pecile, were hidden behind great curtain walls.

The same effect can be discerned in the plans of each individual building, for example the Small Baths. Every room was a different shape and bore a roof of individual height, offering a different perspective of light. The octagonal *calidarium* appears to have had at least six entrances, all of which led to rooms of different shapes and heights. The effect must have been labyrinthine. Conversely, it can be no coincidence that the Palazzo Imperiale, the remains of the old republican *villa* and hence the most traditional area of the complex (that is to say the most open, symmetrical, and visibly accessible) appears to have had the most restricted access. Here is a new era of imperial building where the reality of emperor is hidden beyond the curtain walls, curves, and *cryptoporticus* of the villa. The covering up of what once was open and the disorientation implicit in the abandoning of symmetry were central to the process of revealing the true nature of emperorship by creating an impression of unsurpassable power.

INTERNALISATION OF EMPIRE AND PALACE

The architecture of Tivoli can no longer be thought of as "Roman" but, rather, as explicitly "imperial." All the buildings within the *villa* were put to the service of the emperor. The effect on architecture of being commandeered by the emperor is best demonstrated by the famous buildings apparently recreated in the *villa* complex. The *Historia Augusta* gave a whole list of such recreations: the Tempe Valley, the Canopus, and the Poecile for example. The archaeologists who first explored the site at Tivoli were eager to find these areas. In conferring these names on parts of the *villa*, however, they were forced to call on their own imaginations.

The Canopus provides a prime example of such an identification. The complex consists of a semi-dome fronted along its flat, open side by four columns and extending into a long corridor at its back. The walls are niched, alternately for the display of sculpture or with steps for the play of water, which appears to have cascaded down the steps of the main hall to a transverse channel in front of the building. The view looks onto a further water channel, curved at the far end and surrounded by sculpture. It is named after the port of Canopus outside Alexandria from which flowed a famously corrupt and luxurious stretch of the Nile.[75] According to Strabo, the area was dominated by a great temple of Serapis, reached by a canal tributary of the Nile called the Euripus.[76] Despite the lack of cult images or any archaeological evidence from the original site in Egypt, the first excavators of the *villa* identified the complex as the Canopus, labelling the channel, the Euripus (Figure 20), and the semi-domed structure, the Serapeum (Figure 21). The *villa* was beginning to be understood as a collection of souvenirs, memoribilia of Hadrian's travels and a microcosm of the empire.[77]

The identification of the Canopus was seemingly bolstered by the high incidence of Egyptian sculpture found in the *villa*. A great deal of these have been attributed, at one time or another, to the Canopus. However, the twentieth-century excavations of the area imply a much wider scope of sculptural themes, including the Dionysiac: a Satyr and Dionysus group, a head of the god, a tragic mask, an *oscillum*, and panther head.[78]

However, the possibility of an Egyptianising Canopus complex has remained very attractive. Hadrian had a close personal association with Egypt, the Nile, and the Egyptian god, Osiris (Serapis), with whom he was linked through the tragic death of his young Bithynian lover, Antinous. The story goes that Antinous drowned in the Nile during an imperial visit, and Hadrian consoled himself by devising elaborate civic rituals and extraordinary divine honours for the boy. Gossip concerning the death, treating it as a voluntary or inflicted suicide, hinted at an occult magic rite; Antinous had been offered to the Nile in order to protect Hadrian's own health on earth or to ensure his immortality.[79] In any case, Antinous's death was of immediate cultic significance. All the victims of the Nile were said to enjoy resurrection, in the manner of Osiris who had entered into eternal life after being thrown in the Nile in numerous pieces.[80]

If Hadrian's obsession with Egypt was thought to have been triggered by the tragedy of Antinous, then many scholars have presumed that the Tivoli Canopus evoked Egypt simply as a means of evoking Antinous. The

20. Tivoli, Villa of Hadrian, Euripus. Photo: SJH.

21. Tivoli, Villa of Hadrian, Serapeum. Photo: SJH.

Euripus has been described as a mini Nile in which Antinous's death could be enacted before his resurrection was celebrated in the Serapeum. Kähler suggested that the whole area was designated as a memorial to the youth and that the tomb of Antinous was situated in the immediate vicinity.[81]

22. Tivoli, Villa of Hadrian, Caryatids and Sileni along the
Euripus. Photo: SJH.

There is no real evidence to support this theory though others have chosen
to attribute a collection of sculptures on Egyptian themes, such as sphinxes,
to a monumental tomb.[82]

More recently, Grenier has proposed a detailed reconstruction of the
Canopus sculptural programme by gathering up the Egyptian sculpture
found in and around the *villa*.[83] In combining all known sculpture from
this area, he proposed an intricate programme of the celebration of the
eternal cycle of death and resurrection through the myths of Osiris, Isis-
Demeter, and Antinous. He also saw geographical connotations; the layout
of the Canopus followed a cultic map of Egypt and the Serapeum. The
channel represented the Mediterranean, bordered by Athens, symbolised by
Caryatids modelled on those of the Erechtheum (Figure 22) and by Ephesus,
represented by two Amazons from the Temple of Artemis. Unfortunately,
this scheme relies on presuming that the Egyptian sculpture, which is largely
unprovenanced, comes from the Serapeum and on passing over the eclectic
selection of sculpture, which does seem to come from the immediate area.
The Dionysiac sculpture, in particular, is ignored as unrelated to the desired
Osiran theme.

But what of the sculpture that does have a definite provenance, excavated
along the edges of the Euripus? Along the left side stood the four Caryatids.
On the Acropolis, supporting the porch of the Erechtheum, these women
were potent symbols of service to Athens and her gods, yet at Tivoli they
supported an architrave with no other purpose than architectural frippery.
To add insult to injury, they shared their task with a couple of mythical

beasts, Sileni, servants of Dionysus. Possibly from within the pool came sculptures of two exotic sea monsters; the crocodile from the banks of the Nile and the Scylla. The fact that these monsters – one from the real world, one from myth – share the same waters confuses the identification of the Euripus and even questions that it should be sought in the real world. The issue of geographical location is further clouded by the river gods, Nile and Tiber, who appear to have been arranged at the curved end of the Euripus, overlooking the same stretch of water. Between them stand a pair of Amazons flanking statues of Hermes and Ares displayed under an alternately flat and arched architrave. Many attempts have been made to impose order here. The Amazons might link with the Caryatids, both coming from Greek temples. On the other hand, perhaps they should be understood thematically in connection with Hermes and Ares in that the Amazons and the Greeks were arch-enemies. The opponents are somewhat reconciled here; the Amazons have retired from the fight, wounded. That Ares has finished fighting is suggested by the presence of Hermes, the god of travels either of the living or of the dead, himself an appropriate deity to look over the exhibits from the corners of the Hellenistic world.[84]

Such observations apart, however, finding a coherent link has proved frustrating for a succession of investigators. Might this not be because such a link simply does not exist? These opposing subjects are all brought together in Hadrian's fantasy world despite their particular differences. The surreal fantasy world that their fusion creates all goes to forge an impression of communion brought about by service to a higher authority – the owner of the *villa*, the emperor himself. Images from different worlds were here set loose, and every conceivable boundary between them is imploded. Hadrian's "real" ownership of everything in the empire was a rather mundane reality – he did not have to prove it. The structures of the *villa* are not merely reflections of that reality but fantastic distortions, pressed into service as exhibits for the emperor's delight acknowledging, whilst robbing them of, their original, provincial location and function. The fantasy complexes of the *villa* hinted at the splendours of the empire but remained in thrall to the whim of Hadrian.

Hadrian's rule over the images of the Euripus is expressed in the architecture of the Serapeum (Figure 21). Its hemicycle appears to have housed a large masonry *stibadium*, a semicircular dining couch. This form of couch was rapidly gaining popularity at the time, providing an alternative to the three *triclinia* couches that traditionally furnished dining rooms. Its shape allowed all the diners to be accommodated on one couch. More importantly, the design also made it particularly appropriate for use in those palaces and

23. Sperlonga, Polyphemus group. Photo: Singer, DAIR 72.2416.

*villa*s adopting new forms of curvilinear architecture as it fitted tidily into apses. Its presence here tells us that, whilst the form of the Serapeum might possibly reflect a temple in Alexandria, its function is typically imperial – an extravagant dining room. The use of the Canopus as a dining suite would certainly allow the re-inclusion of the considerable amount of Dionysiac sculpture found in the surrounding area.

As an elaborate dining room, the Canopus has much in common with a peculiar monument type, the dining grotto.[85] The first and most famous of these still extant is the so-called Grotto of Tiberius at Sperlonga (Figure 5), a natural cave decorated with sculpture and fronted by a *triclinium*.[86] The sculptural programme featured large tableaux of the adventures of Odysseus, including Scylla attacking the hero's ship and the blinding of Polyphemus (Figure 23), alongside a range of apparently unconnected sculpture, including Dionysiac motifs. As at Tivoli, these latter pieces are usually detached from the Odyssean sculpture by their attribution to an earlier phase of the grotto's use. However, the grotto is well suited to eclecticism and disorder, a liminal environment at the most elemental level where sea meets land and civilisation meets chaos.

Whilst Tiberius's ownership of the Sperlonga grotto is largely speculation, it is easy to see how such a dark, fantasy world might appeal to an emperor. The maritime grotto at Baiae, which appears to have belonged to the emperor Claudius, features a *triclinium* surrounded by sculpture.[87] The blinding of Polyphemus took centre stage, flanked by statues of Dionysus. In a further six side niches, the imperial presence is made permanent with statues of the emperor's family. The portrait of his mother was accompanied by a small child – a Cupid? – giving her the air of Venus, matronly overseer of the Julio-Claudian line. In the decadence of Baiae, perhaps Claudius could enjoy the quasi-divine status, and hence the divine and mythic company, he was under obligation to disguise at Rome. It would take Nero apparently completely to misunderstand the liminal power of the grotto type and to recreate a grotto, complete with Polyphemus mosaic, in the Domus Aurea itself.[88] Domitian reverted to tradition by restricting his grotto to a lakeside spot in his *villa* at Castel Gandolfo where he could dine with Polyphemus and Scylla in peace.[89]

From these beginnings, the Canopus can be regarded both as development and departure merging functions and types to create imperial novelty.[90] Succeeding again where Nero had failed, the artificial hood of the Serapeum shelters the Euripus, the ultimate condensation of the ocean. The most liminal and hybrid of structures becomes one of the key structures of a *villa*, which paraded the emperor's triumph over boundaries and limitations. The Dionysiac and Odyssean themes, in which past emperors had indulged, were brought together with images from around the empire. Hadrian had envisaged the most wide-reaching impression of imperial power yet, realising an unlimited fantasy that straddled the world of the gods and of empire. Disparate geographic locations were united within a jumbled, cultic, mythic, and imperial world in which the city of Rome, represented by the river god Tiber, was simply another fantastic component in the service of Hadrian.

But if Hadrian was the centre of attention in the Tivoli Canopus, where did that leave Antinous? Previous explanations of the complex have all taken the boy's death as their focus even though the Serapeum appears to predate his death. However, that is not to preclude the significance of Antinous's presence here or throughout the *villa*. The image of Antinous accounts for the majority of sculptural subjects found at Tivoli, far exceeding the incidence of portraits of Hadrian. This is a significant fact given the self-aggrandising project that Hadrian had initiated at Tivoli. The portrait of Antinous (Figure 24) is generally understood as the summation of the second-century perception of beauty, the idealism of his smooth, regular features offset by a head full of long curls.[91]

Antinous's bland portrait reflects the vague details about his life, which circulated the empire. His birth in Bithynia and death in the Nile are the only personal details that can be reconstructed. It would seem that his postmortem mythologising, rather than the realities of his life, caused his celebrity. His fame was not confined to the *villa*: all over the empire Antinous became a familiar figure as cults sprang up in East and, perhaps rather more surprisingly, West.[92]

24. Antinous, portrait bust, British Museum. Photo: Copyright © The British Museum.

As if to reflect its lack of personal identity, the Antinous type is often found in a range of disguises, perhaps as Osiris (Figure 25) or Dionysus. In these images Antinous becomes the leader of the mythic and geographic realms alluded to in the sculpture found throughout Tivoli, particularly in the Canopus. He fulfils each fantasy expressed in the *villa* in the position of authority, which we might expect to have been held by Hadrian himself.

Antinous could not have attracted such adulation by himself, his persona simply was not strong enough. His popularity depended on his close affiliation to the imperial family, particularly Hadrian, and the imperial cult. Antinous could never escape his dependence on and subordination to the imperial family. Of all the outrageous costumes that he is dressed in, he is never represented in any familiar emperor guises. Even his divine disguises do not interfere with imperial affectations. Emperors chose traditional Roman gods to emulate. A Claudius-Jupiter or a Commodus-Hercules, comic as they might seem to us, could be considered a dignified identity

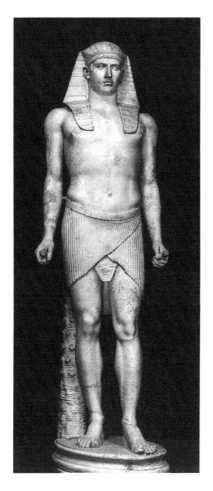

25. Tivoli, Villa of Hadrian, Antinous in Egyptian costume, Musei Vaticani, Rome. Photo: Photo Alinari (Anderson).

for an emperor. On the other hand, it was impossible for an emperor to cavort around Rome as Dionysus or Osiris. As much as the emperor had the power to overhaul his personal image, he was also constrained by the generic imagination of his populace.

The restrictions of the imperial image may well explain why Antinous was so important to Hadrian. Antinous was an empty cipher who could be dressed to be anybody and anything. The versatility of his image allowed him to take on guises that Hadrian could never have been seen to assume. The imperial icon of Hadrian, even with added beard, could only be understood in the terms of traditional, Romanocentric rhetoric and visualised in stock, imperial guises. But this same rhetoric sat awkwardly with the *villa*'s emphasis on divorcing the emperor from any specific, worldly, geographical location. So it is Antinous who becomes the icon of the Hadrianic age. He is the perfect scapegoat for un-Roman activity – close enough for Hadrian to garner his successes, distanced enough to disclaim any adversity.

In this context, the legends of Antinous make more sense. The myth that Antinous drowned to ensure Hadrian's immortality demonstrated the synthesis in their relationship. The death and subsequent deification of Antinous allowed him to embody Hadrianic ideology in a way that Hadrian himself could not. The popular portrayal of the couple as lovers also expressed the relationship. The paedogogue Hadrian was in thrall to, but still master of, the "other." In this respect, Antinous must be the perfect guardian of the sculpture and fantasies of the Canopus, the entire *villa* complex, and an empire that was creating within itself new geographical, economic, and intellectual centres to rival that of Rome.[93]

This interpretation of the *villa* can perhaps only be fully appreciated with hindsight. The empire-wide interest expressed at Tivoli marks an important shift in the ongoing transition from the Romanocentric view of the early Principate. The *villa* presents an idea of emperorship that embraced and collapsed the poles of centre and periphery, recognising and reconciling the tensions between the two extremes by acknowledging a series of alternative centres. The magnetic force that bound the provinces to Rome was not unbreakable, and the impression of Hadrian's power is enhanced, not least through Antinous, by harnessing the explosive energies on the periphery which threatened to blow the empire apart. During the third century, military emperors from the frontiers, empowered by increasing conflict on the borders, finally negated the city of Rome's role as centre of the empire. When Diocletian reached the throne at the end of the century, he acknowledged the changes within the empire with a whole new legislature and a tetrarchy, distributing imperial responsibility around the empire.[94]

CONCLUSION

Hadrian's Villa at Tivoli was the ultimate expression of the fantasies fostered by the Roman, republican elite in the impressions they created in their home. Like that elite, the imperial family used their palaces as depositories of *memoria* and to provide expressions of their political ambitions. In this pursuit, they were helped by senatorial insistence on retaining the traditional rhetorics of domestic space. In the House of Augustus, the *princeps* adjusted this traditional code for a new imperial super-elite, carefully doing so within the established framework of wall painting. But emperors were clearly able, perhaps even expected, to realise the painted fantasies of ordinary households. It was because of the need to convey an impression of limitless power that such lavish estates as the Domus Aurea and Hadrian's Villa at Tivoli were increasingly necessary. These estates were not mere amplifications of traditional house types but their anti-types.

The palaces of Rome show us how power allowed the emperor to overcome and to collapse those dichotomies, which the republican elite had had to balance so carefully in order to demonstrate their *Romanitas* and to participate in Roman public life. Emperors were beyond this need to conform. They paraded their difference by collapsing tensions; the gulfs between mortal and divine, *rus* and *urbs*, centre and periphery were gradually overcome. The very nature of the palaces reveals this – they are *domus*, *horti*, and *villa*s all in one. The emperor showed the tensions between different levels of identity to have been similarly collapsed. Both personally and professionally he was Rome.

Above all, the person of the emperor and his palace began to collapse the distance between Rome and the provinces. He made the entire empire his audience. The inhabitants of the empire would have to fall in line under their ultimate patron, the emperor. They had both to be seen to conform and to be worthy of participation in empire. Two issues thus confronted the imperial elite. One was the need not to transgress, not to be seen to threaten the power balance. It was not for them to realise their fantasies of authority. Second came the need to participate, to express a Roman identity, a participation that would depend precisely on the ability to challenge and to compete. Whereas in the emperor we see layers of identity reconciled, beyond Rome we might see them at their most stretched as provincials struggle to make their personal, ethnic, and local civic identities coincide with their new status as members of the Roman empire.

The palaces of the emperor have brought us as close to the domestic centre of the Roman world as we could possibly get, but still the definitive statement of *Romanitas* seems elusive. The emperors focussed their attention on the fantastic and the peripheral in visualising their power in their houses. As such, they remind us of the important role that the world beyond the city played in making Rome. In the rest of the book we will be exploring the houses beyond Rome, first in Campania and then in the distant provinces, to see how these populations coped with being Roman and how Romans coped with the reality that inspired their fantasies.

PART TWO

POMPEII – THE LIVING HOUSE

4

Finding a Way into the Pompeian House

I f the texts of Rome can give us insight into the ideal of the *domus*, then the archaeological evidence of Pompeii (Figure 26) is often taken as presenting us with the reality. As the best-preserved Roman site in Italy, for several centuries Pompeii has been used as a microcosmic model of life in Rome herself. In fact, some might consider Pompeii's part in the history of Rome to be somewhat overplayed. We must remind ourselves that she was, in the larger scheme of things, fairly insignificant, a prosperous market town in Campania, famous only to the people of Rome for her amphitheatre riot and, of course, the eruption of Vesuvius, which destroyed her along with Pliny the Elder on 24 August 79 A.D.[1]

It is essential to bear in mind the differences between Pompeii and Rome if we are to benefit fully from her evidence. Pompeii was not a Roman town, becoming so only when it was made a colony in 80 B.C. after its defeat in the Social Wars. As a busy harbour town on the River Sarno, Pompeii had been populated by the Samnites since the third century B.C. and received much Hellenistic influence through contact with Greek merchants and the population of the nearby Greek colonies. Her oldest building seems to have been a Greek temple built overlooking the sea. Open to many outside influences, Pompeii absorbed social and architectural practices from central Italy, Rome, and the Hellenistic world with which she traded. Rome was neither the only influence nor the filter through which foreign influences reached Pompeii. It is important to remember this because the many similarities between Pompeii and the capital can cause us to overlook the fact that Pompeii had its own independent identity as well as that thrust on it by the colonists.

Arriving in colonial Pompeii, a Roman would have little trouble finding his bearings. Just as at Rome, the approach roads to Pompeii were lined

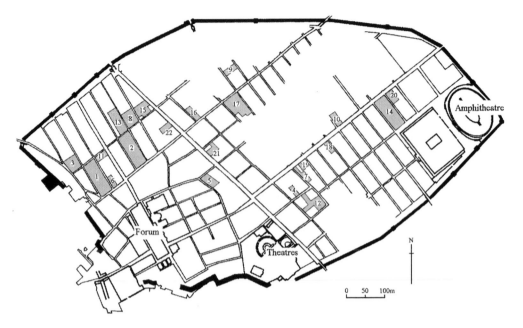

Key:

1. House of Pansa (VI.vi.1)
2. House of the Faun (VI.xii.2)
3. House of Sallust (VI.ii.4)
4. House of the Ceii (I.vi.15)
5. House of Caesius Blandus (VII.i.40)
6. House of the Tragic Poet (VI.viii.3)
7. House of Paquius Proculus (I.vii.1)
8. House of the Vettii (VI.xv.1)
9. House of M. Lucretius Fronto (V.iv.a)
10. House of Trebius Valens (III.ii.1)
11. House of the Small Fountain (VI.viii.23)
12. House of the Menander (I.x.4)
13. House of the Labyrinth (VI.xi.10)
14. House of Octavius Quartio (II.ii.4)
15. House of the Gilded Cupids (VI.xvi.7)
16. House of the Silver Wedding (V.ii.1)
17. House of the Centenary (IX.viii.6)
18. House of the Fruit Orchard (I.ix.5)
19. House of the Priest Amandus (I.vii.7)
20. House of the Marine Venus (II.iii.3)
21. House of Marcus Lucretius (IX.iii.5)
22. House of Orpheus (VI.xiv.20)

26. Pompeii, plan.

with tombs, and all these roads led from the city gates to the Forum. The Forum was built before the coming of the Romans, and pre-colonial Pompeii also boasted its own theatre and baths, to which the colonists added the amphitheatre.[2] Throughout the colonial city were temples, most to recognisably Roman gods but also to gods from the Hellenistic world, including the Temple of Isis, which enjoyed a prominent place in the town at a time when the eastern goddess was still eyed with suspicion in Rome. At points, then, it is possible to see where Pompeii's self-identity and its imposed Roman identity might diverge. Again, we are given an insight to the formation of identity in the Roman world. Just as an individual could achieve *Romanitas* through participation and behaviour, so too could a city be accommodated within empire if she appeared to accommodate a sufficient number of Roman practices and adopt appropriate ideals. This system allowed the empire to expand effectively and economically; the local was incorporated into, rather than rejected from, the centre. The extent to which the Temple of Isis was incorporated into civic life is evident from the inscription over the precinct entrance, which testifies that N. Popidius Ampliatus erected the temple on behalf of his son Numerius Popidius Celsinus.[3] This example straightaway prepares us for the complex layering of identities we will find in Pompeii. The donation allows the family a tenuous public profile usually denied by their freed status. The local platform and the alien cult are used as a vehicle for acceptance into the Roman social system.

More importantly for us, Pompeii boasts street after street of rich *atrium* houses, many with complete ground-floor plans, decorative programmes, and even, occasionally, some furniture or sculpture still in situ. The earliest houses of Pompeii of the third century B.C. appear to have been *atrium* houses backed by simple, working gardens. During the second century, Hellenistic influences began to be reflected through the adoption of the peristyle, usually replacing those back gardens to become an integral display feature of all the larger houses. The planted peristyle was probably a distortion of the peristyle courts of Hellenistic houses, such as those on Delos, and may well have been a distant imitation of the palaces of Hellenistic kings, several of which were planted as gardens.[4] Given that the *atrium*-peristyle house type was established so early in Pompeii's history, it is perhaps remarkable that the houses of Pompeii so clearly parallel the Roman house as laid out by Vitruvius. The very fact that the House of Pansa (VI.vi.1) (Figure 1) has already been used as an illustration of his design shows us how similar in appearance the houses of Pompeii seem to have been to those of Rome. They were probably not deliberately based on them, rather both cities developed their houses through exposure to similar ideals and influences and in response to similar practical and social needs.

When investigating the Pompeian house, it is necessary, too, to realise that, as with the remains of the House of Augustus, in applying Vitruvius to the archaeology, we are applying the ideal to the real. Architects had to rework the dream house to fit irregular plots or downgrade it according to space and resources. We must be aware that we are looking at works in progress. No occupied house is ever finished, and the city had not prepared for its internment. On the contrary, it was a living city in constant flux. A number of houses have walls that were stripped and prepared for a new painting scheme, and many homes have cemented doorways. Most houses standing in A.D. 79 were probably much changed from their original appearance. Different owners had different tastes, resources, household members, and trades. All these factors could entail alterations. Wall paintings faded, the elements attacked the structure – the earthquake of 62 caused immense damage across the whole town. In the aftermath, individual houses and even whole neighbourhoods were transformed. That several *atrium domus* were converted into fulleries has often been taken as a sign of Pompeii's economic decline after the earthquake. However, localities within the town were probably constantly changing status and inhabitants even without the impetus of seismic activity. The final occupants, whether aristocrats or tradesmen, were living in houses that were amalgams of years and years of habitation.

Pompeii was not built in a day. The residential areas developed over centuries under different social circumstances and according to the fashions and practices of the time. Even within one *domus*, modern paintings graced old walls, and peristyle extensions were added to traditional *atrium* houses.[5] On the other hand, we should acknowledge that fashions simply did not change as fast as today. Although it is clear that when innovations, such as the peristyle, arrived in Pompeii, they were widely adopted, such innovations were few and far between. Although there is an opinion that the *atrium* house was becoming outdated by A.D. 79, it is possible to argue the opposite that the *atrium domus* continued to be the dominant domestic type as it had been for centuries.[6] Certainly other houses were built on different plans, but they stood side by side with traditional houses.

The matter of different houseplans reminds us that Pompeians were not all identical. Quite apart from the question of personal taste, the inhabitants were not all of the same status or origin. They would have included Pompeians, Roman veterans, freedmen, and immigrants who may well have harboured different domestic ideals. Although occasional attempts have been made to distinguish between inhabitants (Zanker proposes that the homes built on terraces on the western edge of the city were built by colonists[7]), no such split has yet been convincingly observed. In fact, the upheaval in Pompeian society, which certainly must have occurred with the imposition of a new population in 80 B.C. and is reflected in a proliferation of building projects in the public arena, for instance the amphitheatre, is hardly traceable in the domestic sphere, at least not to our modern eyes. Given the importance of the house in conveying *Romanitas*, this must imply that the houses of Samnite Pompeii were considered Roman enough for their new roles, Roman enough to house the veterans, and, perhaps more importantly, Roman enough to allow Pompeian occupants to participate successfully in the life of the colony.

Having observed these difficulties, however, we should not be beaten by them. Given all the variations that a city the size and age of Pompeii could display, the overall conformity of the houses is remarkable. The homeowners of Pompeii seem to have been much more eager to demonstrate their conformity to, and participation in, local traditions than to assert their individuality. The phenomenon might be explained on two levels: first, competition for public recognition was so fierce that nobody dared go out on a limb in the way they presented themselves, and, second, the cult of individualism, paramount in the modern west, is very different from Roman attitudes. A Roman identity depended on adherence to the family and to the community as much as on the self. To be seen to stand alone would be a disaster.

Another difference between literary and real homes is that a real house has to accommodate those who live in it. We have only met ideal representations of these inhabitants – Lucretia weaving in the *atrium*, for example. We have not had to worry where the loom was stored or how the room was lit. We have only looked at daily life as it was lived in ritual; we have not considered the chaos of a room commandeered for childbirth or for the confinement of a last illness, only the appropriate decoration of the *atrium* when it is all over. The house must find ways of coping with our most intimate activities: sleeping, eating, defecating, and copulating, in addition to dealing with birth, illness, and death. These are the realities of family life behind the image that the house radiates to the outside world. The aim of this chapter, then, is to investigate how the houses of Pompeii were created to cope with their two major functions: the idealistic role of the house as signifier of the family's public presence and Roman identity and the practical needs of housing the family and their daily lives. We might start by ascertaining how the inhabitants of Pompeii coped with Roman demands of being permanently on display. How did their domestic architecture reflect this pressure?

THE POMPEIAN AND THE URBAN LANDSCAPE

The extent to which public and private mingled can only truly be observed by examining the houses and their occupants within the wider context of Pompeii. The domestic arrangements of Pompeian houses directly depended on the facilities provided in a Roman town. The household would visit one of the three public baths, making domestic provision of bathing a luxury rather than necessity. It was only because the *paterfamilias* left the *atrium* after the *salutatio* for the *forum* that the *atrium* could be freed up for other domestic activities. A more permanent reminder of the link between the family and the landscape was afforded by the connection between the houses within the walls and the tombs outside the gates.

Whilst the persons of the household were a living link between house and town, men who had achieved public positions were honoured with a more permanent civic presence. In Augustan Pompeii, Holconius Rufus used his money to make such an impression. His name is preserved on inscriptions in the amphitheatre and theatre; in return for his services, he was hailed *pater coloniae*, and a statue was dedicated to him at a busy crossroads in the heart of the city.[8] The *forum* was his *atrium*, and he entertained guests in the amphitheatre and theatre, which he had financed.

Many of the public benefactions in Pompeii reflect family structures as well as individuals. So, for instance, the inscription at the Isis temple records both father and son. The imposition of the household in public territory is, perhaps, most emphatically demonstrated in the Augustan period with the Building of Eumachia, a portico fronted by a deep porch, located in the Pompeian Forum.[9] The building was put up to commemorate the filial piety of Eumachia's son but appears to have been ostensibly dedicated to the Concordia Augusta and Pietas. Augustus's wife Livia had recently dedicated her portico in Rome to this cause as a means of celebrating the triumph of her own son, the future emperor Tiberius. The porch of the Building of Eumachia is decorated with a statue of Romulus bearing an inscription, which reflects that of the image of Romulus set up in the Forum Augustum back at Rome. Within the portico itself was discovered a headless statue of Concordia bearing a *cornucopia*. Richardson believes that it once flanked a lost statue of Livia, whilst Zanker makes the link even more implicit by proposing that the statue was Livia in the guise of Concordia. In the *cryptoporticus* beneath the portico stood a statue of Eumachia inscribed with both her name and that of her son. This complex demonstrates a family's attempts to publicise its strength and presence through the adoption of a public, imperial building type. In effect, they too had made themselves at home in the city. Eumachia's presence throughout the city is also demonstrated by her apse-shaped tomb just outside the Nucerian Gate. This set of monuments shows that local elites were just as eager to make the city their home were as their counterparts in Rome.

THE POMPEIAN HOUSE – FIRST IMPRESSIONS

If we want to find expression of the Roman understanding of public and private in the Pompeian *domus*, then it is pointless to confine the search to within the house. The extent to which the family lived its life beyond the threshold of their home is demonstrated by the extent to which the physical house itself is fused with the outside. The façades of these houses show us

27. Pompeii, House of the Faun, façade. Photo: Kate Gilliver.

the physical, visual boundary of the house, if not the conceptual limits of the family who are equally eager to be projected in the town.

The façades of the House of the Faun (VI.xii.2) (Figure 27) or the House of Sallust (VI.ii.4) are typical of the larger *atrium* houses of Pompeii. Both open directly onto busy thoroughfare streets. The House of the Faun, in particular, is part of a block of old, grand houses that enjoy close proximity to the Forum. Front gardens, so important to us as a way of distancing ourselves from the public street, were unheard of in Pompeii. Instead the façade of the house brought the public world directly to the homeowner. The positioning of houses alone confirms the complete inversion of modern ideas of privacy.

The façades were broken by shops that flanked the front door of the houses and receded into the house and that, sometimes, even had entrances into the *domus* behind. The shops mingle not only public and private but also status divisions. These were not smart boutiques; there was a *thermopolium* in the shops in the façade of the House of Sallust, which may well predate the possible conversion of the house into an inn. Such shops would have been frequented by the urban poor who did not enjoy their own facilities. The careful provision of kitchens away from the public space within the house is rather undercut by the proximity of cooking to the front entrance of these homes.[10]

The decoration of *domus* façades further elided public and private. Throughout Pompeii, two types of façade decoration predominate. The first, popular around the imposing streets of regio VI north of the Forum, is similar to First Style wall painting, with moulded plaster work imitating large ashlar blocks. These walls hide the brick of which most of the houses are built and give the impression of major public building work. The second style is more simple; the wall is covered with stucco, and the bottom half of the wall is painted red. The House of the Ceii (I.vi.15), located down a side street near the theatres is decorated in this way (Figure 28).[11] Generally, such painting is shared over several houses, seemingly contributing to the public, open community of the street, which overrides the individual identities of each *domus*. The amount of electioneering graffiti painted on the walls of houses would indeed suggest that people in the street regarded the walls as part of the public domain rather than the preserve of the house-owner. Walls were a free-for-all, defining the parameters of the public street as much as the individual property behind. Homeowners seem to have respected the nature of their front walls and allowed them to remain public property. Few tried to impose their own presence onto the walls. Images such as the frescoes of Romulus and Aeneas, which flank the entrance of House IX.xiii.5, are in the minority.[12] More generally, only commercial premises used their façades to advertise their wares. The famous image of Venus and her elephants on the façade of the Shop of Verecundus is fairly typical of such self-promotion.[13]

For the homeowner, there appears to have been only one acceptable place for self-promotion in his façade. The door, as the only possible method of direct ingress, was the one component of the exterior façade that could be seen by passers-by as linking with the interior. This was the only spot in the house boundary where it was evident that there was a house behind. Every time the door was opened, it afforded a glimpse into the homeowner's domestic world. The door was, therefore, an indisputable part of that world and an opportunity to impress. That Pompeians took this opportunity is easy to discern; enormous doorways were hung with great wooden doors fitted with bronze bolts, locks, and insignia. The threshold to the private was marked with great pomp in the realm of the public.

The majority of older houses have impressive portals flanked by half-columns or pilasters, an architectural component borrowed from public architecture, particularly, of course, the temple. The great door of the House of the Faun provides a good example (Figure 27). Other houses complement this architecture with further elaboration. House II.ii.4, for example, has a relief of a commemorative wreath over the portal, reminiscent of the

28. Pompeii, House of Ceii, façade. Photo: SJH.

honours awarded to Augustus and displayed at his threshold. The entrance of the House of Epidius Rufus (IX.i.20) goes much further in commanding the entrance as public space for the household. A huge tribunal platform runs along the façade like a mini Rostrum at Rome.[14]

The platform of Epidius Rufus is a rare expression of private penetration into public space. Even the House of the Faun, one of the foremost houses of the town, lays claim to the public space in front of its huge doorway merely through the Latin inscription, *Have*, set in the pavement rather like a welcome mat. The greeting indicated the owner's command of *Romanitas* and his public accessibility, giving the impression that everyone is invited, every potential voter can get near the great man inside. From the inside looking out, however, the entrance appeared much more impressive, flanked by the three-dimensional decoration of the *fauces*. The walls of the *fauces* are decorated with miniature stucco sculptures of second-storey grand, columned portals (Figure 29), as if the house had an upper level of further halls.[15] This palatial impression is kept strictly within the house, although open doors would have allowed a tantalising glimpse from the street. The opulence of the house is ultimately the preserve of the inside.

Despite the apparently public view of the façade, the rest of the house remained sheltered behind the outer walls. These walls surrounded the property, punctuated occasionally by small windows set high out of reach.

29. Pompeii, House of the Faun, vestibule. Photo: SJH.

With the obvious exception of shop fronts, there is no precedent for large picture windows in the ground-floor walls of the houses of Pompeii. The most simplistic explanation for this might be shelter from the weather. Such explanations, however, are rather disproved by the proliferations of wide openings inside the house, particularly the *triclinia* and *tablina*, which face onto the open peristyle. It must be concluded that the houses themselves are deliberately secretive – whether for security against crime or against the forces of vituperative rhetoric (either through failure to keep up with or overeagerness to surpass their neighbours) remains to be seen.

The walls and high windows of Pompeian houses indicate to what extent the complicated relationship of public to private actually permeated architecture. The rectangular house plots offer barely a clue to the architectural articulations that might lie within. For the Roman senator, the importance of building a house in a prominent, busy location was to be seen. It might seem odd, then, that the owners of the houses at Pompeii who appear to have shared their enthusiasm for a central situation, seem to have hidden away from public gaze their most potent displays. The Pompeian homeowner is restricted in impinging his own ideas on the public by the bounding of his territory by that public realm. Only through the entrance can the owner project his presence onto public space.

THE VIEW – FROM PUBLIC TO PRIVATE

Given the restricted imposition of the *domus* onto the public arena, the entrance became a crucial space where the homeowner and the outsider could communicate. When the doors were open, they admitted to the viewer a thoroughly planned view. From the doorposts, it looks as if the Pompeian house fulfils Vitruvian demands.[16] The viewer sees the symmetrical and sequential arrangement of *fauces*, *atrium*, and *tablinum* around the central axis and, in the "better" homes, a peek through the *tablinum* to the peristyle beyond (Figure 30). The central axis gives the impression to the viewer standing on the threshold that the whole house has been arranged around his standpoint (Figure 31). The house appears to open up to the viewer, giving access to the public, ceremonial areas of the patron's domain. The axis cuts straight through the house. The house is laid bare and made public.

Unfortunately, to read the view from the threshold as evidence for the prescriptive architecture of Vitruvius is to misread the remains. The combination of *atrium*, *tablinum*, and so on, as seen from the front entrance, is precisely that – just a view. It is what Drerup described as "bildraum" rather than "realraum" as far back as 1959. The view does not reflect the reality of the space beyond the door but presents the viewer with an aspect of that space, carefully framed as if it were a picture. The appearance of axial symmetry is also the consequence of this framing. The long, narrow dimensions of the *fauces* channel the viewer's sight to a very restrictive path through the house. The appearance of openness and publicness that meets the viewer might not bear any relation to the real use of the space. This is merely evidence for the appearance of conformity to Roman, Vitruvian doctrines, not their consistent application.

The role of the view in the Pompeian house is quite distinct from that of architecture. Drerup was the first to endow the view with a life of its own and to explore the effects of his bildraum phenomenon on the way the visitor experienced the Pompeian *domus*. He takes as his starting point the traditional view from the vestibule, which appears to have originated as a means of framing the *tablinum*.[17] In the days before peristyles, the *tablinum* is thought to have been the most crucial room in the house – the master bedroom. The union of the head of the household and his wife was both practically and symbolically placed at the heart of the house. The idea of the marriage bed as bedrock of the household has a long heritage – Odysseus himself built his and Penelope's bed around a living tree at the centre of his *oikos*.[18] As the *domus* developed, the *tablinum* seems to have become more of an office, but it was still closely connected with family history, a depository of family records. As the *paterfamilias* worked in this office,

30. Pompeii, House of Tragic Poet, view from entrance.
Photo: A. Crafer.

he was displayed to the viewer as the current, public representative of his *familia*.

Both the view into the *domus* and the architecture of the house begin at the threshold. However, there is an instant tension between the two media as both promise different levels of access to the visitor. On one hand, the view appears to open up the house to the viewer on the threshold, inviting him to participate in the riches of his patron. However, the architectural reality of the space rather works against his quest for access. The *fauces*, which connect door to *atrium*, generally take the form of a high, narrow corridor that acts as a highly restrictive, easily policed entrance. For the viewer who

31. Pompeii, House of the Vettii, view from entrance.
Photo: Kate Gilliver.

remains on the threshold, the length of the vestibule is effective in distancing
him from the interior, the often upward sloping nature of the floor adding
to the effect. The interior looks as distanced and as superior as possible,
making the *paterfamilias* who seemed so near suddenly both physically and
socially remote.

The decoration of the vestibule is instrumental in mediating between
reality and fantasy. Many vestibules are covered in mosaic which faces the
viewer on the threshold.[19] The mosaics present static images that invite the
viewer to stop and consider. All this would seem to suggest that the mosaics
are offering specific information to the visitor. On one level, it might be possible to see these mosaics as offering a splendid chance for the homeowners

32. Pompeii, House of Caesius Blandus, vestibule mosaic.
Photo: SJH.

to assert their personalities and interests, to make their home a reflection of
themselves. The mosaic of the bear, which fronts the eponymous House of
the Bear (VII.ii.5), for instance, might reflect the owner's interest in bears, a
family association with the creatures, or perhaps, more practically, a commemoration of supplying bears to the amphitheatre. The vestibule of the
House of Caesius Blandus (VII.i.40) is decorated with a heraldic design of
dolphins flanking a crossed rudder and trident (Figure 32). In this case, it
might be sensible to assume that the design was commissioned to reflect on
the owners – presumably to convey their success through shipping links.
It would not be the only direct allusion to financial gain at the entrance
of a Pompeian house as the *Salve Lucru* (Greetings Profit!) imprint on the
pavement outside House VII.i.47 would attest.[20] Wealth afforded its owner
participation in a society governed by patronage, both civic and private.
Such advertising of his wealth or desire for it would demonstrate a houseowner's aspirations or achievements. But if the mosaic advertises the owner's
success, does it invite the viewer into the house to share in the delights of
luxury? This might be doubted if we consider the iconography of two other
vestibule mosaics. Both the Houses of the Tragic Poet (VI.viii.3) and of
Paquius Proculus (I.vii.1) (Figure 33) have mosaic guard dogs.[21] They are
not inviting images and the first, in particular, carries a clear warning to the
uninvited guest – *Cave Canem*, Beware of the Dog.

These mosaics, facing and tilted towards the outside viewer, emphasise the
participation of that viewer. The master of the house has clearly invested
some expense in entertaining the visitor from the door and introducing

33. Pompeii, House of Paquius Proculus, vestibule mosaic. Photo: Photo Alinari.

him to his family. However, the possibility of access is blocked in reality. In several cases, the threshold between the *fauces* and *atrium* beyond is marked by a strip mosaic that not only delineates the beginning of the next room but also enforces a pause. The House of Caesius Blandus follows up its heraldic design with closed city gates (Figure 32). The nature of the shape of the grid forces the craftsman to create a composition that reads side to side rather than sending the viewer's sight forward. The effect is to break the impetus of travel along the central axis and to mark the practical terminus of the outsider's access.

The lessening welcome offered to the viewer is particularly visible in the case of the House of Paquius Proculus. Beyond the vestibule mosaic (Figure 33) lays the *atrium* threshold mosaic of centaurs and, beyond that, the elaborately patterned mosaic carpet of the *atrium*.[22] Motifs of animals and weapons appear at various places throughout the geometric design, and, importantly, they face several different viewpoints. This mosaic is crucial in implying that, beyond the vestibule, the space is no longer the sole preserve of the outside viewer and that this viewer no longer occupies the mosaicist as his main priority. For the first time, the mosaic of the *atrium* hints at a circulation within the house, at the participation of the *paterfamilias*, *familia* and invited *amici* and *clientes*.

However, all is not lost for the visitor on the threshold. Just as his chances of physically entering the house are dashed, he is offered a view that takes a privileged path through the house, which those inside cannot physically follow. The axial view of the *atrium* passes straight over the *impluvium* and onto the *tablinum*. This view is highly symbolic in passing through the apparent centre of the home and the traditional *locus* of the house's prosperity, ensured by the collection of water through the *compluvium*. Those inside the house are forced to walk around the *impluvium*, keeping to the edges of the *atrium*. That area of movement in the *atrium,* and the wall decoration that frames it, is largely lost to the viewer because of the narrow framing of his vision. However free-roaming the view into the *domus* may be supposed to be, the fact is that the long walls of the vestibule act as blinkers, channelling the sightlines into a much narrower scope around the central axis and shutting off visual access to the areas of the house that flank that axis.[23]

As a result, the viewer's sight is whisked through the empty middle space and onto the *tablinum* and through that to the peristyle. The effect is again one of a passage that is impossible to recreate – the real path from *atrium* to peristyle lies to the side of the *tablinum* in narrow corridors. Again the viewer gains an insight into a symbolically central area of the house but cannot hope to sustain it in reality. Here, the viewer could be afforded the symbolic vision of the *paterfamilias* in his study. However, his eye could not rest here as the axis again passes through the room, its decor obscured by its oblique angle. The extent to which the eye passed through, rather than looked at, the room is evident from the House of the Vettii (VI.xv.1) (Figure 31). The view into the house appears to conform to the traditional configuration. The view between *atrium* c and peristyle m is framed by the half-pilastered entrance to the *tablinum*, which is flanked by the entrances to the corridors. However, there is no *tablinum* (Figure 34). This lack is only really evident from the point of view of someone inside the house. To the outsider, nothing appears to be missing.[24]

The view now travels to the peristyle, facilitated by the large picture window of the *tablinum* and the widening of the intercolumnations of the colonnade. By altering the sequence of columns in the peristyle, the viewer was again privileged in his view of a perfect symmetrical axis, which was, in fact, only in his own perception. The focussed view again missed out the sides of the peristyle, people moving around in the colonnades, and the rooms beyond. The fact that the outside viewer was much in mind for those planning even the deepest areas of the house is clear from the fact that many houses do not have full peristyles but just enough architectural detail to convince the viewer there must be one. This is true of both the House of the Tragic Poet (Figure 35) and the House of Marcus Lucretius Fronto (V.iv.a) (Figure 36).

At the end of the peristyle, the view ended on the rear house wall. The visual impression created at this point was, therefore, of crucial importance. The eye had travelled over the *atrium*, the *tablinum*, and the peristyle but came to rest at the end of the axis on that which closed the view – the framed picture. The view through the House of Trebius Valens (III.ii.1) culminates in the *triclinium* where, against a somewhat uninspiring painted, tile-effect backdrop, the true view is presumably the owner and his guests at table (Figure 37).[25] The choice of scene that crowned the view reflected the personal tastes and resources of the owners. Many houses provide a visually splendid centrepiece for the back of the house. The Houses of the Small Fountain (VI.viii.23) and of the Large Fountain (VI.viii.22) are named after the fountains covered in glass mosaic and shells that can be seen at the back of the house from the entrance (Figure 38).[26]

The positioning of the *lararium* in the peristyle of the House of the Tragic Poet indicates just to what extent these features were situated for the benefit of the outside viewer. Although the far side of the *lararium* shrine is hidden behind the west colonnade of the peristyle, the niche itself is positioned exactly along the central axis (Figure 30). The viewer at the threshold looks beyond the loyal guard dog in the *fauces*, to the distant *lararium* framed by the peristyle. For the initiated insider, however, the reality of the peristyle is somewhat different (Figure 35). There is not a full peristyle, only two sides of a colonnade. The *lararium* itself appears wildly off centre, thrust into the corner behind the lateral row of columns. The experience of the house was deliberately differentiated between insider and outsider. Even where insider and outsider looked on the same object, they did so from a different perspective.

From the entrance of the House of the Tragic Poet, the *lararium* is viewed as a culmination of a vista that incorporates a particularly Vitruvian *domus*. The *fauces*, *atrium*, and *lararium* hint at the proper duties of the *paterfamilias* safeguarding his *familia* and *clientes* through his observance of appropriate social and religious ritual. The house, or rather this view of the house, reflects the public status of the virtuous owner as a member of the elite responsible for the political and religious welfare of the town – as in the *forum*, so at home. Similarly, the *triclinium* of the House of Trebius Valens (Figure 37) is set, by virtue of the entrance vista, within the context of the official duties of the house owner, alluding to the formal connotations of the entertainment of *amici* and *clientes*. This element of the dining ritual is emphasised here by its visual relation to the *atrium*, where the same *clientes* were received in the morning, during the *salutatio*.

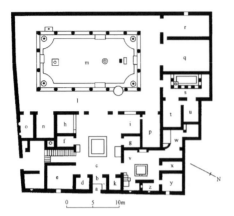

34. Pompeii, House of the Vettii, plan.

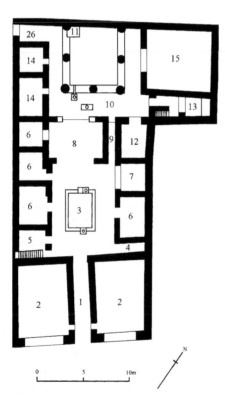

35. Pompeii, House of Tragic Poet, plan.

From the point of view of the outsider, the house gives an impression of *gravitas* and *pietas* appropriate to the elite family – a true Vitruvian house. It is the house of a family of *virtus*, open and symmetrical. However, this is not the view from the inside. In both cases, the immediate visual context of *lararium* and *triclinium*, as seen by the insider, is not that of the traditional ritual area of the *atrium* but of the garden peristyle, presumably putting a

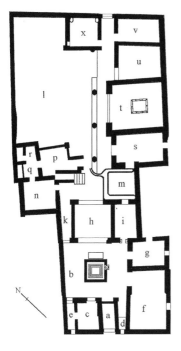

36. Pompeii, House of Marcus Lucretius Fronto, plan.

37. Pompeii, House of Trebius Valens, view of summer *triclinium*.
Photo: Photo Alinari.

38. Pompeii, House of the Small Fountain, fountain in peristyle. Photo: SJH.

quite different slant on the participant's experience of worship and dining there than that of the viewer looking on.

Even where the view from the outside looks onto material more challenging to Roman *austeritas*, it is justified by its inclusion in the moral framework of the view. The resplendent mosaic fountains in the Houses of the Fountains represent a love of private material splendour that would seem to be in direct opposition to traditional "Roman" values and public life. However, again, the fountains are carefully related to the *atrium* and the owner's official duties by means of the view axis travelling through the house. This luxury is seen to have been won through success and proper application of civic rituals. Inside, however, is another story. In their immediate contexts, the *aedicula* fountains are viewed within highly decorated pseudo-peristyles.[27] In the case of the House of the Small Fountain, in particular, the fountain stands within a two-sided colonnade and is surrounded by garden paintings on the lower walls and great scenes of sacro-idyllic and maritime landscapes above (Figure 38), scenes that carry us far from the experience of the outsider.[28]

The surroundings of the viewer at the heart of the house do not return the gaze of the viewer outside nor follow that gaze. The central axis loses its central importance as the wider context around that axis gains dominance. From within the house, particularly around the peristyle, new concerns affect the viewer. The large reception rooms looking over the peristyle often enjoy a privileged view.[29] These views, which begin from reception rooms deep inside the house, accommodate the inside viewer and reward that viewer with a spectacular picture to admire. Just as with the view offered to the outsider, architectural elements that hamper sight are easily moved. The intercolumnations of the peristyle are widened in front of the great hall 18 of the House of the Menander (I.x.4) (Figure 39), and the perspectives in the Corinthian *oecus* of the House of the Labyrinth (VI.xi.10) are clearly tailored for insiders (Figure 40).

The Corinthian *oecus* of the House of the Labyrinth offers a superb example of the extent to which these interior views detract from the axial view to/from the street. The *oecus* looks onto the peristyle through a broad opening, and its walls are painted with a Second Style perspective view. Behind an *aedicula* with broken pediment stretches a colonnade, in the middle of which rises a small round temple. Within the "real" space of the room itself, the colonnade effect is strengthened by the columns of the Corinthian *oecus* formation that run around the three closed sides of the room. The painting perspective has been tailored so as to accommodate specifically the viewpoint of those on the inside of the room. These viewers can enjoy the fantasy of the sacred complex, which has been designed for them with them at the centre. For those outside, this *oecus* is only distantly visible along the one traditional, restrictive entrance axis (Figure 41). Yet for those inside, the wall painting affords the viewer a range of complex views within his immediate physical range, immersing him within the room instead of projecting his gaze back out onto the street. The outsider looks into a house; the insider finds himself within a sacred enclosure.

The garden of the House of Octavius Quartio (II.ii.4) (Figure 42) is generally hailed as a classic, intricate example of the introspective view. The numerous, isolated perspectives of an "unreal" world abandon and transcend the more mundane singular view from the threshold.[30] This garden begins with a water channel that runs along the back of the house to a *biclinium*, k. Another long channel runs the length of the garden decorated with fountain structures, platforms, and pergolas (Figure 43). Different elements of the water channel and fountain structures are best admired from a series of vantage points.

Some would argue that the natural conclusion of the development of these more complex, pleasurable viewing systems led to the growing unpopularity of the traditional *atrium* house. For Jung, the House of the Gilded Cupids

39. Pompeii, House of the Menander, plan.

40. Pompeii, House of the Labyrinth, Corinthian *oecus*. Photo: SJH.

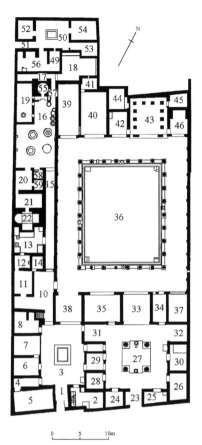

41. Pompeii, House of the Labyrinth, plan.

(VI.xvi.7) (Figure 44) demonstrates the natural conclusion of this development. The charmed vistas of the peristyle F (Figure 45) predominate to such
an extent that the *atrium* view is almost completely sidestepped. From the
fauces A, the view from outside leads over the small *atrium* B and ends at
the *tablinum* E. The real heart of the house is the great peristyle alongside,
rather than behind, the *atrium*, which now becomes the centre of the viewing
systems of the house, rather than the culmination of them.

All this would seem to complicate the usual conclusions concerning the
view. The outsider's view of the Pompeian house was indeed carefully
contrived. His sight axis through the door of the house was privileged,
sometimes at the expense of the true symmetry of the house interior, or
regardless of its asymmetry. However, the aim of this central view axis was
apparently not to lay the house open to his scrutiny. The view presents to the
outsider a barren space that is, in reality, nontraversable. On the one hand,
this reinforces the privilege of his experience. On the other hand, the viewer
is denied visual access to the rooms off the central space or even the

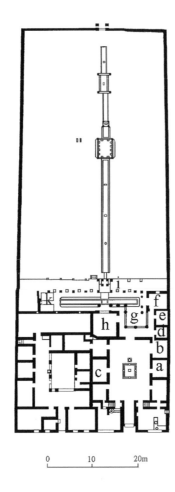

42. Pompeii, House of Octavius Quarto, plan.

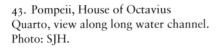

43. Pompeii, House of Octavius Quarto, view along long water channel. Photo: SJH.

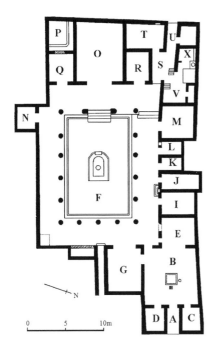

44. Pompeii, House of the Gilded Cupids, plan.

45. Pompeii, House of the Gilded Cupids, peristyle. Photo: Photo Alinari.

decoration of that space. The luxuries of the house are hidden except at the culmination of the vista. The view from outside gave a somewhat standard scheme of the Pompeian house that largely hid the idiosyncracies of each home. Meanwhile, within the house, new views open up which engross the viewer and lure him away from the outside world.

It was once believed, even by Drerup, that, as with the development of wall painting, the development of views followed a chronological pattern. Viewing systems began with the straightforward axis through the house as in the Samnite House of Pansa (Figure 1) and developed into the myriad individual vistas of the House of Octavius Quartio (Figure 42).[31] The *atrium* house configuration gave way to houses dominated by their peristyles, like the House of the Gilded Cupids. This need not have been the case. As complicated as the garden vistas of the House of Octavius Quartio might be, the house is fronted by a vestibule, *atrium* configuration. Instead, these two conflicting methods of viewing are seen to exist within the same system, designed to be seen by different audiences and to different effect. From the inside, the view becomes a tool in the construction of fantasy that serves to negate mundane reality. Conversely, the view from outside was instrumental in hiding the realities or, perhaps more importantly, the fantasies of the house.

Jung draws attention to the nature of this integration of appearance and reality at the culmination of views. The real is found to be interchangeable with the impression of reality.[32] Pliny himself, talking of the view from his Tuscan *villa*, endorses this principle – the viewer will not be able to tell if he is viewing a framed reality or a beautiful picture.[33] The house that appears to reinforce Vitruvian emphasis on the open, public reality of houses, actually uses its architecture and space to undermine that reality. Vitruvius himself cannot escape the fact that the viewing of architecture is subjective and open to permutations of perspective.[34] It is inevitable, if much played down, that the view, as a vehicle for fantastical impression, becomes a part of the system that appears to revile it.[35] Bek sees view planning as a fundamental aesthetic principle of houses – it would seem that it was also instrumental in the political and moral arrangement of space.[36]

INSIDE THE ATRIUM HOUSE

In concentrating on viewing systems, it has become clear that views were awarded not only to outsiders but also those on the inside. There was obviously an audience inside the house that merited attention. This would imply that we should seek the public not just on the threshold of the house but also inside. Consequently, we must expect the interior of the *atrium* house to deal with public and private boundaries, and we must learn how to recognise them.

In learning to do so we might take advice from modern anthropological studies. All houses in every society have to work with similar antitheses, visualising social distinctions between classes of people and between the poles of dirty and clean activity.[37] The house, as medium between the family and the world beyond, is where the household can attempt to come to terms with the outside. Two modern influential studies on houses – one by Roderick Lawrence who works primarily with houses built after the industrial revolution and the other by Bourdieu who studied the Berber houses of North Africa – understand housing practices in this way.[38] Whilst in the Berber houses, the house was preoccupied with elemental oppositions – female and male, darkness and light – the modern council houseowners of Lawrence's study were preoccupied with ideas of space, which divided the house into front and back, upstairs and downstairs and provided a way of separating the social and domestic functions required of the house. Both sets of owners were preoccupied with ideas of cleanliness and pollution, although the Berber houseowner was affronted by the invasion of his male, civilised space by cattle and the Cambridgeshire housewife by the sight of dirty saucepans at dinner. The homeowners of Pompeii equally had to deal with these oppositions in their daily life and resolve them in their domestic architecture.

Traditionally, the syntax of the Pompeian *domus* has been understood as being very simple. Vitruvius tells us the crucial rooms; the rest are clearly unimportant. The rooms definitively labelled on the house plans are *atrium*, *ala*, *tablinum*, peristyle, and *triclinium* – the rooms associated with male, social activity, in particular the morning *salutatio* and the evening *cena*. These are the public rooms of the house where the interdependency of *familia* and *clientes* are played out everyday.

In the past decade, several attempts have been made to make a more sophisticated analysis of the movement around the Roman house, moving away from the text of Vitruvius and instead bringing modern anthropological techniques into play. At the same time, the evidence itself has been assessed on its own merits. How can wall painting or architectural layout help to guide us around the domestic remains?[39] However, any new scheme aimed at presenting a sophisticated analysis of movement around the house will fail if it is based on a very modern understanding of public and private. Most models depend upon each room having a set function and status and presume that that status is reflected in material remains in a way we can

grasp today. Most also take a modern viewpoint that the conceptual location of the visitor was on the threshold, whilst the family's was deep within
the house. Given the interpenetration of guests into the house, however, it
is just as likely that invited guests were conceived of as being equally part of
and within the house, even if they had originally arrived from outside. So,
for example, if we took the visitor's conceptual location to be in the heart
of the house at the *tablinum*, then the model of the levels of access between
him and the rooms of the house would be quite different. In overlooking
this likelihood, we are back to applying modern antitheses to an ancient
setting. If we are to appreciate the complex boundaries between public and
private, we must tackle these problems of function and decoration.

STATUS AND GENDER

One of the most universal desires in partitioning space within houses is
to divide up the inhabitants, to shield some from outsiders but also to
draw boundaries between insiders. In the modern world, we are familiar
with the highly segregated "upstairs downstairs" homes of Victorians and
Edwardians. In ancient times, we have only to look to the Vitruvian concept
of the Greek *oikos* to see the separation of women in the *gynaiconitis*.[40] It
would seem improbable that in a highly patriarchal, status-driven society,
Pompeians would not have been likewise preoccupied with distinguishing
between gender, status, and cleanliness. However, the difficulties of interpreting room function within the *domus* makes it uncertain where we should
find the household.[41]

The biggest distinction we might expect to find in a slave-owning society
would be between the family and its servants.[42] However, in most houses,
it is impossible to find space that seems to have been specifically designated
to the slaves. Only the very biggest houses have a clearly differentiated area
for what we might term servile activities; for example the backyard in the
House of the Menander (Figure 39). These areas, often well separated from
the main house, are the *locus* for the dirty or polluted activities of the house.
The kitchen is often found here and so is the latrine. Recent surveys point
out that the nature of the decoration in these areas of the house contrasts
sharply with that found in both the main reception rooms and the *cubicula*.
Often the walls are just plain plaster. In the House of the Vettii (Figure 35),
a small room off the kitchen has crudely executed pornographic sketches.
As the principal preparers of food and so on, it is likely that many slaves
would have spent a great deal of time in these areas. However, there is no
hard evidence to confirm they were hidden here.

On the other hand, there is plenty of literary evidence to suggest that slaves were constantly on hand throughout the house proper. They were always present, whether on social occasions, such as the *cena*, or at more intimate moments of dressing or illness. Despite the harsh rhetoric that divided master and slave, in physical terms it would be hard to separate them. They lived, worked, and even slept in the same space, the slaves sleeping at their owners' doors. Although elite families might have grown accustomed to looking straight through the slaves that surrounded them, it is also likely that slave presence was all part of family display. In this case, it would seem more plausible that the "service quarters" of these grand homes were not designed to separate certain members of the household as much as to demarcate certain activities. As much as possible, the mechanics of daily life were removed from view.

Perhaps some evidence for this suggestion can be found in the use of water in the houses of Pompeii. Most of the large *atrium* houses of the town were connected to the mains via lead piping in the Augustan period. Rather than use these supplies to feed kitchens, the extensive lead piping in houses such as the House of the Vettii leads to fountain displays in the *atrium* and peristyle. The training of water is typical of the Roman's interest in inverting nature as a form of display, a typical luxury.[43] Most toilets, meanwhile, had to be flushed with buckets of water.[44] Slaves working in the kitchens and latrines would have to fetch water from these water features and take them back to the service areas. A resource such as this would be largely lost in the invisibility of the kitchen.

Once the slave was in clean space, however, his presence was able to be integrated in the larger house. The Pompeian answer to solving rhetorical tensions seems to have been to let them clash wherever possible and only separate them in extreme instances. The presence or otherwise of the free members of the household within the *domus* reflects the experience of the slaves. None of the houses in Pompeii appear to have any space that can be identified as female, by virtue of location, architecture, decoration, or content. The simple explanation for the lack of such space in Pompeii might be that women have a much higher, visible status in the Roman world than in the Greek and so do not have to be separated from the rest of the social intercourse of the house. The woman of the house is seen to be in full, public view.[45]

Lisa Nevett has recently suggested that the Greek woman was, in fact, not much better served with her own space.[46] The woman's place in the Greek house is not so much a particular place but simply any space that is not specifically male, like the *andron* where the head of the house entertained

46. Pompeii, House of the Menander, *exedra* 25. Photo: SJH.

his guests. In Pompeii, the houses are public to the extent that all the family are on display. The town has yielded no evidence of nurseries, nor is there literary mention of them. Given the intertwined functions and relations between the members of the household, this lack of distinction is not so surprising. Women and slaves shared domestic tasks such as weaving, children were fed along with slave children by a wet nurse. The entire household worked together to ensure the ongoing success of the family. When the *paterfamilia*s invited his clients into the *domus*, the visitors could view him against the backdrop of his family. Even those who could not make a physical appearance had a part to play. The ancestor busts in the House of Caecilius Iucundus (V.i.26) and the figurines in the garden *lararium* of *exedra* 25 of the House of the Menander (Figure 46) made sure that the ancestors were always present in the lives of the current generation.

The likelihood that none of the household were allocated specific rooms has great ramifications for the use and function of space. How was the status of a room decided if not by its occupants? Recent work begun by Allison on precisely this problem has, for the first time, attempted to investigate the artefacts found in Pompeian houses.[47] The technique has already underlined the multiple uses of *atria* in Pompeii. Whilst high decoration and marble artefacts stress the display capacity of this important space, strong boxes and cupboards demonstrate the area as a storage space for the house and the many whorls and loomweights attest to its use as workroom. These finds suggest that in addition to being the social and spiritual centre of the house, the *atrium* was, at other times of the day, a centre for the women and even slaves to work. Eleanor Leach's investigation of Roman texts suggests that Romans are more likely to use names that reflect the architecture of a room rather than its function, implying that the two were not mutually dependent and that functions were not fixed.[48]

This new approach to understanding the houses of Pompeii would seem to hold the key to understanding exactly how the house worked. Of course, there were still sharp distinctions between the activities and people in the house, but these distinctions followed the activities or people not the room.[49] If this were the case with major reception rooms, then it is even more likely to have been so with the undistinguished minor rooms. Most so-called *cubicula* seem to serve no definite function. Sometimes, niches in the walls, as in cubiculum I off the peristyle of the House of the Gilded Cupids (Figure 44), confirm their use as bedrooms, but generally there are neither architectural nor decorational clues as to their function. Because of this, they have generally been overlooked as of little consequence. However, in this light, their versatility might be assumed to be crucial in accommodating both public and private within all aspects of the house. They could be bedrooms, workrooms, or intimate entertaining rooms at will.

DECORATION AND FUNCTION

The idea that the rooms of the *domus* had no set function and so, presumably, no set status, has great implications for our understanding of the distribution of architectural and painted effects around the house. We are often told that the architecture of the large, "public" rooms reflected the public sphere. The use of columns referred to civic buildings in both Rome and Greece. Temples, *stoas*, *gymnasia*, and *palaestras* all relied on columns. Colonnades framed the Forum. The adoption of columns recalled these civic examples in the *atrium* as well as in reception rooms such as the *oecus* in the House of the Silver Wedding (V.ii.1) and the Corinthian *oecus* in the House of the Labyrinth (Figure 40).[50] Pediments too reflected public architecture, particularly temples. They appear on the major reception rooms overlooking the peristyle, 18 in the House of the Menander (Figure 39) and O in the House of the Gilded Cupids (Figure 45).[51] Within rooms, vaults recalled public, utility architecture. The reconstructed columns in *oecus* 4 of the House of the Silver Wedding bear a large barrel vault which hides two thirds of the flat ceiling above it. Every domestic ritual now assumes a guise of civic import, apparently played out within a public *locus*. Little more could be done to remind the viewer of the civic implications of rituals such as the *salutatio*, which was really a daily affirmation of the civic status of the participators.

However, public architecture can be found beyond these rooms. The technical needs of the bathsuites of the biggest houses necessitated the vaults and domes of their public counterparts. Such baths can be found in the House of the Menander, House of the Silver Wedding, and House of the Centenary (IX.viii.6) as another aspect of the house's allusion to the public sphere.[52] Even the tiniest rooms show an interest in participating in public architecture. Although none of these rooms has space enough for columns, many have barrel vaults. This is the case of the famous painted *cubicula* of the House of the Fruit Orchard (I.ix.5) and *cubiculum* I in the House of the Gilded Cupids.[53] Practically, the tiny size of these rooms preclude their use from large-scale public activity.[54] Nevertheless, these smaller rooms appear to rise to the challenge, giving the impression that they are more than equipped to challenge their larger counterparts.

This same blurring of boundaries can be observed in the distribution of wall painting. Many *atria* were decorated in the so-called Pompeian First Style, painted stucco that appeared to imitate ashlar masonry (Figure 47). By itself, this was symbolic enough as ashlar masonry was only used on the most prestigious public building projects, particularly temples.[55] In addition, the Basilica in the Pompeian Forum was similarly decorated in First Style, giving the *atria* of the town a specific link to the city's public space.[56] In the House of Sallust, the *atrium*, *alae*, and *tablinum* are all decorated in First Style.[57] A similar relationship can be detected in the decoration of *atrium*, *alae* 4 and *tablinum* 8 of the House of the Menander (Figure 39) where a very similar red and yellow scheme is repeated in each room. The wall paintings of the *atrium* 5 of the Villa of Oplontis reveal how the First Style was felt to be appropriate decoration for this space (Figure 10).[58] The frescoes depict a First Style wall punctuated by doors. Around a painted cornice run golden shields with busts, the *clipeatae imagines* of the ancestors, apparently confirming the general opinion that wall painting reflected the function of the space it decorated.[59]

It was not just First Style that allowed interiors to give an impression of the public sphere.[60] The Second Style of Pompeian wall painting generally depicts public architecture, breaking down the reality of the wall to show temple colonnades and suites of receding rooms. The Corinthian *oecus* of the House of the Labyrinth is decorated in this style (Figure 40), implying to

47. Pompeii, House of Sallust, *atrium*, First Style wall painting. Photo: DAIR 31.2757.

48. Pompeii, House of Marcus Lucretius Fronto, *tablinum*, wall painting. Photo: SJH.

the viewer that he is in the midst of a rich temple complex. Third Style wall painting closes up the wall again and focusses attention on mythological panels at the centre of the walls, often framed by *aediculae*. These walls have been interpreted as imitating *pinacothecae*, public picture galleries that displayed "old masters" to the public.[61] The *tablinum* h of the House of Marcus Lucretius Fronto (Figure 48) is decorated in this style, featuring panels of Mars and Venus and Dionysus and Ariadne.[62] Fourth Style, meanwhile, remains an elusive and somewhat arbitrary category. It is probably most readily understood and described as a conflation of Second and Third Style, combining an architectural structure with flimsy floating motifs. The *atrium* and *alae* of the House of the Vettii (Figure 31) demonstrate the sumptuous nature of this decoration.[63] The paintings of the *atrium* show people leaning out of high windows to feed birds. The scheme literally turns the house inside out, implying that the *atrium* is the outside space in which these birds live and fly.

The distribution of these painting styles, though, follows no discernable pattern. The small rooms are decorated with the same schemes as the so-called public areas. The *cubicula* of the House of the Faun are decorated in First Style, and Second Style open wall schemes are also found in smaller rooms. The House of Marcus Lucretius Fronto's Third Style *tablinum* h is easily matched by the decoration of *cubicula* g. The intricate painting of the *atrium* c of the House of the Vettii seems more than a match for the schemes of imitation marble dadoes and mythological tableaux in the *oeci* p and n around the peristyle (Figure 49). If mythological panels denote elaboration in inner reception rooms, then it should equally be noted that the *atrium* of the House of the Tragic Poet had a series of panels depicting episodes from the Trojan War. In a paradoxical fashion that is becoming increasingly familiar, many of the smaller rooms boast the most public or extravagent schemes of all, for example the *cubiculum* m of the *villa* at Boscoreale with its fantastic architecture (Figure 9) or the splendid "Blue Bedroom" in the House of the Fruit Orchard (Figure 50).[64] If smaller rooms were denied the columns or marble of the larger spaces, their fantasies were just as amibitious.

These examples show that, for all the literary insistences on order and division in the house, the real *domus* was intent on defying all these categories. The decor of the greatest and smallest rooms cut across their practical differences, defying their separation. Such tricks are even observable in the relation between those areas of the house usually thought (contrary to Vitruvius's advice) to be inherently opposite, the *atrium* and the peristyle.[65]

The impression that the wall paintings of the House of the Vettii *atrium* gives of being open, outside space is complemented by the *compluvium* in the ceiling, which opens the *atrium* to the sky (Figure 31). Both *atrium* and

49. Pompeii, House of the Vettii, *oecus* p. Photo: Photo Alinari.

peristyle, the two major circulatory parts of the house, are open air. The two areas are linked in sequence by the natural light that floods them, distinguishing them from the darkened side rooms. Whilst Elsner has attracted criticism for designating these spaces as "outside," it is surely the case that *atrium* and peristyle are brought together by the invasion of the natural elements.[66] The peristyles of Pompeii, perhaps merging the paved Greek peristyle and the Italian *hortus*, emphasised their "outsideness" at the same time that they brought the garden inside.[67]

Both *atrium* and peristyle use architectural features, painted effects, and even real plantings to give an impression of public space, and both merge inside and outside. In terms of function, the similarities also override the modern antithesis. In the House of the Tragic Poet (Figure 30), the House of the Menander (Figure 46) and the House of the Gilded Cupids, there are *lararia* in the peristyles, despite their all having *atria*.[68] They work together in contributing to the overall impression of the house. The way in which the *atrium* and peristyle both appear to obey rhetorical demands of their separate identities yet similarly undermine them seems to be typical of the manner in which the Pompeian *domus* coped with the demands of

50. Pompeii, House of the Fruit Orchard, "Blue Bedroom,"
wall painting. Photo: SJH.

being open and accountable whilst also avoiding charges of arrogance and
tyranny. The houses managed these dual, seemingly incompatible, needs by
ensuring that none of the rooms were, in fact, definitively either public or
private but could serve as both at short notice. Rear or front, small or large,
their fantasies ensured an impressive backdrop for the family wherever they
might be in the house.

PUBLIC AND PRIVATE

The use of views in the Pompeian *domus* might explain further the ambiguous conception of the house. The experience of viewing the house from

outside sets up a dichotomy that is no longer between a public *atrium* and private peristyle, but between the aspect of *atrium* and peristyle available to outsiders and the aspect accessible to those inside. The distinction of public and private is not between visitors and family but between those members of the public admitted to the house and those excluded. Inside the house, almost every room appears to have had the capacity to become public at any moment. Of course, real life did go on in the house; it was the house's main function to shelter its family. However, its secondary function of promoting the identity of that family appears to have dominated. The decor and architecture of the house was planned with the public in mind; retreat into privacy behind doors, screens, or curtains was a temporary resort. Lawrence understands privacy as entailing the management of social interaction to enable the development of self-identity.[69] The houses of Pompeii show that the whole domestic pattern was shaped around defining the status of the family so that the living generation, particularly the head of the household embarking on a political career, could benefit from an enhanced reputation.

The idea that levels of privacy and publicness are tied to the acquisition and maintenance of self-identity and status is clearly demonstrated in Pompeii. In many ways, the privilege of the richest houseowners was to win more privacy. The poorer members of Pompeian society were doomed to live their whole lives in public, eating at taverns, bathing in the town baths and using the public latrines. The owners of the villas and rich *domus* of Pompeii bathed in private suites and ate at their own *cena*. The ultimate dichotomy here seems to be that the very rich were able to withdraw into their own private worlds and draw in the outside world with them. The poor remained invisible and "private" even when living in public.

Those members of the public who were admitted through the front door of the *domus*, were admitted to the world of their patron. Once within the house, the internal viewer is faced with an impression of civic grandeur. His experience of the house becomes very different from that of the outsider as he is brought into the owner's private world. The *paterfamilias* could use the house as a stage on which to project an impression of himself, supported by the *memoria* of his family, in the same way as the public buildings of Pompeii did so for him and his contemporaries in their public capacity as the local ruling elite.

Conveniently hidden behind the façade and axial view of his house, the patron can present himself to his own public in the manner he would truly wish. Hence the preference for creating impressions of public life. In the Forum itself, the houseowner was just another citizen among many. At home, the houseowner had no competition – his own private city, the gates of which he opened to a select audience, his own public, had only one leader in each generation. The control that he exercised over this little world (and the greater the impression the better), the more he might appear fit to lead the urban community. His ambition would be to make the *forum* his *atrium* during a term of office. Holconius Rufus, as *pater* of his hometown, completely merged his private and public responsibilities in a way his fellow citizens could only do in their fantasies and in their homes.

The houses of the Pompeian elite show us one elite's attempts at projecting an impression of themselves through their houses. One of the most enduring features is their eagerness to implode rhetorical dichotomies rather than to categorise and obey them. The implosion of public and private brought with it the simultaneous rejection of difference between inside and outside, religious and secular. In the drive to present themselves to the public, the family were prepared to overlook deep social and moral divisions between gender and status. Such an attitude demonstrated a double response to the rhetoric we have met in Latin texts. On one hand, the Pompeian house reveals just how artificial some of those boundaries are. On the other hand, perhaps these schemes reflect the attempts of elites to balance the extremes policed by those boundaries so as to avoid condemnation on any front. Of course, one of the dangers of doing this is inviting chaos as civilised categories are broken and invalidated. Just like the emperors back at Rome, Pompeians coveted both Romanness and its antithesis, but could they, like emperors, control chaos? The next chapter will investigate how exactly a Roman identity could be won through transgressing the very rhetorical boundaries that were presented as safeguarding Rome and her empire.

5

The Art of Impression in the Houses of Pompeii

The viewing systems of Pompeian houses have led us to the interior of the *domus*. It is here, at the culmination of the view, that we should expect the family to be revealed. Today, we can only trace the family through the image they projected in their interior decor, particularly the wall painting that survives in great quantities in the *atrium* houses of Campania. Studying this wall painting, however, is no easy matter. There are all sorts of obstacles in our way that we need to consider before we can look at the iconography. What did Pompeians think of their paintings? What factors governed the choice of designs? To what extent was personal choice subject to the skilled labour available in the immediate vicinity?

To some extent, the Four Styles of Pompeian wall painting were invented to deal with some of these issues. By dividing them into a dated progressive set, some common order is imposed on the diverse designs. In inventing the Four Styles at the close of the nineteenth century, August Mau followed the opinions of Vitruvius who charted the medium's rise and decline (as he surveyed it during the lifetime of Augustus) according to its faithfulness and abandonment of reality as a model for its art.[1] Mau viewed the paintings of Pompeii as a closed set, with the Fourth Style conveniently running out of steam precisely at the time of the eruption. It may well be the case that Mau was not altogether unaware of the limitations of his categorisations. Indeed, when faced with such a large body of new material, the chronological system may have appeared the most immediate way of bringing some order to the finds without having to address the problems of the content of the paintings.

Unfortunately, of course, wall painting neither started nor ended at Pompeii, and subsequent finds throughout the empire, those at Ephesus in particular, have forced the extension of Fourth Style's chronology over several centuries.[2] Even within the confines of Campanian painting, numerous refinements of the Mau system have only demonstrated the inability of the chronological tables to provide a satisfactory means for considering the evidence. Every quirk of style within a certain chronological limit or even every anomaly of chronology within a certain style threatens to blow the whole system of categorisation apart.[3]

Given these limitations, it is now more usual to consider the paintings of Pompeii as mixed ensembles.[4] A fair few houses still had some First Style decoration in A.D. 79, and very few houses were decorated consistently in one style. Instead, as with the architecture, we are dealing with houses in flux, decorated and redecorated by different owners and at different times. New owners might have read the interior decor they inherited in a completely different way than those who had originally commissioned them. Think, for example, how the Hellenistic owner of the brand new House of the Faun might have considered the great Alexander mosaic and then what it might have meant to subsequent owners who used it as a showpiece. The likelihood of constant change is, in itself, argument enough against the suggestion that houses were decorated according to complex, cohesive programmes. The homeowner who had time to think all this through would be very much in the minority, an exception to the general norms of decor in the house.

When we use these paintings to construct a picture of the *familia*'s identity, we must always remember that there is a whole history of different identities contained in the decoration. We can only look at how the ensembles, as they existed in A.D. 79, may have worked together. But we can look for recurrent generalities. It is possible to see themes that were adopted across the town again and again. The basic concept of wall painting seems to have remained remarkably constant during Pompeii's life; however, fashion must have played some part in the history of wall painting. Paintings were relatively easy to replace and, as we noted before, several rooms show evidence of refurbishment at the time of the eruption. Even though we may never be able to understand the nuances of painting enough to say, for the sake of argument, that the summer of 58 was THE season of salmon pink, it is occasionally possible to watch a fashion sweep Pompeii. A simple example can be found in the animal hunt scenes that appear in a small sample of houses, including the House of the Ceii (Figure 51) and the House of Lucretius Fronto. The extreme similarities in the choice and rendering of the animals would seem to suggest that they were painted by the same hand, perhaps a visiting artist who inspired a flash trend before moving on.

51. Pompeii, House of the Ceii, *viridarium*, wall painting. Photo: SJH.

It is not surprising, given the competitive nature of local politics and the openness of houses, that popular fashion trends would catch on quickly. Nor is it perhaps surprising that there was widespread repetition of designs across richer and poorer houses. So, for example, we see that the mythological panels of Polyphemus and Galatea and Perseus and Andromeda, which graced a room of the Villa at Boscotrecase, appear again in the *triclinium* of the more modest House of the Priest Amandus (I.vii.7).[5] On a more general level, the use of mottled paint to create an impression of marble, popular in wall painting throughout Pompeii, a good example being *oecus* p in the House of the Vettii (Figure 49), would seem to suggest conscious imitation of a more lavish medium.

However, it is not necessary to presume that, through such dissemination, all meaning of the iconography and the practical function of the medium were lost. In other words, that whilst the Roman super elite, who invent new fashion trends, use them to their socio-political advantage, those of lower status who imitate them are happy to exist merely as pale imitations of their betters. In Pompeii, such a chain is easily constructed. Luxuries originate in the pleasure villas of holidaying Roman senators and are passed on to the *villas* of local landowners and from there to their townhouses and eventually to the houses of their clients.

Zanker, in particular, believes that the realities that inspire wall paintings can be found in *villas* where the schemes are realised and articulated by greater wealth and scale. The difficulties of this viewpoint are clarified in a much older discussion of the link between *villa* and house decoration that emerged in the 1950s when Phyllis Lehmann attempted to consider the famous paintings of bedroom m at Boscoreale as they had been set up in the Metropolitan Museum of New York (Figure 9).[6]

These paintings are classic examples of Second Style wall painting. The centrepieces of the main walls are the monumental sacred arches and *tholos* temples that rise up behind low walls, flanked by colonnaded precincts. The sides of the walls depict a vista onto monumental gateways, towers, and balconies, which vie for space in the crowded landscape. For Lehmann, having laboriously justified the appropriateness of each element of the composition, the presentation was clearly that of a *villa*. These painted buildings were fully realised in the great *villas* of prominent Romans. Unfortunately, this does not provide an answer – it simply shifts the question to a different medium. It does not question how a temple complex comes to have a place in the *villa*. The debate only serves to demonstrate that architecture can play as much a part in creating fantasy as wall painting and that the *villa* had as much need for fantasy as the *domus*.[7]

The belief that wall painting imitates a reality that the houseowner does not have the resources to realise is a persistent one. As we saw, the Four Styles are all based on a reference to architectural reality. When they are given a functional value, it is to aggrandise the owner through reference to that, often public, model. They provide a public, Roman backdrop to the activities of the Pompeian *domus*. But what if these paintings are not about realities at all? Inasmuch as they represent an unattainable reality, could they not just as easily be defined as fantasies?

Thinking of them in this way frees the wall paintings of Pompeii from the constraints that have dogged the study of the medium. The possibilities of fantasy are endless as we have already suggested in the case of the paintings of Augustus. There is literary evidence that wall painting could be perceived as embracing the fantastic. Vitruvius's attack on the medium is concerned precisely with the unreal elements of its designs – capricious monsters, vegetal columns, both of which can be observed in the Pompeian corpus.[8] This attack is somewhat limited; it is not an attack on the use of wall painting, merely of elements of the iconography. As such, it does not establish the contention that wall painting was thought of in terms of constructing fantasies. However, the possibility remains intriguing. If the owners of these walls were seen to be using aspirative fantasies, transgressing the boundaries of their own status, then we could see them actively engaging with their investment. Rather than passively adopting other people's identities, we could regard them as building impressions of their own.

TRIMALCHIO: IMPRESSIONS AND TRANSGRESSION

We are helped in our efforts to understand how the homeowners of Pompeii used their houses as a mode of self-display by a literary treatment of a particular Campanian house by a Roman writer. The author is Petronius, and the work in question is the episode known as Trimalchio's Dinner Party from the *Satyrica*.[9] The satire is of particular interest here in its commentary on the Italian, freedman milieu by the Roman, elite centre. The author Petronius, as he is usually identified, was a privileged member of the Neronian court, the emperor's *arbiter elegantiae*, and he was famed, though apparently not reviled, for a life lived in indulgence and pleasure.[10] As if most pertinently to demonstrate his upsetting of Roman *mores*, Tacitus describes Petronius as sleeping through the day and coming to life at night, a most basic inversion of the norm. Petronius was thus in a good position to write satire, a genre of literature that particularly seeks the transgressive. However, under the reign of that baddest of emperors, Nero, transgression becomes a complicated issue; the living centre transgressed, or rather was presented as having transgressed, every rule in the Roman rulebook. When Petronius earned Nero's disapproval and was forced into suicide, his reputation was necessarily rehabilitated, and he mustered one final masterstroke, apparently writing a composition of all Nero's debauched activities – the ultimate satire that did not have to resort to fiction in order to record the most extreme transgressions.

The (anti)hero of the *Satyrica*, Encolpius, on the run from the wrath of the god Priapus, arrives in Puteoli and somehow ends up with an invitation to Trimalchio's house for dinner. Trimalchio, a local freedman millionaire, proceeds to transgress Roman *mores* in every way imaginable and in ways inevitably similar to (but also crucially different from) Nero at Rome. Just as Nero overstepped every civic, familial, moral, sexual, and sacred boundary in Rome, so Trimalchio is shown to blunder his way through the niceties of Roman social conventions, shattering the careful balance maintained between collective restriction and individual megalomania, overturning rhetorical norms. To this extent Trimalchio, regardless of the identity of his creator, is a mini Nero, his delusions are satiric rather than tragic, and we immediately meet the sense of distance that distinguishes the ruling centre of Rome from the ruled communities of the rest of the mainland. Nero's transgressions threaten Rome and result in mass loss of life; Trimalchio's, in gross lack of taste.[11]

So who is Trimalchio or what exactly does he represent? Whether the old man could have been modelled on Nero (and the diminutive context of Trimalchio would have been the perfect insult to Nero), the work ostensibly points a finger to Campania and uses this specific context for Petronius's *exempla* of transgression. Trimalchio is an eternal outsider. As a freedman, he is attempting to escape the stigma of his origins and with his new found wealth is now attempting to take his place in the world of competition and display (a social situation often attributed to the owners of the House of the Vettii[12]). As a freedman, however, he will find himself permanently excluded from a share in civic power. His aspirations, through impotence, are therefore turned inwards to his house and his immediate circle as he compensates for his lack of real authority by using fantasy to create an impression of power within his own home. This impression is effected by assuming an identity of Roman convention, an identity that can compensate for his (unexplained) ethnic origins and his maligned, ex-slave status. The satire is, therefore, indicative of the plight of the freedman. But, from the ultimate centre, Rome itself, it might seem a typical dilemma of all provincial elites, covering their lack of power with a collective, public and individual, private impression of potency that provided them with a fantasy of significance. They, like freedmen, were essentially struggling to contend in the Roman circus of competition and display, and they, too, were adapting their local, civic identities to create a persona that would allow them to participate in that circus.

As a character in satire, where transgression becomes a norm, it is understood that Trimalchio is a man who has failed to balance his perception of fantasy and reality. His fantasies, lived out in every medium at his disposal, have swallowed up his life completely; he really feels entitled to the purple robes and five gold rings he wants to be depicted in on his tomb.[13] This belief is constantly underscored throughout the text – Trimalchio's confidence in his ability to transcend everyday living is demonstrated in his wall decoration, which dispenses with mythical allegory to depict his own life cycle.[14] The tendency is reinforced by a steady stream of disguised foodstuffs, such as eggs made from pastry and hares dressed as Pegasus.[15] In taking advantage of the occasion of the opening of Trimalchio's house to us and to his guests, we can see the nature of these fantasies and the transgressions from which they spring. In doing so we might expect to gain some insight into the norms of Campanian consumption.

Trimalchio knows of the norms expected of a Roman *domus* and its *paterfamilias*, he just cannot resist going further. Take, for example, the link between domestic and civic cult. The Roman house was the focal point of a family's religious life; the fire of Vesta burned in the domestic hearth as it did in the Temple of Vesta, hearth of the city. The political vagaries of the word *aedes* reflected this link.[16] Trimalchio acknowledges, but exceeds, this practice by remarking that his house, which was once a mere *cusuc*, is now a *templum*.[17] Nor must Trimalchio concern himself with the ambiguities of a familial *genius*, a conflated spirit of ancestors that neatly avoided the specific deification of any one individual. His *lararium* boasts a golden statue of himself, which guests are expected to venerate.[18] The old man has made the mistake of literalising a delicately balanced set of euphemisms and comes down on the wrong side. Of course, he has no choice. Trimalchio has no family of his own, and his patrons are dead. He cannot rely on a familial identity to justify his person and so has to depend on his own efforts.

The aim of Trimalchio's fantasy is clear. When we first meet Trimalchio at the baths his (un)dress is unremarkable, but back at home, in private, the old man is resplendent in purple striped napkin and gilt ring, coming as close as he can to assuming the robes of a Roman senator.[19] Elsewhere, Trimalchio proudly displays symbol of rank, the rods and axes for example, traditionally associated with the Senate and now extended to the one freedman office, *sevir augustalis*.[20] The satiric *exemplum* reveals the mentality with which the centre distributed its symbols around the empire to encourage a sense of participation amongst provincial populations of every rank. The Roman nobility and provincial freedmen are united by a common Roman appearance, despite their racial and status differences. The Roman empire remained a deeply divisive society, but it had found mechanisms both to acknowledge difference and stimulate community. Art allows Trimalchio to build on this permitted fantasy to create an impression of further potency. This being satire, Trimalchio cannot help himself and ends up wearing five gold rings on his tomb relief.

Trimalchio's greatest problem is that his potency remains strictly private. His dining guests are mainly fellow freedmen – Petronius gives him no role in the social network of clients and patrons, a role that would entail a public profile as much as a private one. Without that role, Trimalchio remains trapped in the private sphere. Is this why the threshold is so highly demarcated with signs threatening any slave who dare leave? Such self-aggrandisement in the safety of the home is remarked upon by one of the guests, Ganymedes, who acknowledges that men are lions at home, foxes outside.[21] In the space of the house, Trimalchio must create as much of the outside world as he can. In his peristyle, a real troop of athletes literalise the impression of a *gymnasium* or *palaestra*.[22]

Trimalchio's excessive preoccupation with his death is a reflection of his stifled public voice. Without a family history or public face, Trimalchio only has a presence in his own person. He has no means of *memoria*, and the chance of achieving any rests with him alone.[23] The funeral procession is the one chance a freedman gets to be publicly paraded through the town, and the tomb, safely outside the town's order, is his one public monument. His death becomes a crucial moment, his sole chance to create a public impression, to create a *memoria*, the one goal of the true Roman. Before Trimalchio reveals his own funeral plans, the funeral of Chrysanthus is discussed, and its display value assessed – top marks for draped bier, less for restrained distress of the widow.[24] The desperate freedman knows no restraint in his bid for maximum impact.

Petronius uses this apparent lack of restraint as his main attack on Trimalchio, the permanent outsider desperate to crawl his way into a centre. His eager anticipation of his death must somehow be deferred. For now, Trimalchio channels all his aspirational energy into his house, in which he attempts to assume the rituals of the Roman elite – preserving the clippings of his first beard, for example.[25] However, the old man consistently gets the environmental and temporal context for such rituals wrong. His failure demonstrates just how precise prescriptions for acceptable Roman behaviour really were. It serves to remind us that learning these prescriptions would entail some effort and that it would have been difficult for outsiders to pick them up by accident.

Trimalchio's authority can only exist within this Roman house gone wrong, within the fantasies he creates through the visual world around him.[26] When Trimalchio argues with his wife, Fortunata, he orders that her image be removed from his lavish tomb design, permanently excluding her from the *memoria* of his life.[27] Invisible in the real world, Trimalchio and his entourage can only exist within the inverted Rome they invent for themselves. The power of this fantasy world should not be underestimated – while they are in his world, Encolpius is convinced by the impressions, even though he mocks them. On entering the house, Encolpius is overcome with fright on encountering a fierce hound bearing down on him. His friends are merely overcome with amusement. The dog is, in fact, "only" a wall painting, and they obviously cannot believe that Encolpius could so mix representation and reality.[28] On attempting to leave, the chained hound appears unquestionably real, barking at them so ferociously that both Encolpius and Ascyltus end up in the water before the hall-porter rescues them and the dog is pacified, like Virgil's Cerberus, with some tasty morsels.[29] By now, the guests are so caught up in Trimalchio's fantasy that the elements of that fantasy are real to everyone. Petronius thus acknowledges the power of impression as conveyed by Trimalchio's display, hinting at the effect of the transgressions of those in power, an all too contemporary reality. Trimalchio's fantasy, however, is impotent beyond his front doors. Nero's unfortunately stretches much further.

It is this diminution that seals Trimalchio's fate. In Rome, Nero's overreaching self-aggrandisement through visual representation included the Golden House, a complex that threatened to engulf the city and was composed of drastically innovative designs. Even during the Republic, the ambitious Roman senator, or would-be senator, surrounded himself at home with lavish marbles or even edifices modelled on temples.[30] Trimalchio's house, although large (as he is proud to boast), does not appear to compete in any of these categories.[31] We do not hear of any evidence of imposition on the outside world, lavish marble schemes, apses, or vaulting. Instead, Trimalchio concentrates his efforts into small details – silverware, food and, of course, wall painting.[32] These media bear the brunt of Trimalchio's fantasising, where he is shown at his most transgressive. It is in this sense of transgression and diminution, a sense of both overreaching and underachieving, that Petronius views and mocks the peripheral from the centre of power at Rome. Trimalchio may be idiosyncratic and far-fetched, but his aims to create a Roman persona can be identified with a much wider, provincial population.

THE HOUSES OF POMPEII – LOOKING FOR THE REAL TRIMALCHIO

The sense of dimunition, which distances Trimalchio from his archetype, Nero, is easily traced in the different methods employed by the wealthy homes of Rome and the houses of Pompeii to trace the public sphere within their boundaries. In Rome, elite homes could build an extension in the form of an entire civic structure (Pompey's theatre); however, in Pompeii such architecture had to be built within the main house. This is true, for example, of the baths in the House of the Centenary. However, although they may be architecturally indistinct, the owner's wish to convey an impression of a true bath house is realised in the decoration. The strip mosaic along the threshold to the baths from the peristyle features a large bath building complete with vaults and dome. The strip mosaic of closed city gates in the *fauces* of the House of Caesius Blandus similarly asks viewers to see their domestic setting in terms of a private city (Figure 32).[33] Both homeowners must create an impression of civic status through decoration rather than architecture.

Like Trimalchio, then, these Pompeian houseowners seem to have acted like mini Neros in wanting to pull the city inside out and relocate it within the walls of their own homes. Although they may have to rely more on impression caused by two-dimensional iconography than on architecture, the aim seems to have been similar, to make the *familia* the centre of its own city, led by its *paterfamilias*. The more control that he exercised over this little world and the higher the calibre of its inhabitants, his *familia*, the more he might appear fit to lead the urban community of the real city outside.

To this extent, the members of each competing Pompeian family had to show themselves to be the best members of their colony. They must project the strongest impression of their elite *urbanitas* to show that they were competing with the Mediterranean elite at large. In this respect, they did not necessarily wish to assume a Roman identity at the expense of their own ethnic identities but rather a cultural identity shared by the elites within the Roman empire. This collective identity had its roots in the Hellenistic *koine* of the third and second century B.C., of which Pompeii had been a part long before the arrival of the Romans. Mythological panels demonstrate knowledge of Greek culture. *Oeci* p and n in the House of the Vettii boast perhaps the most famous examples of painted wall schemes designed around central mythological panels. The three walls of *oecus* p featured Daedalus and Pasiphae, the Punishment of Ixion, and Dionysus and Ariadne (Figure 49).[34] This practice permeated society; we have already seen how the same mythological subjects could appear in both the wealthy Villa at Boscotrecase and the modest House of the Priest Amandus. A more general impression of the owner's aspirations to intellect was provided by the sight of painted muses floating across walls, such as those of the peristyle colonnades l of the House of the Vettii (Figure 52).

However, wall painting was not simply about coldly adopting cultural symbols. The decoration of Pompeian homes brought the family's own history to life. The painting of the *atrium* of the Villa at Oplontis included *clipeatae imagines*, images of ancestors arranged about the upper wall (Figure 10). The painted *lararium* in the House of the Vettii depicts the *genius* of the family in his veiled toga, and elsewhere the family's procreative force is signified as a snake. Although these images fall short of depicting living members as Trimalchio did, they do provide a hint of how wall painting and reality interacted. The images promoted the presence of the ancestors

52. Pompeii, House of the Vettii, peristyle, wall painting of muse. Photo: DAIR 53.630.

as a way of bolstering the identity of the *familia*. They somehow bridged the threshold between the living and the dead. The paintings act as a visual manifestation of the dichotomies with which we saw literature wrestling in Part I. The house was the *locus* where these dichotomies were resolved.[35] Homeowners appear to have enjoyed choosing wall painting designs that exploited those boundaries.

As much as wall painting and decoration allowed the blurred distinction between past, present, and future generations of the family to be expressed and resolved, it also invited the presence of other members of the extended household, the gods. We tend to think of images of gods in an intellectual way, distanced in the mythological tableaux we discussed previously, but their presence could also be manifested much more immediately. In the ancient world, the threshold between divine and mortal was not as imbreachable as today. The wall painting in room 9 of the House of the Ephebe features the accoutrements of Jupiter (Figure 53) and Minerva in the middle of white panels. The paintings imply that Jupiter has put aside his thunderbolt, Minerva her helmet and owl, as if after a hard day's work. They are relaxing somewhere in the house. The impression that human and divine are living together is further given by those walls, such as the Corinthian *oecus* of the House of the Labyrinth (Figure 40), which appear to transport the viewer to the heart of a sacred complex. The real colonnade of the *oecus* echoes the painted architecture; the experiences of being and

53. Pompeii, House of the Ephebe, room 9, wall painting of
Jupiter's attributes. Photo: R. Ling 83/20A.

viewing are effectively collapsed. It is not clear whether the sacred space is
beyond us or includes us.

The wall paintings that depicted the gods at home in Pompeian houses
made explicit the concept of the ongoing mediation between mortal and
divine in Roman life. Pompey's dedication of his theatre to Venus Victrix
and the consequent erection of his own image in the immediate vicinity of
that of the goddess set himself up on a par with the deity. Similarly, Clodius
lived next door to his shrine of Liberty. In Pompeii, too, houses and shops
seem to have been eager to invite the company of the gods in order to
assume a little divine favour. If the owner of the House of the Ephebe went
straight to the highest level, Jupiter himself, most other attempts were less
aggrandising.[36] The occupant of the House of the Marine Venus (II.iii.3)
chose the local patron deity, Venus, to adorn his back wall in her conch
shell (Figure 54).[37]

However, it would be wrong to see the Pompeians as obediently taking
their place in the Roman cosmos. In many other paintings, they seem to have
given into the appeal of more exotic deities. The Dionysiac megalography
of the Villa of the Mysteries (Figure 55) represents the fullest alignment of a
Campanian house with exotic cult proceedings but minor Bacchic elements
appear throughout Pompeii.[38] So, for example, the gold bands that separate
the main panels in *tablinum* h of the House of Marcus Lucretius Fronto
feature tiny panther heads and theatrical masks (Figure 48).

The Isis cult was one of the most popular exotic cults in Pompeii.
Although the cult was largely of Hellenistic derivation, stripped of its

54. Pompeii, House of Marine Venus, peristyle. Photo: Kate Gilliver.

55. Pompeii, Villa of the Mysteries, Mysteries frieze. Photo: Kate Gilliver.

most dangerous, alien attributes, it remained to the Italian imagination resolutely Egyptian. In the room at the back of the House of Octavius Quartio (Figure 42), the so-called Isiac *sacellum*, f, the wall painting included a white-robed, shaven headed priest of Isis.[39] The inclusion of the

Isiac cult within domestic iconography might appear to challenge Roman authority at the deepest level, striking at its very gods. Both Dionysus and Isis had rocky relationships with authority in the mid-Republic and the early Principate. The wall paintings of Pompeii, however, seem unconcerned with such troubles and, perhaps most strikingly, allow a clash of cultic extremes in the same space. Many houses throughout the town play host to a variety of reactions to the divine within their decoration. In the House of the Menander (Figure 39), the precise civic nature of the Roman pantheon is at first only slightly undercut by the apsed *exedra* 24, which features Venus displayed in a rustic shrine.[40] In the baths, reverence for civic cult is, momentarily, completely abandoned in favour of the caricatures of figures from Graeco-Roman mythology in the frieze of the small *atrium*.[41] Elsewhere, the clash between Roman and exotic religion is brought into close proximity. In the House of the Gilded Cupids (Figure 44), the same peristyle F plays host to both a *lararium* featuring the Capitoline triad – Jupiter, Juno, and Minerva – and a shrine to an Egyptian triad of Isis, Anubis, and Harpocrates.[42]

Of, course, it would be foolish to suggest that the presence of foreign deities should be interpreted as a threat to Roman religion. Rather, these wall paintings allowed homeowners to express the full variety of responses to concepts of religion circulating at the time. By embracing the Roman and the exotic simultaneously, the wall paintings play with suggestion. The presence of foreign gods begins to question the most basic assumption about the house and the identity of its colonial owner. Is this even Roman space? The implications for cosmic order are far-reaching – for the Romans, places like Egypt and their cults were signified exactly by their entire lack of order, a chaotic antithesis to Roman norms. If Augustus could be trusted to rein in his Egyptian desires, could Rome trust her peripheries likewise? The family's interaction with the exotic questioned issues of Roman and alien to the same confused extent as their open house muddled understanding of public and private. As with public and private, there seems to be no strict space where the one ends and the other begins.

Fantasy allowed homeowners to explore the full range of points between opposite poles. On the one hand, Pompeian families identified themselves as Roman by distancing themselves from slaves and foreigners. In the House of the Menander, a mosaic of a caricaturised, simplified slave marks the entrance to the *calidarium* in the bathsuite off the west side of the peristyle.[43] Here, a wreathed and macrophallic black man, holding out the strigil and oil flask – tools of his subservient trade – occupies the narrow passage in front of the arriving bather as if he were about to perform his duties. Inside the *calidarium* itself, the central mosaic features a number of marine creatures swimming around a central roundel with vegetal motif. Included in the marine scene are a further two African figures, one an ithyphallic swimmer and the other attacking a squidlike creature with a trident (Figure 56).[44] In all three cases, the black men are very clearly made inferior, crude in terms both of appearance and rendering. Their ithyphallic form may be apotropaic or may reduce them to figures of fun. Their simple black silhouettes contrast with the detail and colour used for the marine creatures, further belittling the men's inferior status.[45] Demeaning the subjects even further, the entrance figure is preparing to serve the viewer in a very Roman ritual, the act of bathing. This distances him even further from the bathers and propels the bathers deeper into the camp of the Roman. He becomes a mediatory figure, a point of contact between the Roman world and the wilderness beyond.

However, whilst Africans might be considered liminal, laughable figures, the continent from which they came was a source of enduring fascination to the Italians. Fantasies of Africa invariably were visualised as Egyptian scenes. The dichotomy between the ridiculous inhabitants of the area and the majesty of Egypt is presented throughout Pompeii. Two very similar mosaic inserts in the floors of the Green *oecus* 11 (Figure 57) of the House of the Menander and room f off the peristyle in the House of Paquius Proculus demonstrate this tension.[46] Both scenes feature pygmies sailing on the Nile, encountering crocodiles. Although, as the physically deformed pygmy, the African remains laughable, the interest in recreating the environment of the Nile setting is much more detailed. The observation of the fauna and flora of Egypt creates a definite, foreign setting for the pygmies.

The most extensive treatment of the Nile can be found in the painting that decorates the sides of the *triclinium* couch in the garden of the House of the Ephebe (Figure 58).[47] The masonry couch was set in the middle of a pseudo-peristyle and set under a pergola lit by the bronze ephebe holding a candelabra, which gave the house its name. Its sides depicted various aspects of an imagined Nilotic life where pygmies attend to Egyptian cult, sail, fish, and even fornicate, all against the background of a landscape, which convinces of its authority by its carefully observed details of flora, fauna, and buildings. Such landscapes, repeated throughout Pompeii, might suggest that, in the midst of attempting to distance themselves from the peripheries, both artist and patron are drawn in and their covert desires are beginning to show through. The detailed temples and shrines on the couch are an appropriate reflection of the collective desires of a town that enjoyed its own public Isiac cult, apparently fully functional within the

56. Pompeii, House of the Menander, *calidarium*, mosaic.
Photo: DAIR 69.2076.

57. Pompeii, House of the Menander, *oecus* 11, pygmy
mosaic. Photo: DAIR 72.794.

community's wider social and political context. As far as Pompeians were
on the road to becoming Roman, they carried the peripheral with them, or-
biting around alternative centres. In this respect, they were not unlike those
elites back at Rome who raised themselves above their colleagues by appealing to the exotic world of Egypt. Augustus himself had looked in this direction. His attempts to fit Egyptian motifs within the wall painting designs of

58. Pompeii, House of the Ephebe, garden *triclinium* with pygmy scenes. Note remains of animal hunt on rear wall. Photo: Photo Alinari.

his Palatine home are particularly reflected in the Villa of Mysteries, where pharaohs and Egyptian gods float on the black walls of the *tablinum*.[48]

These wall paintings have begun to create fantasy worlds that seem a light world from Rome. The painted world of the Pompeian frescoes is not that of the Roman *domus*, but of exotic fantasy. The possibilities opened up by wall painting allowed the Pompeian to invite the whole world into his house. Rather than accept their place in an ordered, Roman, philosophical view of the nature of things, they seem deliberately to challenge it. Roman literature tried to define what it is to be Roman by appealing precisely to nature, their gods and Italy, all of which are overturned by these frescoes.

The fantastic nature of wall painting allowed homeowners the run of their imaginations. Wall paintings exploit every tension at the heart of Roman identity. The threshold between nature and civilisation is likewise provoked. Again, the House of the Menander demonstrates the contradictions within domestic space. The civic architecture of the bathsuite gives an air of urban impenetrability, which is first undermined by the painted plantings in the *atrium* dado. These plants, seemingly sprouting from the floor, appear to let the wild creep into the urban house. The vulnerability of the *domus* to such

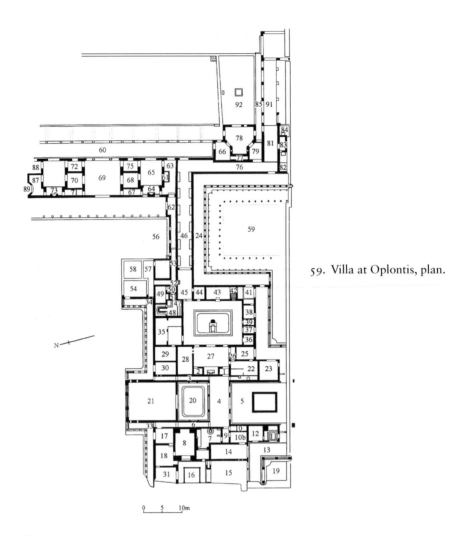

59. Villa at Oplontis, plan.

an attack is fully recognised in the peristyle where painted wild animals appear to race around the inside of the low peristyle wall.[49]

Villas, too, already set in the hinterland, must play out this dilemma. The *atrium* (5) of the Villa of Oplontis (Figure 59), so urban in its painted fantasy of a traditional First Style *domus atrium* (Figure 10), is undercut by the decoration of the *viridarium* (20) behind it. The east and west walls of this small planted area reveal garden paintings between half columns, furnished with fountain basins lifted on sphinxes and craters and visited by birdlife. This cultivated garden is itself dragged further into the wilds by the animal scenes that grace the entablature.[50] Each successive fantasy is here crystallised by their visual proximity – the descent from civilisation to wild can be observed from one vantage point. Yet each fantasy continues to instill an impression on the viewer at the same time as its reality is clearly disproved. Both the power and impotence of fantasy is revealed. It gains limitless possibilities through its aversion to reality but is rendered powerless by those, Vitruvius particularly, who attempt to profess that only reality counts.

THE GARDEN – THE TRIUMPH OF THE LIMINAL?

The work of Jashemski, in cataloguing the gardens in the homes of Pompeii and Herculaneum, has drawn attention to the pivotal place of these gardens within domestic space.[51] Gardens are found as decorative elements within the confines of the peristyle in the House of the Vettii (Figure 34) or the House of the Menander (Figure 39). Occasionally they exist as true, agricultural *horti* (as at the rear of the House of Pansa, Figure 1). Even more frequently they occur as painted luscious landscapes known from a myriad of houses, particularly the Blue Bedroom of the House of the Fruit Orchard (Figure 50) and the garden rooms, 64–74, of the Villa of Oplontis.[52] All these forms seem to have references back at Rome itself. They invite comparison with the literary sources relating to the suburban *horti* and the famous garden scenes from Livia's Villa at Prima Porta (Figure 6).[53]

Within these spaces, real or painted, all the different levels of negotiation played out within the house might appear at their most explicit. Here was a space that was seemingly incontrovertibly "outside" and "rustic," negating its wider context as part of a cultivated, domestic interior. The liminal status of the garden made it a natural haven for what was restricted by the norms of ordinary life, the perfect environment for toying with the transgressive and stretching the blurred boundaries between civilisation and chaos to their very limits.[54] At the same time, the peristyle, which marked the limits of this liminal space, reinforced the public, urban aspect of the rest of the *domus*, making sure that the garden did not get out of hand.

The freedom afforded by garden space may well explain the immense desire to own a garden, which is demonstrated throughout the houses of Pompeii. Whilst houses such as the House of the Faun had two huge peristyles, other houses simply created an impression of such a garden. This is a particularly popular tactic in houses that were simply too small to build a full peristyle.[55] The peristyle of the House of Priest Amandus is surrounded on two sides by real, architectural columns and on the remaining sides by half columns on the house walls, allowing the impression of a full peristyle in

60. Pompeii, House of Priest Amandus, peristyle. Photo: Photo Alinari.

a small and irregular plot (Figure 60). In the neighbouring House of Fabius or Amandus (I.vii.3), where space was even more restricted, the garden is basically a planted lightwell.[56]

Similarly, all houses appear to have coveted the garden painting. Paintings of wild gardens, dominated by small trees and bushes, visited by birds and bound by fencing are found throughout Campania, both in peristyles and interior rooms. In the House of Priest Amandus it could perhaps be argued that the garden painting in the pseudo-peristyle was designed to extend the tiny area.[57] However, bigger gardens also use the device: the south and east walls of the garden of the House of the Marine Venus are painted with lush vegetation and garden ornament (Figure 54).[58] The content of these paintings as simply illusion is questioned by the complex levels of fantasy within the painting itself. The garden painting seems to be a straightforward representation of a normal garden. The figure of Mars stands on his plinth as an indication that he is a statue, not the real thing. But how should we understand the Venus in her shell? Is she a painting on the wall of this painted garden or our real one? Or is that really her?

The use of garden paintings in interiors, such as those in the "Black Bedroom" of the House of the Fruit Orchard (Figure 61), further question the illusionistic function of the theme. The painting above the dado is divided into two registers on a black ground. The lower features a trellice fence with recesses in the centre for a fountain and behind which grow flowery bushes. The tall, upper register is divided into three panels, each filled with a single tree with bushes at their trunks and birds flying around their branches.[59] This flat, divided scheme would serve to suggest that the painting here has a worth that transcends an illusionistic extension of space.

The row of rooms 64–74 that flank the pool in the Villa at Oplontis (Figure 59), decorated with a complicated interaction of garden scenes and real indoor fountains, would also seem to question the imitation motive.[60] After all, the *villa* owner could have easily planted a real garden since space and money were of no object to him – as they were certainly not to Livia, at whose *villa* at Prima Porta the style gains one of its earliest expressions (Figure 6). Garden paintings must, then, have served their own intrinsic function.[61] They are doubly transgressive, bringing fantasies of horticulture into interiors where they could not possibly be realised.

As fantastic liminal spaces, both gardens and garden paintings became prominent centres for flaunting transgressive display. Visually, the garden gives the scenes a certain autonomy, free from an immediate Roman context. Egyptian subjects were popular for garden sculpture. The garden (18) of the House of Marcus Lucretius (IX.iii.5) (Figure 62) featured ibises around its fountain pool. The inventory from the peristyle of the House of the Silver Wedding included a toad, a frog, and two crocodiles.[62] The garden was also the place to celebrate Egyptian ritual through the Isis cult. Real or painted Isiac shrines give an air of explicitly sacral ritual in the House of the Gilded Cupids and the House of the Amazons (VI.ii.14).[63] In the House of Octavius Quartio (Figure 42), the garden takes on the role of a grove dedicated to Isis-Diana. Sculptures found in *viridarium* g, alongside the *sacellum* f, include a marble ibis and terracottas of Egyptian deities.[64] In paintings of gardens too, as in the Blue Bedroom 8 of the House of the Fruit Orchard (Figure 50), the garden becomes an Isiac grove, punctuated by images of pharaohs and *pinakes* of cult scenes and symbols such as the Apis bull.[65] More generally, sphinxes and ibises inhabit the seemingly most innocent painting, such as the sphinx that bears a *labrum* in the garden painting in the *viridarium* (h) of the House of the Ceii.[66] At the same time, of course, however carried away with this fantasy wilderness, the viewer is still safely hemmed in by the peristyle columns. Imagine the diner in the House of the Ephebe (Figure 58), seated outside, surrounded by painted pygmies but experiencing it all from

61. Pompeii, House of the Fruit Orchard, "Black Bedroom," wall painting. Photo: Koppermann, DAIR 64.2256.

the safety of the *triclinium* as he partakes in the most Roman of rituals, the *cena*.

In the illusive freedom of the garden, fantasies confined to paint in the rest of the house appeared to come alive. The world of Dionysus, so apt for a wild, bucolic setting, was particularly popular. Sculpture of a Bacchic nature appears everywhere. Sileni often serve as fountain figures, such as the drunken Silenus who stands in the niche fountain in garden 18 of the House of Marcus Lucretius, kept company by the other satyr figures who disport themselves around him (Figure 62).[67] The sculptural arrangements in peristyle m of the House of the Vettii and peristyle F of the House of the Gilded Cupids (Figure 45) consist of a wide range of Bacchic sculpture. The latter's great inventory includes *oscilla* featuring maenads and satyrs and double herms of Dionysus.[68]

One of the most important aspects of gardens is their ability to accommodate many different worlds simultaneously. Garden 18 of the House of Marcus Lucretius, for example, features both Bacchic and Egyptian sculpture. The sculptures surround the two major water features of the garden, the niche fountain and a central pool. In addition to the satyrs, Silenus, and ibises already mentioned, there are also herms of Bacchus, cupids riding dolphins, and various animals. Similarly, the Egyptian theme of the *viridarium* area g of the House of Octavius Quartio shares space with the Dionysiac statues in the main garden. The sculptural motifs that pop up in

62. Pompeii, House of Marcus Lucretius, garden. Photo: Photo Alinari.

Pompeian gardens are not designed to re-create any one setting. Themes and worlds are merged in a fantastic confection that predates and anticipates the empire as imagined by Hadrian at Tivoli.

Wall paintings of gardens and landscapes were even freer to ignore reality and bring different worlds together. The *viridarium* at the rear of the House of the Ceii is of particular interest in this context. Three sides of the narrow, rectangular room are decorated with landscapes framed by thick, painted garlands and bordered with hanging *paterae* and other offerings. Below the landscapes are garden paintings featuring fountains in the forms of nymphs, vegetation, and the usual trellice fencing. The landscapes themselves take the viewer past the fantasy of the civilised, tended garden to even more exotic worlds.[69] On the west wall, pygmies populate a Nilotic landscape, and the east wall keeps up the Egyptianising theme with a rural landscape dotted with palm trees and a sphinx. The scene on the north, rear wall, however, plunges us even further into the wilderness. In a rugged landscape, lions and leopards hunt boars, deer, and oxen (Figure 51). The animals are wild and exotic, and the barrenness of the rocky landscape provides another indicator of how far the viewer has strayed from the cultivated, garden setting. These animal hunt scenes appear to have enjoyed a sudden popularity in Pompeii and are repeated throughout the city, in the garden of the House of Marcus Lucretius Fronto and on the low wall between the columns of the peristyle of the House of the Menander.[70]

These hunt scenes appear to take the viewer to a place where the human, let alone the Roman, can have no control. Do the owners of these houses really surrender control to the beasts prowling at the back of their homes? The way in which Pompeians expected to interact with the paintings is hinted at by their composition. The animals are shown in the wrong geographical terrain with domestic and wild animals sharing the same feeding ground.[71] These paintings, then, do not intend to create an illusion that could ever be experienced in reality. We are not transposed to any specific location. Instead the houseowner is able to manipulate nature in bringing his menagerie of painted animals together regardless of natural habitat. In this respect, these hunt scenes are often thought to have parallels with the animal shows in amphitheatres which brought together exotic beasts from all over the empire. As a consequence, it has been suggested that such scenes served as reminders of shows that the houseowner had sponsored (or dreamt of sponsoring). The exotic nature of the game reflects the extent of his wealth and authority.[72] This, of course, need not be the case. Rather, these scenes demonstrate the link between collective and private fantasies of the wild. Both attempt to exert control over the elements of chaos and danger through the medium of the hunting animals.

The seemingly innocent plantings in gardens and paintings of gardens must be seen in the same light. Although highly decorative and well groomed, the garden was not merely to be looked at. Taking his cue from the great number of fruit trees and market gardens found throughout the town, Jung has considered the likelihood that the long symmetrical rows of postholes that run down the length of the garden of the House of Octavius Quartio were to support plants that could be usefully harvested and consumed.[73] Again, the emphasis is on control over nature, which is diligently arranged for both appearance and utility. Far from accepting the order of nature, the peristyle forms a place where nature is effectively bound.

A similar control is revealed in the garden paintings that are generally more adventurous than the real plantings, depicting a greater range and density of flora and fauna. The different approaches to taming this real and painted nature seem to typify the double-edged Pompeian reaction to their own domestic fantasies. They reveal both confidence in overwhelming and trepidation at being overwhelmed by these forces they have invited into their homes. The revelation that the plants and birds of the garden scenes

63. Pompeii, House of Orpheus, rear wall, wall painting of
Orpheus. Photo: DAIR 58.986.

from Prima Porta (Figure 6) were in fact incompatible, that they flowered
at different seasons and inhabited different terrains, has now been extended
to the garden paintings of Pompeii.[74] These are not real wildernesses but
manipulations of nature by artist and patron. They are fantastic confections that cannot be confused with reality but at the same time bolster the
impression of the real authority of the houseowner.[75]

The homeowner of Pompeii, then, is a man who is seen to live in an
Elysian paradise where animals, birds, and flowers appear at his whim –
a true Orpheus.[76] Orpheus himself appears on the back wall of the House
of Orpheus (VI.xiv.20) (Figure 63). In a T-shaped panel, surrounded by
conventional garden paintings, the eastern, mythic hero plays his lyre,
enthroned on a rocky outcrop and surrounded by the wildlife he has
charmed.[77] All the different boundaries between centre and periphery are

here brought together and exposed – the outside, the wild, the alien, and the mythical. Most importantly, this most succinct exposé of marginality is not situated in the garden in order to remain hidden. In fact, it forms the culmination of the view from the entrance; transgression and *Romanitas* are both publicly feted, equally dependent. It appears to the outsider that this is the home of Orpheus, the true identity of the owner becomes conflated with that of the hero himself. Put this way, we must consider where we should find Dionysus in the peristyle of the House of the Gilded Cupids and who the consort of Isis in the House of Octavius Quartio is. Could it, in fact, be the houseowner himself? The answer, of course, is left to the viewer's and the patron's imagination. However, consider the importance of the view of these idyllic spaces in the house.

In the House of the Gilded Cupids (Figure 44), the peristyle F acts as a forecourt for a raised platform on which rests a large reception room, O, the front of which is articulated by a gable (Figure 45). This architecture heightens the impression that we are in a sanctuary and that here is the temple in which the cult image will be revealed.[78] The room in which the family are entertaining their guests is, effectively, a temple *cella*. The connection between the two spaces is assured by the viewing axis that binds them. The guests in the reception room find themselves, not in an urban house, but in a Dionysiac idyll. Dwyer's work on the House of Marcus Lucretius (Figure 64) demonstrates that the sculpture around the fountain and pool in garden 18 (Figure 62) was placed slightly off central view axis so as to be more easily observed from rooms 16 and 25.[79] The view into a Romanised, domestic space is everywhere tempered by a view out onto an exotic, wild space, both of which were ruled over by the family, led by the *paterfamilias* who governed the bizarre fantasy world that was his home.

These wall paintings are much more than simply reflectors of status or luxury decoration, although both are doubtless subsidiary motives. Wall paintings are an inextricable part of the house and household; they appeal fundamentally to the very identity of the family themselves. The wall paintings of Pompeii set up a variety of thresholds between public and private, Roman and alien, and so on, but they do not force us either way. We are always teetering between the two, aware of and seeing both depicted in the wall paintings around us. They question every aspect of a family's life by playing on concerns that were constantly debated in the literary rhetoric of what it was to be Roman. To be Roman was not simply to be urbane at the expense of rusticity or to be purely Italian in ignorance of the East. To understand *Romanitas* in this way is to take too simple a view of how the Roman empire found room to accommodate so many different

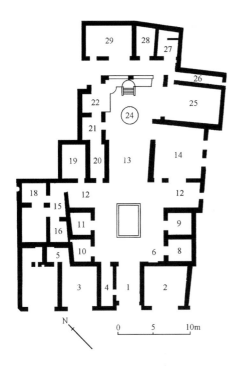

64. Pompeii, House of Marcus Lucretius, plan.

identities. Wall painting helped to realise identities within the house by es-tablishing a *locus* for the inhabitants within the universe. Whether slave or *matrona*, regardless of their disadvantaged status or gender, the familial identity provided a group persona with which they could participate in Pompeian society.

Of course, it was the *paterfamilias* who benefitted most from this familial identity. He remained the focus of the family, its living, public person. The visitors invited into the house saw their host leading the family in struggling and overcoming elements of chaos. They could not fail to be impressed with the impression that their would-be magistrate shared a home with the gods and exercised a quasi-divine power over the fantasies he concocted around himself. The Pompeian *paterfamilias* may well have acted like a little emperor in a similar way as the satiric invention, Trimalchio, resembles a little Nero. All his transgressions and inversions, however, are carefully con-fined to fantasy where the impression remains both resolutely indefinable and eminently imitable. Everybody can indulge in their wildest dreams of both civilised *Romanitas* and life on the edge. By declaring the environment as fantasy, the houseowner avoids responsibility. He cannot be to blame for the impression that is given to the visitor.

This elusive quality may well be the reason for Vitruvius's fear of these confections. Although they are harmless in that they can never be realised, unlike schemes that are realised, they can never be pinned down. Consequently, they are able to withstand any twist of rhetoric. This is the beauty of fantasy; it triggers the imagination. Only Trimalchio would dull the fantasy by making it explicit.

THE ANTHROPOLOGY OF THE POMPEIAN HOUSE

Far from being problematic, these attempts to override the realities of domestic life with painted fantasies of other worlds reveal the true nature of the Roman house. The whole house acted as a threshold between different long-established rhetorical *topoi*: public and private, town and country, mortal and divine, Roman and alien. The entire *domus* was transitional space; there was no unambiguous space where visitors, or indeed the family, could finally imagine they had arrived at the heart of the house. Instead, they found themselves constantly on the threshold of a fantasy world, the architecture and decor simultaneously confirming and undercutting expectations.

In this respect, Pompeian houses might appear to have conformed to a practise recognised by anthropologists in many societies. At its most crude, the house becomes a cosmological symbol with various parts of the house representing opposing parts of the universe.[80] The Pompeian *domus* invites in the elements as a means of facing and exerting control over them.[81] All the threatening forces that lurked outside the house, beyond the city limits and without the empire met and mingled within the *domus*. In every domus those forces are represented by stock motifs of socially prescribed "others." The family must allow their imaginations to grapple with these pre-ordained dangerous elements in order to carve a place for themselves within the Roman world. In political terms, their desire to explore forbidden worlds and exert control over them can be explained as an effort to show extreme power. By inviting the public into the house to watch the *paterfamilias* exert control over these peripheral environments, an impression is conveyed of his ability to cope with the demands of being Roman and hence his suitability for public office. Wall painting was the best medium in which to play out this struggle. It could, with least expense, bring these other worlds directly into the house but at the same time keep them safely at bay. The overreaching impression that the *paterfamilias* sought to give, as king of these worlds, was proclaimed as fantasy at the same time as it conveyed a very real impression of his might. The power to realise and to act on those fantasies was handed over to the emperor, the living *exemplum* of *Romanitas*. In this model, these other worlds were as crucial to Roman identity as a toga.

The evidence seems to remind us of the complex way in which the empire became Roman. Even in the literature from Rome, it became clear that there was no absolute definition of *Romanitas*. Similarly, the houses of Pompeii would seem to suggest that there was no simple domestic package that made a house Roman. Instead, a successful Roman house was a house that was seen to wrestle with the different tensions inherent in *Romanitas*. It was the house that provided an arena for combining and layering personal, familial, and civic identities. *Romanitas* depended on the successful interplay and balance between these identities; Pompeians were ethnically Italian and culturally Mediterranean as much as they were politically Roman. The Roman system of imperialism allowed room for these different identities as long as they could be intertwined with more familiar characteristics.[82] This was the process of acculturation that bound the empire. To appreciate fully the way in which Roman identity building could accommodate difference, we must travel to the farther provinces. Here we might expect the tensions of *Romanitas* to be stretched to their very limits and the role of fantasy in constructing impressions of belonging to be at its most potent.

PART THREE

THE ROMAN HOUSE ON THE
PERIPHERY OF EMPIRE

6

The Houses of the Western Provinces

The *De Architectura* seems to echo other contemporary texts when it implies that the ideal *domus* affirms its owner's Romanness. Vitruvius makes clear his Romanocentric views in the first chapter of Book Six. From 6.1.1–2, he discusses the effect that climate plays on housing needs. The cold north calls for a closed, vaulted architecture, whilst the south needs an open, airy architecture. Of course, this advice would necessitate some deviation from the ideal elite *domus* he is about to describe, but his lack of concern over this problem is indirectly revealed by 6.1.3–12, which assures the audience that climate affects the nature and appearance of men as well as their homes. Having lamented the defects caused by either under- or overexposure to the sun, it becomes clear that only those who live at the centre of the world – the Romans, of course – are born with the kind of perfection that would require the ideal house.[1]

Whilst this attitude might be fairly typical of Roman snobbery, it raises interesting questions about what makes a house, or a person, Roman. As the empire (Figure 65) expanded, more people were becoming part of the Roman empire and living as Romans. But they were not Romans by birth or location, and their domestic traditions and native climate required non-Roman solutions to housing problems. How could they stand a chance of competing within the literary and visual rhetoric of self-representation that had been created for a small elite living in the city of Rome?

It should be no surprise to learn that building techniques varied over the vast space that comprised the empire in the first couple of centuries of imperial rule. It might seem logical, for instance, that the houses of Roman Britain do not feature peristyles or that, in North Africa, peristyles might be located in cool basements.[2] Similarly, the availability or otherwise of

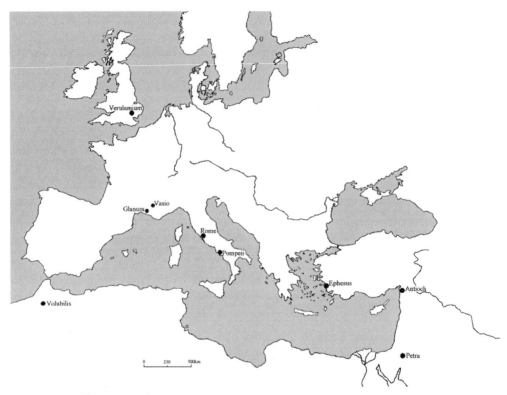

65. Roman empire, map.

certain building materials must dictate appearance; the dense woodland of the northern provinces is reflected in the choice of wood or wattle and daub for early urban developments across Britain and Gaul. In the eastern deserts, as in Petra, houses were carved out of the rockface.[3] None of these houses replicated the *domus* of Rome. Nevertheless, they were the homes of legitimate inhabitants of the Roman empire.

The aim of this chapter is to examine how houses might demonstrate the provincial elites' understanding of their new Roman identity. The task is not necessarily easy because the study of the spread of Romanisation has usually been understood in terms of public, civic amenities. It is generally in sites where little remains of the monumental centres that the archaeologist's attention is drawn to the domestic remains. As a result, the cities that we will meet in this chapter are not always the most famous, either to the ancient or the modern visitor. However, that these examples are not all highly celebrated in Roman texts is perhaps to our advantage. There were thousands of urban communities in the Roman empire, most of which the average Roman back in the capital would never have heard of. The cities discussed in these chapters were all locally important centres (Verulamium was a local *civitas* capital) and were, at times, of imperial-wide significance (Volubilis was capital of Mauretania Tingitana), but they were not among those exceptional cities that were well known to people all over the empire. As a result, they are places where we can observe the norms rather than exceptions of acculturation. It is also important to stress, before we advance further, that the next two chapters are not intended as full surveys of the domestic types of the empire.[4] Instead, by looking more closely at several sites, we can investigate the peculiarities and idiosyncracies of each city's encounters with Rome and, from there, begin to identify any wider common experiences and strategies of the process of negotiation between local and Roman, once known as Romanisation.

ROMANS AND THE PROVINCES

The construction of the provinces, it might be said, relied principally on the local response to the centre. However, it is also true that the entire concept of empire was shaped by the Roman reaction to those peripheries it seemed to desire so much from the safety of Italy. It is quite clear that the bravado demonstrated in the homes of Italy, where homeowners delighted in wrestling with painted fantasies of exotic worlds, was much less in evidence when Romans abroad were confronted with the reality of alien chaos. The need to instill recognisable *Romanitas* on alien landscapes was the inspiration behind the organisation of empire. The overriding ethic of the Roman presentation of geography was the creation of order where before had been chaos. Cicero specifically understands the duty of the Romans to be to spread order and civilisation the world over.[5] Barbarian lands were incomprehensible; anarchy of language, organisation, and terrain demonstrated their lack of *mores* and *forma*. The world outside was so extremely alien because it allowed no lynchpin upon which familiar Roman culture could be secured. To venture into chaos required caution. Caesar's first overture to Britain was to send Volusenus to observe the country without disembarking from the safety of his ship.[6] Tacitus emphasises his father-in-law, Agricola's, role in the province of Britain with the information that although others began the subjugation with invasions and battles, Agricola was the first to circumnavigate the island and therefore to define completely its *forma*.[7] This was the seal of the nation's defeat as if he had sailed around bestowing *forma* on the coastline as he went. The organisation of *forma* became a symbol of victory. Agrippa's greatest project was the preparation of a map of the world. According to Pliny he had collected measurements of all the provinces in order to chart the map, which was displayed in the new Porticus Vipsania.[8] The whole empire was bound and captive, on display in Rome. The world now lay well in the realms of the experience of every Roman citizen.

Perhaps inevitably, though, it was seen to be Augustus himself who set the seal on the *forma* of the empire. Rather than compile a map, the *Res Gestae* confined the world within the parameters of the Latin language. Just as the careful ordering of the various areas of Rome had demonstrated Augustus's appropriation of the city, so this tactic was extended over the whole empire. The text travelled all over the world, bringing each territory within popular Roman experience and *forma*, defining victory for Rome and for the Principate.[9] The *Res Gestae* would become the definitive expression of world power, not least because, unlike Agrippa's map, the *Res Gestae* travelled back across the empire to Asia Minor where, displayed on temple walls, it served as a physical reminder of the greater scheme of things. Not just Romans but the whole empire could learn of the extent and organisation of the Roman world. With the whole world subjected to Roman organisation, Roman omnipotence was inevitable.

The bringing of order and of *forma*, implicit in Agrippa's map and the *Res Gestae*, was a very real consideration in the life and travels of a Roman citizen. The absence of *forma* was totally dehabilitating. The lack of familiar, Roman culture brought about complete disorientation and dysfunction. Writing under Augustus, Ovid composed his *Tristia* and *Ex Ponto* from the point of view of a man in exile on the shores of the Black Sea.[10] These poems afford the rare chance of seeing how a Roman might react when he is jettisoned from Rome, the centre of political and natural order, to a land of "shapeless riverbanks."[11] He cannot even recognise the seasons, which not only are climatically different from those at Rome but also are celebrated in alien ways; he can only conceive of spring through the rituals enacted in Rome.[12] Without these signposts, spring is nothing; indeed, life is nothing. Ovid frequently uses funerary images to describe his ejection from Rome.[13] When Ovid celebrates his wife's birthday according to the Roman ritual of lighting incense, he imagines the incense wafting to Italy, a frail but tangible link with Rome.[14] It is through the enaction of such ritual and the recognition of symbols associated with that ritual that a Roman can feel at home in the empire. If provincials were to be recognisable as Romans, then they would have to participate in this rhetorical language and ritualistic practice. Otherwise, the distance between centre and periphery would deny any communication between the two.

By the time the western provinces gained literary voices – for example, the novelist Apuleius in second century North Africa and Sidonius Apollinaris, a member of the Christian elite of fifth century Gaul – these voices begin to provide us with evidence that local elites had indeed come to regard themselves and their homes as Roman. Apuleius's *Apologeia* presents a man fully integrated into the public, social life of a Roman elite, attending dinner parties, presiding over the *salutatio*, and participating, willingly or not, in elite competition. Offering an excuse for marrying in his *villa* rather than his townhouse, Apuleius explains that he did so because he and his bride, Pudentilla, did not want to be bothered by the crowds gathering for another generous dispersal of *sportula*.[15] Apuleius himself became the victim of the rhetoric of the house when he was accused of practising magic whilst in the home of Junius Crassus. The otherwise secret rituals were only "revealed" to the outside world by a household slave.[16] It would seem that, whatever the visual expression of it might be, the elite of North Africa were fully aware of the potency of rhetoric surrounding the house and the consequences on public life that could result from flouting, or being seen to flout, those conventions that were required of the Roman.

The presentation of the domestic life of these men is clearly based on that of the Roman elite. Just as Cicero had done long ago in Rome, Sidonius boasts of the number of visitors crowding his house.[17] As in Rome, such social activity bore heavy implications in public life; Sidonius presents a candidate for a bishopric wining and dining his way into office.[18] Seemingly oblivious to the barbarian chaos threatening Gaul, he discusses the progress of his building projects, appropriating a discourse which Cicero had once used to report on the villas of his brother.[19] Another of his letters, following a Roman tradition that had thrived several centuries earlier in the works of Statius and Pliny the Younger, is composed as a description of his *villa*.[20] His literary "description" is vital in indicating the link between the socially important areas of the home as places of Roman ritual and their visual realisation.

The tour begins with the baths and then proceeds to the main building and its ladies' dining room, the dining area of the children and dependents, and finally Sidonius's own winter and summer dining rooms. It is inconceivable that this mounts to a full tour. The *villa* presumably had service areas and *cubicula* if nothing else. The author briefly mentions bedrooms but explains them only as contrast to the suites he is describing; the bath and dining suites must be special. They are the rooms of specific Roman ritual and apparently public; he talks of outside friends as fellow-bathers.

As for the decoration of his baths and *triclinium*, the author ensures that both appear to conform to Roman practice. The baths boast porphyry columns and coffered ceilings. His second dining room opens on to the lake; the dining rooms of Lucullus with their fish cascades and aviaries immediately spring to mind.[21] Sidonius, it would seem, had arranged his (literary, if not physical) dining room as part of a long tradition of appropriate display.

The description of this *villa* indicates that the most important rooms are those that accommodate Roman ritual and create an appropriate *locus* through the use of Roman decoration. The letter implies that such rituals were carried out in an ambiance suggestive of Rome, perpetuating the *ethos-locus* link between behaviour and environment. The creation of the correct ambiance was essential; ritual and its setting are interdependent, a lesson we have already observed in the failures of Trimalchio.

There are, of course, problems in using the letters of Sidonius as evidence for domestic Romanisation, not least because of their late date. Whilst it could be claimed that this provincial literature is largely motivated by Roman literary conventions rather than everyday experience, this does not necessarily preclude its use as evidence for the use and appearance of provincial houses. Might it not be equally likely that Sidonius's peers should turn to these same conventions when building their homes? Both text and art could likewise serve the same purpose of building an impression of *Romanitas*. In turning to the physical remains of the houses of Vasio in Gaul, Verulamium in Britian, and Volubilis in North Africa, we might investigate how barbarian peripheries came to be reconciled to the rhetoric of the centre and to become centres in their own right.

VASIO: THE *ATRIUM* HOUSE?

The impossibility of considering only the Vitruvian *atrium* plan as a proper Roman house is emphasised by the lack of evidence for its spread beyond Italy. There are some isolated examples: Augusta Emerita in northern Spain, a colony of Augustan veterans founded by Publius Carisius in 25 B.C., had several large *atrium* houses.[22] The town also had all the amenities of a Roman urban centre, and the theatre was dedicated by Augustus's right-hand man, Agrippa himself. The fact that the inhabitants were all Roman might well explain their choice of house type, which did not spread through the rest of the Iberian peninsula.

However, the *atrium* house does occasionally appear in other contexts, famously at Vasio in southern Gaul. Vasio (modern Vaison-la-Romaine) was a capital of the confederate tribe of the Vocontii. The Romans first made

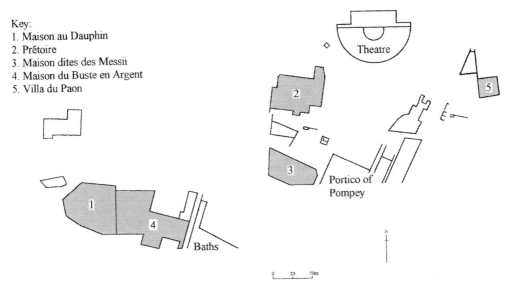

Key:
1. Maison au Dauphin
2. Prétoire
3. Maison dites des Messii
4. Maison du Buste en Argent
5. Villa du Paon

66. Vasio, plan. After Carrien.

inroads into the area in the mid second century B.C. and faced several major uprisings in which the Vocontii participated. However, during Caesar's
Gallic Wars, the tribe remained loyal to Rome; as a result, Vasio was granted
the status of *civitas foederatae*, which gave the city both Latin rights and inde-
pendence. Under Augustus, Vasio underwent far-reaching alterations. Most
importantly, the new city (Figure 66) was built on virgin territory, the pre-
Roman settlement being a hill fort across the river.[23] Unfortunately, much
of the Roman city is lost under the modern town, but the orientation of the
few excavated buildings would imply that the city was laid out on a grid
plan, symbolic of Roman order. Vasio was entered along streets lined with
tombs, and at its heart lay the *forum*, observing traditional Roman ideas of
civic boundaries and concepts of centre and periphery. The city had a theatre, several bath houses, and a porticoed street as well as a good number
of exceptionally wealthy, large *domus*, most of which have their own bathsuites. The extent to which Vasio was Romanised might be understood by
the fact that already by the first century A.D., the citizens were holding high
commands in the Senate, becoming consuls and, in the famous example of
Burrus, praetorian prefect to the emperor Nero.

But perhaps one of the greatest signs of successful and intense Romanisation was the great *atrium* house, the Maison au Dauphin (Figure 67).[24] The
architecture of the house is arranged to address all the complexities of
Roman life that we saw in the houses of Pompeii. The house is oriented
onto a main thoroughfare, a colonnaded street, not far to the south of

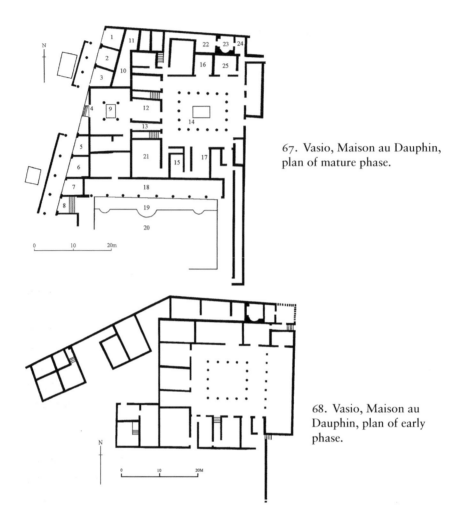

67. Vasio, Maison au Dauphin, plan of mature phase.

68. Vasio, Maison au Dauphin, plan of early phase.

which ought to lie the *forum*. The stepped entrance is flanked by shops, and from the entrance, a central view axis extends from *atrium*, 9, through *tablinum*, 12, to peristyle, 14. As in Pompeian houses, the homeowner offers a second, more luxurious view to those who are admitted access. The viewer in *exedra* 16 can see straight through the intercolumniations of the peristyle, over the pool in the middle of that garden, to the *exedra*, 17. From there, the view extends even further through a window and the intercolumniation of a second portico, 18, to a fountain niche set in a long basin, 19. The skewing of the *tablinum* (12) to accommodate the view from the street demonstrates that these vistas are hardly accidental. Even in the absence of its decoration, it is clear that the house has accommodated tensions between public and private, town and country in its interplay of views and use of natural features.

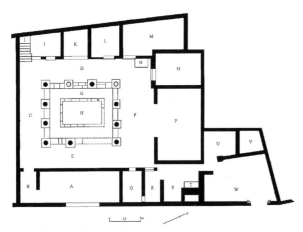

69. Glanum, Maison des Antes, plan.

The Maison au Dauphin was taken as a symbol of the early, thorough Romanisation of the Vocontii. However, when a more detailed stratigraphic analysis was carried out, a more complex picture of the house's development became clear.[25] The house was not an imposed Italian type. Rather than growing from its *atrium* to its peristyles, the house had expanded from its peristyle outwards. In its first incarnations, perhaps as early as 40 B.C., the house had been simply a court, ringed by a single layer of rooms (Figure 68). The alienness of the plan is exaggerated by the awkward placing of the Roman rooms, the bathsuite, away from the main house.

In fact, if we are looking for a model for the houses of early Vasio, we are better off looking for local, rather than Italian inspiration. The inhabitants of southern Gaul had been exposed to Greek culture since the founding of the Greek colony, Massilia (modern Marseilles) in about 600 B.C. The town of Glanum, not far from Vasio, had been under the control of Massilia since the second century B.C. and, as a result, boasted many Greek elements. Its inhabitants lived in masonry peristyle houses in an urban environment that included an *agora*, *bouleuterion*, and porticoes.[26] Two of the peristyle houses built during Massiliote rule have been excavated in the town centre. Although they are small and somewhat irregular because of the tapering house plots, they are recognisable as Greek houses. The Maison des Antes (House 6) (Figure 69) follows that pattern most closely, consisting of rooms surrounding three sides of a peristyle, C–H, which lies along the south wall of the house. Entrance to the peristyle from outside is through a wide vestibule, A, to the east. Directly in front of the peristyle to the north was a wide room, usually known as the *oecus*, P, and there was an open room, an *exedra*, K, to the west side. These are canonical attributes of a Greek house and are clearly influenced by the living arrangements of the Massiliotes.

The Roman attitude towards these houses is enlightening. Agrippa set up a temple in the sanctuary, and the *agora* and *bouleuterion* were replaced by a *forum* and *basilica*, which was built over a housing block. Meanwhile, the peristyle houses, which lay out of the way of the public building works, were left to thrive. Presumably this would imply that their plans were not thought of as inherently anti-Roman. Indeed, the peristyle of the Maison des Antes has been interpreted as serving all the functions of a perfect *atrium* with both an *impluvium*, H, and *lararium*, N. Even the peristyle house based on the Greek model, the very antithesis of the Roman *domus*, might find a role in the empire.

The similarity of these plans to those at Vasio would seem to confirm their relation. Goudineau even sees a large room on the north side of the portico in both the "Prétoire" and Maison au Dauphin. It would appear, then, that a house type derived from Greece was adopted by Gauls attempting to live like Romans. By Flavian times, it is clear that the choice of these houses had paid off. The epigraphic evidence implies the involvement of members of the community as priests and magistrates. Leading families begin to dominate the cityscape. The Pompeius family, presumably once clients of the general, built a porticoed pleasure garden in the middle of town. The epitaph of Q. Pompey, erected by his daughter Pompeia, shows that he was *aedile* and prefect as well as holding several priesthoods.[27] The inscription assures the visitor entering the city that this was Pompey's town. A rich house, again situated on the theatre road, is known as the Maison dite des Messii (Figure 70), due to the family name found on inscriptions found within this house, throughout the town, and in its local environs.[28] The Messii clearly had a high profile, binding their home not only with the city but with its hinterlands as well.

The situation of the houses within the city also demonstrates social interaction. Whilst the Prétoire and Maison dite des Messii opened on to the road taking traffic to the theatre, the Maison du Buste en Argent opened onto the Rue du Boutiques (Figure 71).[29] Like its neighbour, the Maison au Dauphin, it lay on a major commercial road, provided with a colonnade, opposite a major public building, once known as the *basilica* but more likely part of a public bath. In fact, modern taste might find it a little too close to the public latrines of that edifice. The spectacular entrance is not an *atrium* but a grand vestibule, 18, with a tripartite entrance behind a two columned porch (Figure 72). This tripartite view is followed up through the far side of the vestibule, over a peristyle courtyard, and into the room beyond. Again, a second view axis creates a vista from rooms deeper within the house, across the south garden and its water basin.

Unfortunately, little of the interior decoration of these houses has survived. To get some idea of the extent of the decoration in the houses of Vasio, we must turn to the Maison dite des Messii (Figure 70). Its slightly more irregular house plan means that this house does not admit an axial view through from the front door, but it does have several interior views, one unfolding from the entrance across rooms 3–5, all decorated with mosaic.[30] The rear of the house is arranged so that the large room 8 has an unbroken view through its large window and the wide intercolumniation of the peristyle onto the water basin and garden, 9, beyond. The importance of the room is suggested by its *opus sectile* floor. The arrangement of the peristyle further enhances the importance of the room and its painted neighbours 6 and 7. The greater height of the columns on this north side would suggest that this was a Rhodian peristyle, like that of the House of the Golden Cupids in Pompeii (Figure 45).

Throughout Vasio, the remains of decoration and sculpture found in a domestic context recall the worlds invoked in Italian homes. The incursion of the wild is evidenced by the planted peristyles and water features, several of which have provision for housing fish. The pergola in the Prétoire, itself on axis with a fountain, demonstrates a practice of using wild, garden space for social, dining rituals. Nature continues to invade the interior space. The tiny piece of wall plaster from a house on a site known as the Pommeral preserves a plume of foliage again familiar from Campania.[31] The most interesting wall decoration comes from the Maison aux Fresques of which very little survives except two painted rooms to the south of the Maison du Buste en Argent.[32] The frieze from one room features an animal chase including a leaping lion and a man attacking a deer. Throughout the town, too, this rural idyll takes on a religious tone. *Oscillae* featuring Dionysiac themes were found in the *atrium* of the Maison du Buste en Argent, and a herm of Bacchus came from the Maison à Atrium.

The Villa du Paeon, built on the eastern outskirts of Vasio towards the end of the first century A.D., provides architectural expression of the wealthy rural life.[33] It would appear to be much more strictly symmetrical than its urban counterparts, furnished with more lavish mosaics, including the bird mosaic featuring the peacock that gives the villa its name. On its central axis, a stepped niche fountain looks onto the court. This sophisticated, suburban *villa* is the ultimate expression of the interplay between town and country, providing a hint of the extent to which the elite inhabitants of Vasio had structured the world around them according to a rhetoric invented at Rome. The structure of both town and hinterland was diagnosed by Roman convention.

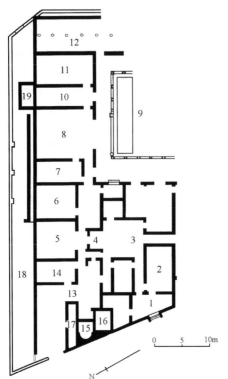

70. Vasio, Maison dite des Messii, plan.

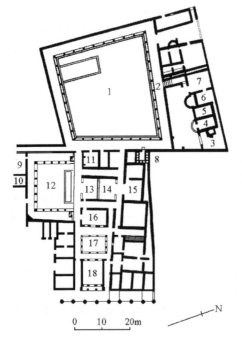

71. Vasio, Maison du Buste en Argent, plan.

72. Vasio, Maison du Buste en Argent, view from street. Photo: A. Crafer.

The houses of Vasio, then, seem to be fully working Roman houses. The local elites seem to have been grappling with all those tensions played on by elites back in Italy. They appear to juggle their rural and civic sides, to begin to explore the wild and the divine. They use their house both to impress outsiders and reward insiders. They are eager for the public gaze. In effect, these elites have made themselves a centre from which to define and to tackle dangerous peripheries. It is also possible to observe how this mini centre related itself to the great centre of Rome by exploiting different layers of its new identity. Many individuals were clearly exploiting a family name in order to secure presence on a local level. As a community, the city could use its status to assert itself to a wider audience, adopting Burrus as its patron or representative in Rome. But between the centres of Vasio and Rome, it is also clear that these elites inserted themselves into an intermediary group on a provincial level, borrowing their house type not from distant Italy but from Graeco-Gallic neighbours. The house types of Vasio, then, reflect the essentially parochial experience of being part of the Roman empire. Elite homeowners grafted Roman decoration and features onto local designs, absorbing the Roman into their own conception of life. The practise suggests that Romanisation was brought about through the co-operation of local elites looking to express their social position in their immediate area as much as to compete within the empire.[34]

In recognising the local nature of the domestic architecture of Vasio, we are not asserting that the city was any more or less Romanised than if she had simply adopted, or been forced to adopt, the *atrium* house at the time of Augustus. The hybrid house type of Flavian Vasio proves itself amply able to wrestle with different identities and conflicting demands; the very architecture is born of this negotiation. We must remind ourselves that, even in Rome, this negotiation "proves" Romanness, not the ability to win any given category. Similarly, the houses of Vasio did not have to be traditional *atrium* houses to compete. The rhetoric of their decoration and the use of space within them built a convincing impression of their *Romanitas*. The citizens of Vasio could fantasise like true Romans. The ongoing success of the city up until its sack towards the end of the third century would seem to be evidence of the success with which Vasio took its place in the empire.

Traditionally, the *atrium* type had proved Vasio's Romanness. But Vasio was not simply a mini Rome, and that was not the intention of Vasio homeowners. Their identity rested on wrestling with their local, ethnic, and social Roman personas. In doing so, Vasio ceases to be merely a periphery; it becomes a new centre where an idea of Rome can be reinvented. Taking themselves as the centre, the elites of Vasio organised the world around their viewpoint and seemingly embraced, as part of their Roman experience, not only all those recognised Roman traits – urbanisation, civic religion – but also all their antitheses – the wild and the exotic. Not only did they entertain Celtic gods, Roman gods, and conflations of the two, but they also took an interest in alien deities, like Serapis and Horus.[35] In embracing these different deities simultaneously, the people of Vasio exposed themselves to the variety of experiences offered within the Roman empire. As such, they found themselves a place on that scale between Roman and alien and, in adopting Roman ideas of the peripheral and exotic, brought themselves into the sphere of the Roman.

BRITAIN

The northern reaches of the western empire are generally thought of as the least Romanised in both Roman and modern popular opinion. The urban areas of Roman Britain, northern Gaul, and Germany – even with the occurrence of such familiar building types as amphitheatres – appear to be largely free of the Classical culture of the ancient cities of the Mediterranean. However, the very alienness of the architecture of these areas makes the investigation into the acquisition of *Romanitas* all the more acute.

In the northern provinces, the majority of Romanised homes are row houses.[36] They are very different from the houses inhabited by the populations of these areas before the Romans came. A typical pattern of change can be seen in the south east of England in the area that would become Verulamium. During the Iron Age, the area was populated by round houses like that found directly under the Roman *villa* at Lockleys.[37] The abandonment of the circular hut was not a natural development; in the farther west country where Roman influence remained minimal, round houses are found well into the fourth century A.D.[38] That so many of the row villas around Verulamium exhibit definite signs of Iron Age foundations beneath shows a clear decision on the part of the landowners to abandon their own building conventions in favour of those that better appear to conform to the local interpretation of a new life that we would recognise as Romanised.

Before the invasion of Britain by the emperor Claudius in A.D. 43, the site of Verulamium was the *oppidum* of the Catuvellauni tribe.[39] The settlement consisted of an area of sub-rectangular houses and animal pens enclosed within a dyke system. The tribe were fiercely anti-Roman and, under the leadership of the notorious Caratacus, they fought to resist the Roman invasion. As a result of his defeat, a fort was built along the site, and the Roman city (Figure 73) developed, becoming a regional capital.

The Catuvellauni, like the Vocontii, begin their careers in Roman history by vigorously opposing political domination. However, even at this early stage, they were familiar with Roman forms of display. Before the conquest of A.D. 43, the tribe were already adopting symbols of Roman superiority. Coins of Cunobelinus, whose leadership of the tribe is roughly contemporary with that of the emperor Tiberius in Rome, do just this. Some coins present us with a portrait of a moustached and bearded, long haired male with elliptical eyes shown face on, a defiant chieftain (Figure 74). However, others show a typical Augustan profile, a *princeps* crowned with laurels.[40] The deliberate decision to use Roman iconography cannot be regarded as bowing to Roman superiority since the Catuvellauni were not famous for their love of Romans. Instead, it should be understood as an attempt to express local pride through symbols most effectively equated with power and success, inevitably those of Rome. In adopting such symbols alongside indigenous images, the Catuvellaunian elite imported foreign culture as a means of enforcing local control. Even before the arrival of the Roman army, Roman material culture was already within the grasp of the local elite. A divorce in provincial minds between the city of Rome and its culture was predicated by the determination of elites on the edges of the empire to assert themselves as alternative centres. Britons might build an impression of living like Romans to give expression to their resistance to Rome. By adopting the guise of imperial power for themselves, the Catuvellauni cast

Key:
1. Ins.1.2   7. Ins.4.10
2. Ins.27.2   8. Ins.1.3
3. Ins.3.2   9. Ins.2.1
4. Ins.28.1   10. Ins.28.3
5. Ins.4.8   11. Ins.22.1
6. Ins.21.2   12. Ins.14

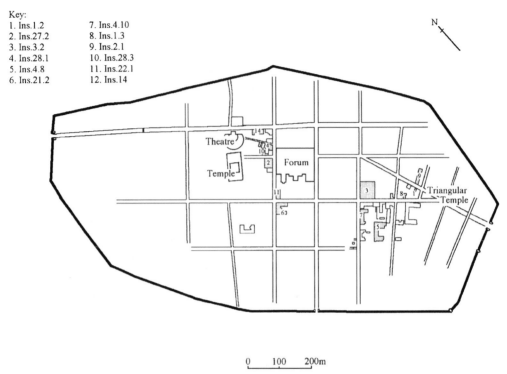

73. Verulamium, plan. After Frere.

the Romans as the outsiders, the enemy. This ploy in itself gives a small hint at how complex motives behind acculturation might be.

As a *civitas* capital, Verulamium was an important focus for the local landscape and was early on ringed with *villa*s, among them Gadebridge, Gorhambury, Lockleys, and Park Street. The main thoroughfare was Watling Street, the road travelling north from London, which joined the city to other major urban sites such as Silchester and Colchester. Although early Verulamium was sacked by Boudicca in A.D. 61, the city recovered to be further formulated. An inscription suggests that the *forum* was dedicated in A.D. 79. A large masonry *forum*, surrounded by colonnades and a huge *basilica* must have marked the city out as very impressive at such an early date in Britain's Roman history. However, the city's heyday was not to arrive until another disaster threatened its existence; a terrific fire caused intense damage around the city centre in the mid-second century. It was in the period of recovery that the city reached its full expression. The city was decorated with three arches, a relatively rare architectural type in Britain. Although no baths have been found within the site, it is suggested that there was a large establishment just beyond the walls.

74. Coin of Cunobelinus, British Museum. Photo: Copyright © The British Museum.

The many Roman components of the city, however, were not simply imposed on a local populace. It is easy to see acculturation at play in the Romano-Celtic temples, an amalgam in which it is hard to see precedents in either culture but which clearly formed a solution, however unintelligble to us, whereby the demands of both Roman and local religion could be to some extent satisfied.[41] The presence of the theatre is worth noting in this context, too. The close correlation of the building with the temple in Ins 16 would imply that it was built as a specific adjunct to religious activity and not simply (if at all) as a place of dramatic entertainment.

The architecture of Verulamium not only shows the interaction of local and Roman in the Romano-Celtic temples but also sheds light on the changing interactions and negotiations between centres and peripheries as we travel around the empire. The triangular temple along Watling Street, apparently built in the second century, is often identified as a temple of Cybele and Attis. Cybele was a Phrygian mother goddess from whom all nature emanated; Attis was her unfortunate lover, whose fidelity was finally forced by being driven to self-castration. Several features point to the pair's occupation of the sanctuary. First, the offerings of pine cones have been found in pits associated with the site. Grafitti found elsewhere in the city also mentions a *dendrophoros*, an agent in the cult of Attis. The two pits in the precinct might find some parallel in the pits that seem to have flanked the steps of the Cybele temple at Ostia.[42]

The identification is not altogether certain. Another possible recipient of pine cones could be Dionysus; either way, both represent the dangerous and exotic to the traditional Roman imagination. The cult of Cybele was very much defined as a foreign, though essential, cult in Rome, where she was introduced from Phrygia during the Punic Wars on the advice of the Sibylline Books. Whilst the Sibylline Books granted her legitimacy at the heart of Roman religion as did her Palatine temple, aspects of her cult, most luridly and much played on by the satirists – her eunuch priests – ensured her difference.[43] The possibility that the site was indeed dedicated to Cybele again raises interesting wider questions about the process of acculturation and the interplay of centres and peripheries in Roman culture. Were the Britons who embraced Cybele aware of her peripheral status or did she just appear to them as a component of the Roman package? From the Roman point of view, it would seem to suggest that both central and peripheral were so integral to Roman identity that they had to be exported together in order to spread *Romanitas*. Furthermore, if Britons accepted both Roman and Phrygian cults as parts of the same cultural group, then how might they define centre and periphery? And how might they understand the tensions between British and Roman to fit into the debate? These questions are almost impossible to answer, but the problems they pose demonstrate just how much the peripheral was caught up with the central, how dependent Roman identity was on the expression of both, and, in fact, how elusive is a definition of either.

The urban monuments of the Roman city began the process of Romanising the landscape, but the city could only survive with people. It is telling that when Agricola tried to pacify the Britons as governor of the province, he urged them not only to build *templa* and *fora* but also to build *domos*.[44] Agricola had brought with him the expectation that the rhythm of the city depended on the interplay of public and private, individual and populace. He understood that private architecture would influence successful urban life as much as its civic counterpart. To our eyes, we might expect Agricola to have been disappointed with the results. The first houses in Verulamium are generally simple constructions made of wood. Many of the earliest are shops built along Watling Street. They tend to be strip buildings with narrow frontages, backing deep into the *insula*, perhaps simply partitioned into two like the second century example at Ins 1.2 (Figure 73).

In the rebuilding of the city after the Antonine fire, much greater use was made of masonry and Roman decorational techniques in order to create larger and more complex, winged row houses. The houses present a wide façade to the street, with their short wings turning to the interior of the *insula*. Long corridors run along the front and back of the house; the rooms are arranged in a row between them. Although most of the houses lack familiar architectural features, almost all the houses have traces of mosaic and wall painting. To what extent these houses interacted with the city is hard to say. The majority, as implied earlier, are built with long sides against the street, or even to take advantage of a corner to put two sides along the street – this is true of Ins 27.2 and Ins 3.2 (Figure 73). Further indication of the efforts to interact further with the outside world is implied by the use of porticoes and verandahs by shops, particularly those fronting Watling Street. The houses of Ins 27, which faced the *forum*, were porticoed. It is also the case that 28.1, which also occupied the entire *insula*'s length of the *forum* street, had some public functions.[45] Frere identifies both a possible shop and a public latrine. The domestic end of the house appears to have been located on the other side of the building and at least room 19 was tessellated and served by a hypocaust. However, it is important to put this into perspective. After the original buildings of Ins 28 burned in the Antonine fire, there was a fifty-year gap before the construction of Ins 28.1. Very few other larger houses appear to show the penetration of commercial activity and, indeed, several, such as Ins 4.8, are built deep within the *insula* with no street frontage.

On first sight, the row house seems almost an anti-type to the *atrium* or the peristyle house, looking inward and disinterested in the outside world. Even once inside, the visitor was essentially confined to an outer corridor, which ran the length of the house, unless specifically invited into one of the rooms opening off it. In that sense, the visitor who penetrated one of these houses would not necessarily feel he had arrived in the heart of the house in the same way as would a visitor to a Pompeian household.

The permeability or otherwise of the houses of Verulamium remains something of a mystery in the absence of known entrance points. However, in some cases, it is possible to observe the conversion of these outer corridors into semi-colonnades. Ins 4.8 has a verandah along both its long sides (Figure 75). More generally, the verandah is used between the wings of the house as a means of drawing together house and yard. This appears to have been the case at Ins 4.1 where the verandah ran all around the house, and a fragment from around room 5 would imply that it was painted with coloured panels. The preservation of the ornate painting on the courtyard wall of Ins 21.2 also implies the original presence of a verandah (Figure 76). The use of such painting in itself demonstrates the permeability of the wall and interaction between the occupants and outsiders. Excavators are inclined to see the small square rooms that protrude from many houses into the courts as porches. If this is correct, it would seem that the major entrance was in effect at the back of the house, often on the verandah side.

Although the domestic architecture of Verulamium might seem very alien, its space was articulated by an easily recognisable repertoire of Roman interior decoration. Just as in Rome, Pompeii, and Vasio, wall painting and mosaic provided permanent embellishment. Unlike Pompeii, though, this type of decoration appears to have been restricted to key areas of the

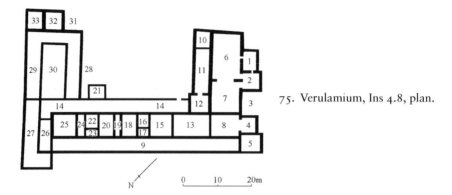

75. Verulamium, Ins 4.8, plan.

76. Verulamium, Ins 21.2, courtyard, wall painting. Photo: © St. Albans Museums.

house. In Ins 21.2 (Figure 77), the excavated parts of the southwestern wing boast some of the most sumptuous decoration in Verulamium. The entire wing was victim to an intense application of tessellated floors and wall and ceiling painting. The culminate in the largest room, 4, which houses a lion

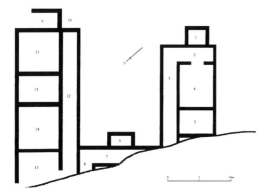

77. Verulamium, Ins 21.2, plan.
After Frere.

78. Verulamium, Ins 21.2, room
4, lion mosaic. Photo: © St.
Albans Museum.

mosaic (Figure 78) set off by painted walls of coloured dadoes surmounted
by large panels. The archaeological evidence would also serve to suggest
that the room had clerestory windows; so it was at least seventeen feet
high. These special features of decoration and architecture, not only of the
room itself but also of the corridor around it, would seem to work as a
signal to the visitor or, indeed, occupant that he was entering an important
part of the house.

Again, it was in the right-hand wing that decoration predominated in
a number of houses of Ins. 4, including 4.1, 4.2 and 4.8 (Figure 75).[46] In
Ins 4.10 (Figure 79), tessellated floors are found grouped in the western end
of the house. At the eastern end, the large corner room has a mosaic of an
urn flanked by dolphins laid above a hypocaust. In Ins 4.8, the southern
wing appears to have been a bathsuite with an extensive hypocaust system.
Almost all the rooms have mosaics. The only figural design, from room 4,
features the head of a sea deity with lobster claws in his hair (Figure 80).
Here it would seem that practice, architecture, and decoration have all coin-
cided to recreate a thoroughly Roman experience. The pattern of elaborate

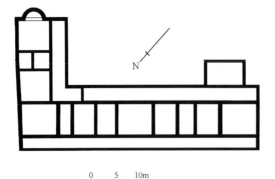

79. Verulamium, Ins 4.10, plan.

0   5   10m

80. Verulamium, Ins 4.8, room 4, mosaic. Photo: © St. Albans Museum.

bathsuites is traceable in the *villa*s around Verulamium, particularly Gadebridge where a self-contained bath house was in place even before the construction of the first masonry *villa*, prompting comparison with the early phase of the Maison au Dauphin at Vasio (Figure 68).[47]

The pattern of a single, large, highly decorated room is confined not only to the big winged houses but also evidently filtered down to smaller houses such as Ins 1.3, which in the late third century took an L-shape, the foot of the L being the largest room of the house and boasting a mosaic.[48] One of the more unusual rooms can be found in the second-century phase of Ins 2.1.[49] The principal room had a panel of geometric mosaic, and its walls were painted red and green. Most importantly, though, the room was not isolated. It had a huge doorway, 7.5 feet wide, which led the viewer's eye over the red tessellated corridor to an apse decorated with a scallop shell mosaic. This pattern is unique in Verulamium and was destroyed in the following century.

Perhaps the nearest to this arrangement would be Ins 21.2 (Figure 77). The fact that the lion mosaic in room 4 faces outwards helps to elucidate the manner in which the elaborate nature of the room affected the building around it. As at Ins 2.1, the room, and the lion, look out through a wide threshold, across a highly decorated corridor to a small porch-type projection. The decoration here was hardly analogous to the apse of 2.1, but it was highly decorated with painted walls and ceiling. It does at least imply a similar attempt at bonding different areas of the house into limited viewing and spatial systems.

The size of these rooms would suggest that they have been made prominent as the focus of the social activities of the household. The suggestion that room 4 of Ins 21.2 might have served as a *triclinium* comes from the position of the lion mosaic (Figure 78), pushed forward to the front of the room. However, it is also the case that the orientation of the lion facing the entrant rather than occupiers of the room, may upset this plan. Frere sees a *triclinium* in room 3 of a late second-century house, Ins 21.1. The room was decorated with mosaic and wall painting, but its function is based on the fact that the room behind it seems to have been used for a kitchen. The position of the mosaic panel in room 9 of the short-lived second-century Ins 28.3 might suggest a *triclinium*.[50] The floor is tessellated except for a panel of patterned mosaic divided into nine panels, eight outer ones framing a central motif of two dolphins flanking a kantharos. This motif faces the back of the room whilst the rectangular panels of vegetal design on either side are faced out to the side walls. The whole panel is centrally situated but pushed forward in the floor. The fragments of wall painting suggest a lavish wall. Although the main scheme would appear to consist, fairly typically, of dado, main fields with panels, and frieze, the area between panels features delicate vegetal detail, and the main field and frieze are separated by an imitation cornice. The evidence of the wall painting would also imply that the room was at least twelve feet high, further highlighting the importance of this room in the overall plan. We might have learned from Pompeii that we should be cautious in applying a precise function to such rooms. Better to note that, whatever uses this room might serve at any one time, the occupants are constantly acting against this backdrop of Roman grandeur.[51]

The forms of domestic decoration used in the houses of Verulamium demonstrate the adoption of an entirely foreign practice.[52] In discussing the translation of cultures across the Roman world, Woolf confirms our suspicions that material goods are exchanged the most readily and need not imply absorption of ideals or practises associated with them back at their point of origin.[53] It is more than likely that Britons interpreted the iconography they adopted according to their own experience. It would be ridiculous to assume that the associations that a Palatine or a Watling Street dweller would bring to any motif would be the same.[54] Acculturation is a complex enough process to accommodate various, simultaneous motives and reactions. On the other hand, the adoption of a cultural language to compete with fellow elites in projecting impressions of power would suggest the ability and intention to compete within that culture. Certainly, social aspiration seems to have been a common element amongst many elites of the empire. Very quickly, it is possible to see the houses of Verulamium begining to exploit the possibilities of wall painting.

Ins 28.3 appears to have been built as an L-shape, though its full extent has not been fully excavated. The house was substantial but, unfortunately, made of wood very shortly before the Antonine fire. It was gutted and never rebuilt, but quantities of the wall plaster survive, particularly in room 3 (Figure 81). Here the marble-look dado is complemented by fields in the upper zone, which are divided by painted marble columns, a deliberate attempt to give an impression of wealth. Room 3 seems to have been a corridor with gravel flooring, and the columns give the impression of a colonnaded gallery running along the building. The evidence is interesting because, as a corridor, it is likely that the room was frequented by outsiders. This would seem to give weight to the idea that decoration was often there to impress an audience, not simply to gratify the inhabitants.

Occasionally, other forms of architectural imitation are evident. We have already mentioned the painted moulded cornice of Ins 28.3 and the ceiling painting of Ins 21.2 would seem to owe some inspiration to coffered ceilings. In Ins 22.1, one scheme involves blue panels with white lattice work (Figure 82). It seems to be a simple form of the trellice fencing found in Pompeian painting. Perhaps it is an attempt to imply an opening through the wall. A small segment of wall painting found in Ins 18.1 had remains of a painting of plants. Whilst these schemes seem simple in comparison with the garden paintings of Italy, they do appear to imply experimentation with the medium's repertoire of motifs and perhaps, more importantly, the ideas behind them.

The use of wall painting and mosaic entailed not only the assumption of Roman media but also Roman iconography. As manifestations of Roman decoration, they are used exclusively for Roman themes. There are no easily recognisable local motifs in mosaics from Britain. This might

81. Verulamium, Ins 28.3, room 3, wall painting. Photo: © St. Albans Museum.

82. Verulamium, Ins 22.1, wall painting. Photo: © St. Albans Museum.

well explain the largely decorative nature of the Verulamium wall paintings. Most of the figural mosaics of mythological and allegorical figures date from late Antiquity, at the end of a couple of centuries of acculturation. However, even the most basic Graeco-Roman symbol held cultural associations. The acanthus scrolls in Ins 21.2 (Figure 76), for instance, feature a Mediterranean plant. The interior decoration does not appear to allow any expression of the local. Of course, there is the possibility that the British commissioner of mosaics saw Celtic significance where we only see Graeco-Roman images. Their decision to express that significance through Roman images would seem to reflect a desire to take on the trappings of Roman power.

But how seriously should we take these trappings? The row house seems to be an indigenous response to Roman urbanisation. It is a reflection of how the people of the northern provinces adapted their own domestic needs to those imposed upon them by the need to participate in Roman life. The type is also used for the *villa*s around Verulamium. Recently, Smith has suggested that each *villa* might be the residence of several family units, implying a social structure based on tribal kingroups rather than Roman *familiae*.[55] The arrangement of suites on which Smith's plan is based is shown very precisely by the second phase of the *villa* at Boxmoor, not far from Verulamium. A main central room is flanked by two thin corridors, which are in turn flanked by two larger rooms, each of which are bordered by a further two rooms. Smith proposes that this plan provides living space for two family units, each occupying a suite flanking a common reception room.[56] Bigger villas might feature three or four repeated suites and so are not to be understood as the large home of an exceptionally rich man but the multiple dwelling of several families.

For Smith, the *porticus* along the front of the *villa*s, which might be said to imitate the empire-wide language of rural architecture and the Italian portico *villa* in particular, is merely an addition that has no integration into the main syntax of the house. Does this necessarily mean, however, that the adoption of Roman decorational or architectural techniques was literally just a façade? The evolution of the row type is not a slow continuous one, and corridors seem to have been a feature from the start. Even if it might not seem immediately clear to us how the new form is any more Roman than its predecessor, these houses were a specific reaction to a new lifestyle. It would be wrong to reject immediately the efforts of the homeowners of Verulamium as being non- or anti-Roman just because they do not fulfill our expectations of what being "Roman" is. To do so would be to presume that the aim of Romanisation was to create a homogenous society where houses all looked the same and to suppose that Roman civilisation depended on that homogeneity.[57] The long-term survival of the row house would rather imply that these houses should not be regarded as any less Roman than any other type. Indeed, it would suggest that these houses could sustain a Romanised way of life to the degree that they could be tolerated within the imperial system. Nor should the row house be understood as a halfway house. Houses of this plan were still being constructed in the fourth century. In Verulamium, only one house, Ins 3.2, ever became a courtyard house.[58] Instead, the row type, first formulated in Britain in the countryside, was translated to the cities.

The townhouses do not follow the tidy arrangement of Boxmoor. Ins 4.8 appears to follow Smith's *villa* plans in that a reverse symmetry can be observed in the main row of the house (Figure 75).[59] Room 19 acts as a corridor between two largish rooms – 18 and 20 – which themselves are flanked by two rooms, 16 and 17 and 22 and 23. Perhaps 15 could take the role of the common reception room – it was decorated with a mosaic and once served by a hypocaust. The southern wing was home to the bathsuite. Whilst it might be possible to assign different groups to each suite, it is also true that the provision of one main reception room (and, perhaps less surprisingly, one bathsuite) would have presented a unified front to the visitor and would seem to accommodate the Roman practice of one household under a *paterfamilias*. So, even if Smith is correct in assigning each house a multiple occupancy, it must also be said that the layout of the house could mould the household into Roman social patterns. It is easy to see how the senior member of the group might have gradually become a *paterfamilias*, the man around whom public/private boundaries revolved.[60]

Perhaps the strongest evidence for the important role played by Roman elements of architecture and decoration is the spread of such embellishment not only between provincial elites but also throughout local societies. Not everybody in urban centres lived in row houses; multiple residencies or not, these were elite dwellings. In Britain, Gaul, and Germany a second rank of urban housing exists in the form of the strip house. They are long narrow terraces whose façades impinge little on public life. A block of these houses, fronted by shops, survives at Verulamium Ins 14.[61] After the Antonine fire, these wooden shops were rebuilt behind a colonnade. In the back rooms, basic Roman decoration, such as wall painting and *opus signinum* floors begin to appear. As with the elite corridor houses, the decorated areas are grouped together in adjoining rooms, which in one case, appear to include a *lararium*. The inhabitants of these homes seem to be equally taking on the symbols of wealth employed by the elite. They too wanted to participate in local *Romanitas*.

Throughout the empire, wall painting appears to tap into a empire-wide desire to aspire to better things, to allude to a wealthier or more magical world. As a relatively cheap way of initiating such display, it was very popular through several strata of society. The fact that the decor of the strip houses of Verulamium reflects the painting of the row houses in the same town demonstrate this competitive aspect of self-promotion and display. Although the wall paintings of Ins 14 survive only as fragments rather than full schemes, it is clear that they followed those of the corridor houses with candelabra and marbling effects. In the later rebuild, when the shop units were divided to become two façades, one room boasted a mosaic featuring a lion, a motif already famous from Ins 21.2 (Figure 78). This should not be written off simply as imitation. Locals would have needed a more pressing reason to invest in such trappings. Instead, we might see smaller householders using Roman decor to their own advantage, buying themselves a place in the competition.

The end of the third century saw some rebuilding in public Verulamium. The temple with the theatre was extended and beautified by colonnades. In the private sphere, several new buildings were going up, and some houses, such as Ins 4.10, received new mosaics. Late in the next century, a winged row house, which embraced a courtyard, Ins 27.2, was built with engaged columns – a late manifestation of Romanness but an exceptionally large and wealthy one. There are several signs of Roman practises being prac- tised in Verulamium during the fourth and even fifth centuries. They cor- respond in date to the rich evidence for elite life elsewhere in the country. Treasure hordes, such as the Mildenhall Treasure, date mostly from the fourth century and are particularly valued for the Classical, mythological designs inscribed on silver plate.[62] They reflect the lifestyles of a wealthy elite eager to display wealth and cultural affiliations on the social occasion of the *cena*.

As at Vasio, the houses of second-century Verulamium are neither British nor Italian, but something entirely different. The houses do not show an attempt to squeeze all the components of an *atrium* house into a new house type. Instead, the houses reveal a peculiarly local take on Roman power; a take that might accommodate a "barbaric" family group but that is never- theless successfully Roman. It was the elite who ultimately stood to win from acculturation; participation in the Roman empire enabled them to secure their local power balance and to spread their nets into a wider arena. But in receiving guests and being viewed, they automatically dragged the wider populace into the scenario as visitors and viewers. A social gulf opened up between those who were, on another level, united through their common ethnicity. The elite made themselves centres around whom their countrymen could only orbit as peripheries. In effect, in becoming patrons, the elite in- vented clients and thus spread the process through society. That aspiration fed through society is clear from the shop units of the city, which reflect the decor of the large row houses. Those clients, finding themselves so cast, set about entering the arena themselves.

The elite *domus* dwellers of Verulamium reshaped the world around their new cultural viewpoint. The ever-shifting relationship between centre and periphery was noted, even in Roman times: the exotic luxuries that appealed to the Britons were not those of the East, which had led Lucullus and Antony astray, but those of Rome herself. Tacitus, deploring the enervation of the Britons, firmly placed the blame on their adoption of Roman fripperies such as bathing.[63] He sees the provinces as newly born Romes that might escape the luxurious pitfalls of the aging capital.[64] Verulamium can be considered as its own centre, desirous of the exotic, immoral world of Rome. The multilocal nature of the empire is assured by a centre that can recognise its own birth in every new foundation. These new cities, however, will not be microcosms of the parent city. They are unique amalgamations that neither repeat a set template nor provide a model for future imperial cities. The provinces are regarded as positive and negative simultaneously; they can be integrated within, or distanced from, the centre on a rhetorical whim. Even Rome herself is cast in different degrees of central and peripheral as new centres observe her from a distance.

The complexities of the relationship between Rome and province is further evoked by looking back at the culture coming into Britain. The Rome that Verulamium received was already an entangled mix of centres and peripheries, bringing with it not just Jupiter but also Mithras and Cybele. The inhabitants of Verulamium was plunged straight into this mix, so as not only to reconcile Rome to their own idea of centre but also to meet the other peripheries. It is often said that the idea of Rome is diluted by being spread over the provinces.[65] In fact, the essence of Rome is refined and honed by the provinces as local elites sift through the multicultural bulk to find how they must use it to make themselves Roman.

NORTH AFRICA

By comparison with Britain, North Africa might appear streaks ahead in the Romanisation game. The scale of her cities range from the splendid remains of Lepcis Magna to the working town of Thuburbo Maius. The extensive decoration of the houses of these cities is evidenced by the thousands of mosaics that adorn museums like the Bardo in Tunis.[66] The abundance of information has led the Roman houses of North Africa to be addressed and investigated as a coherent group, making them the only provincial houses to be brought into recent debates on Roman domestic space.[67] Such studies

Key:
1. Maison aux Travaux d'Hercule
2. Maison au Portique
3. Maison a Cortège de Vénus
4. Maison à la Monnaie d'Or
5. Maison de Flavius Germanus
6. Maison des Fauves
7. Maison à l'Ouest du Palais du
    Gouverneur
8. Maison au Bacchus de Marbre
9. Maison aux Gros Pilastres
10. Maison des Néréides
11. Maison à l'Abside

83. Volubilis, plan. After Luguet.

have been crucial in allowing us to look past Campania and to think about the Roman house in its widest sense.

Volubilis was the provincial capital of the largely unurbanised province of Mauretania Tingitana (Figure 83).[68] The city was an old foundation situated on good agricultural land and in a strategic position for trade, which is probably what attracted the Punic interest that fuelled urbanisation amongst the Berbers. Octavian annexed the area and installed as king, Juba II, who presumably used the city as a base, if not as a second capital. So it was already an urban area with temples and a "palace" before Caligula decided to add to his empire by having Juba's son, Ptolemy, executed. By the early third century A.D., Volubilis had a *forum*, a *basilica*, and a large Capitolium complex. Several baths also dotted the landscape, and a lavishly decorated arch, dedicated by the people of Volubilis to Caracalla, stood along the *decumanus maximus*. During the Roman period, the city was expanded to the north to provide a new residential area. The houses built there represent the high point of Volubilis's prosperity in the end of the second and early third century before it was abandoned by the Romans in A.D. 285.

The builders of the elite houses of Volubilis faced a problem not encountered by architects working in the new cities of Vasio or Verulamium. Within a full urban plan, the homeowner was not free to disport himself where he wished. The building of the new, northeast quarter implies that the occupiers thought that the old site simply was not amenable to them, either in terms of size or organisation. Although several large imperial houses seem to have evolved from pre-Roman sites, the Maison de l'Ephebe for example, most of the big peristyle houses were confined to the new quarter.[69]

The houses had a big impact on the town even though they were slightly removed from its centre. The *insulae* were arranged around the *decumanus maximus*, making the houses part of a busy thoroughfare. The lower half of the main street is colonnaded so those houses at that end receive a particularly civic frontage. Most of the houses along this thoroughfare and on the subsidiary streets interplay with civic life by opening the front of their houses as individual shops, which, as a rule, have no interplay with the house proper. However, despite appearances, the houses were not necessarily, in reality, eager to share their domestic lives with passers-by. A great deal is often made of the Maison aux Travaux d'Hercule's porticoed frontage, which uses transverse columns at either end of the property to mark the boundaries of the house (Figure 84).[70] However, the entrance, 1, itself lies to the side of the property, away from the main street (Figure 85). The porticoes become even more important because they represent the owner's only presence on the main road. The block containing the Maison au Portique and the Maison au Cortège de Vénus was also porticoed along the decumanus sud 1. The first house blends in well with the street, taking advantage of the portico to attract commercial business into its shops. The second, however, takes a much more aggressive stance whereby the portico has been swallowed up to become part of the house proper, a corridor running along the front.[71]

Shops are not the only incursion of commercial life. Many of the *insulae* feature bakeries and oil factories. The corner of the Maison à la Monnaie d'Or seems to have a self-contained apartment that takes a simple corridor plan reminiscent of local building practices.[72] The whole *insula*'s jumbled use as elite home, rented flat, shops, stables, and industrial units is very typical of Pompeian *insulae* (Figure 1). The contrast with the houses of Verulamium is marked and reminds us just how different reactions to the

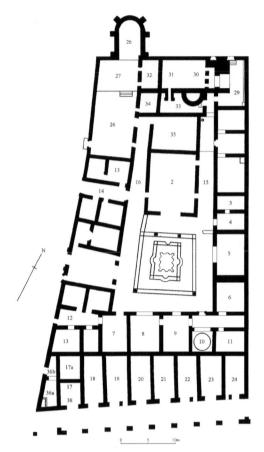

84. Volubilis, Maison aux Travaux d'Hercule, plan. After Etienne.

demands of *Romanitas* could be. As at Pompeii, doorways are crucial as the only aspect of the house visible on the street. The doorways of the district are very standardised, invariably formed of a double entrance – one big, one small – flanked by engaged columns or pilasters. The entrance will lead to a sizeable vestibule, which might offer two possible methods of ingress. A "private" means involves a long vestibule that takes a dog leg turn in order to reach the peristyle, thus keeping the heart of the house concealed until the last minute. Both the Maison de Flavius Germanus and the Maison des Fauves take this option.[73] The entrances show a desire to invite penetration and to make a show but at the same time to control physical and visual access. We might ask whether, by these obscured entrances, homeowners demonstrated their knowledge or their ignorance of Roman, cultural demands on the house? Perhaps they should be credited with mastering a rhetoric that demanded openness for political rather than aesthetic or structural reasons. The inhabitants of Volubilis, then, might be seen to have learnt, as had their counterparts at Rome, how to create an impression

85. Volubilis, Maison aux Travaux d'Hercule, view of entrance.

of obedience and conformity whilst retaining their own private world safe
inside.

The second vestibule type, which was very popular in third-century
Volubilis, involved a more symmetrical arrangement, which opens the peristyle view to the outside viewer. In these examples, as in the Maison au
Portique, the vestibule is placed on the axis of the house, joining the entrance directly to the peristyle. However, the view afforded by this arrangement is not as open as in the *fauces* of Pompeii. The openings at either
end of the vestibule are not lined up; there are two on the street and three
on the peristyle and the doorposts of the inner entrance can obscure the
illusion of unimpaired access. Only in a few houses, such as the Maison à
l'Ouest du Palais du Gouverneur is there a perfectly symmetrical vestibule,
tripartite at both ends (Figure 86).[74] It is presumably no coincidence that it
occurs again in the most richly decorated house, the Maison au Cortège de
Vénus. The symmetrical opening seemingly would allow visual access right
through the house, into the *oecus* (Figure 87). It is worth noting, though,
that this house also requires the visitor to cross more thresholds than any

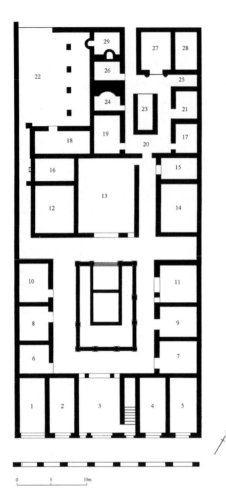

86. Volubilis, Maison à l'Ouest du Palais du Gouverneur, plan. After Etienne.

other before reaching the peristyle. Perhaps the owners can afford to be so visually accessible when they are, in fact, more physically protected.

Once inside, the main part of the house is laid out around a grand peristyle, the major circulatory area of the house and highly ornamental. As well as the columns and fountains, the court of the Maison à la Monnaie d'Or was paved in pink and grey *opus sectile*. The porticoes of the Maison au Cortège de Vénus bore figured mosaic. Almost without exception, each peristyle is bordered on the side opposite the vestibule by an *oecus*, which becomes a dominant feature of the whole area. In several instances, as in the Maison aux Travaux d'Hercule, the peristyle is of Rhodian type, with higher columns along the side of the *oecus*, further articulating the room. The dominant room often has a tripartite opening that might be further emphasised by the use of engaged columns as in the Maison de Flavius Germanus. These rooms are generally also made prominent by their size or

87. Volubilis, Maison au Cortège de Vénus, view from entrance.

their high level of decoration. The *oecus* of the Maison au Bacchus de
Marbre was about twenty-five feet wide, whilst that of the Maison aux
Travaux d'Hercule was paved with marble.[75]

The importance of the room is further demonstrated by the orientation
of the water features within the peristyles towards them. Generally they are
placed along a central axis and also pushed closer to the *oecus*, or perhaps
even engaged with that side of the peristyle as in the Maison aux Gros
Pilastres.[76] The relationship is most closely demonstrated in the Maison au
Portique where the placement of the waterbasin seems odd if considered
from the entrance but makes perfect sense from the *oecus*. The relationship
between basin and *oecus* can be further stressed by decoration. In the Maison
des Néréides, the wall of the elaborate basin, which faces the *oecus* between
two columns, is paved with a mosaic of the head of Oceanus, whilst within
the basin was a mosaic of nereids riding on sea monsters.[77]

The basic articulation of the house, then, is dominated by the great *oecus* and the peristyle. In some of the houses, a second major room is also obvious on another side of the peristyle. These are usually recognisable as *exedrae* by their wide openings. The *exedra* 7 in the Maison de Flavius Germanus was flanked by semi-columns and had a mosaic floor and wall painting. In the case of the Maison aux Travaux d'Hercule (Figure 84), *exedra* 5 seems to have been used as a *triclinium*. It was floored with the mosaic that gives the house its name; twelve medallions featuring the labours of Hercules with a centrepiece of the Rape of Ganymede.

At a most basic level, the houses of Volubilis seem to feature many room types associated with Greek housing and appear to be arranged loosely around a peristyle. So where did this plan come from? The plans of the local houses in the lower city, and the early layout of the Maison de l'Ephebe, are essentially based on Punic ideas and are arranged around an open corridor or court. The typical Punic home in Carthage of the Hellenistic period had a courtyard that was flanked by a few large rooms and could be reached from the entrance by a long corridor.[78] The arrangement of the long corridor survives in the north-east quarter of Roman Volubilis in the Maison à l'Abside.

Greek ideas might also be attributed to African, rather than Roman, innovators. Greek influence was already prevalent in the Punic world during the Hellenistic era. The wealth and contacts built by the Phoenician cities through trade were demonstrated in the domestic architecture of the city of Carthage. By the time of its destruction by the Romans in the second century B.C., Carthage was joining in the common culture of the Mediterranean elites, with houses arranged around paved peristyles.[79] Moreover, *opus signinum*, the flooring utilised throughout the empire was probably a Punic invention of the Hellenistic era. Mediterranean influences such as these would have percolated through to western Africa long before the building of the later Roman houses. Certainly, the Ionic columns in the façade of the palace, which became the governor's under Roman rule, have been attributed to the reigns of Juba II and Ptolemy, and it is possible that the Maison de l'Ephebe gained a portico during this period. It would seem, then, that many of the components of the Volubilis houses can be traced to a local source.

In translation, these Greek and Punic influences have formed a new unit, peculiar to Volubilis. The peristyle has lost its commanding position. The houses have acquired more rooms and elongated beyond the peristyle area. Many of the houses reach out behind the *oecus*, via long corridors, to reach areas beyond the front part of the house. In some of the houses, the peristyle begins to look much more like an *atrium*, receiving an initial influx into the house. The increasing use of symmetry also forces the peristyle out of shape, imposing a central axis that pulls the vestibule, peristyle, and *oecus* into a chain that we are more familiar seeing in Italian houses. The house imposes a syntax of its own on its borrowed elements.

One of the most distinctive features of the houses of Volubilis is the arrangement of one corner of the house around a tiny court, an *atriolum*. This little court, usually with its own mini water feature, is surrounded by between three to four rooms, in which Étienne would like to see a miniaturised repetition of the main peristyle, with *oecus* and *exedra*, an instinct that is best served by the suite in the Maison à l'Ouest du Palais du Gouverneur (Figure 86). This suite is bigger than the similar suites in most of the houses, and its *oecus* is certainly articulated both by substantial size and two engaged demi-columns at its entrance. This secondary unit sets up a much more complex flow of space around the house. Clearly, it was the part of the house with the least capacity for crowds and was furthest from the door, so, it was a privileged area of some description, but whether this was privilege of status or family connection we cannot say. It may well have been both at various times; as at Pompeii, it is more important to note the capacity for a fairly complex layering of access and hierarchy than to attempt to pin down the exact function of the rooms.

The ability of the house both to invite and control access would appear to make it well suited for Roman life. The large reception rooms, the *oecus* and *exedra*, are appropriate in size and elaboration for social functions. Both could apparently serve as *triclinia*. The plain U-shape left by the mosaic of Venus and her marine train in *oecus* 11 of the Maison au Cortège de Vénus suggests that it was appropriate for use as a *triclinium*, just as the mosaic of *exedra* 5 in the Maison aux Travaux d'Hercule marked that room's suitability. However, neither room type is consistently marked out as a dining room, implying that they were not restricted to a set purpose. In the Maison de Flavius Germanus, the peristyle is flanked by a series of rooms with mosaic, which could fulfil any number of functions and to which entrance seems relatively easy. Again, rather than looking for a function for each room, it is, perhaps, more appropriate to regard them as deliberately ambiguous, prepared for any event.

The houses of Volubilis seem to have exploited boundaries between public and private. Both the Maison aux Travaux d'Hercule and the Maison au Cortège de Vénus had private baths. The owner of the latter house allied himself to the wider world of civic leadership through the display of two bronze portraits, one of Cato the Younger, known in Africa as Cato of

Utica, and a second of a Hellenistic prince. Cato, who saved the Phoenician town, Utica, from Roman destruction during the civil wars demonstrates proper Roman *virtus* in an African context as local elites adopted him as their own against a Roman enemy.[80] He provides the elites with an *exemplum* for setting up their own centre, their own idea of Rome, in their own environment. A small find like the statuettes of Minerva and Isis found together, perhaps from a *lararium*, in the Maison au Bacchus de Marbre would imply that, as elsewhere, the "Rome" Volubilis invented was a Rome with all its tensions and diversities intact. Elites impressed their audiences by asserting themselves over the whole range of experiences offered by such a vast and diverse empire.

CENTRES AND PERIPHERIES

The houses discussed in this chapter give some idea of the variety and yet cohesion of the imperial experience in the western Roman empire. The *atrium*, the peristyle, and the row house all show different ways of coping with housing problems. They show the stress of having to shelter the family grouping in a locally appropriate manner but also of having to project a façade that could be integrated with the Roman public world. Far from rejecting *Romanitas*, it could be said that individual house plans represent many ways of reacting to and constructing an identity within Roman society. Ultimately it was the process of wrestling with, rather than overcoming, these tensions that made the houses Roman.

In an absolute sense, it is ridiculous to suggest that Rome meant the same to a Briton as to an African. Certainly, integration into the empire opened a local elite's eyes to a much wider stage. Trade and communication routes opened up, but this was still essentially localised even if on a bigger scale – most imports found in Silchester and Verulamium would seem to have come from an area covered by modern France or Germany. The elites of North Africa may have been geographically fortunate to be able to communicate with the entire Mediterranean basin, but that does not necessarily make them more Roman. Of course, some of the highest men would make it to Rome and the Senate. For them, a truly empire-wide world might open up. The rest would have to rely on the translated experiences of that individual to get their idea of empire. Although it is clear in the literature of Sidonius that Rome the city remained an emotive centre, she had become essentially a metaphor for the local experience.[81] However much a provincial might recognise his geographical distance from the centre, Rome, his perspective put him at the centre of his own Roman empire. In this respect, the Roman empire might be thought of not as international but as multilocal, a myriad of centres.

The whole machine relied on the ability of the empire to convey to these centres some feeling of cohesive identity. Roman literary *topoi* and iconography allowed elites to explore the tensions and negotiations inherent in Roman life, using a common language. Very different experiences were thereby made comparable, allowing a link between each new centre. A recognisable Roman culture, which, in the domestic sphere, can be understood in terms of accommodation of certain rituals, application of architectural and decorational features, and depiction of mythologies and themes, allowed each new Roman to mediate his experiences. The elites of Vasio, Verulamium, and Volubilis all used the same iconographical language to express quite different experiences. Nevertheless, that same language allowed the accommodation of such differences whilst helping various elites to communicate with and recognise each other.

A Roman could feel at home wherever he was in the empire because he was always part of the negotiation of being Roman. Whether he cast himself as the centre or was cast by others as peripheral, he was nevertheless part of the debate. For Woolf, one of the most important aspects of a Romanised elite in Gaul was that they cast the rest of the population in a Roman light. Such a process allowed visiting Romans to recognise chaotic barbarians as clients or country folk, the sort of backward bumpkin they could snigger at, or conversely admire, back at home.[82] In Volubilis, the distinction between settled agriculturalists and the nomad population might become the familiar difference between town and country dwellers. In this way, the entire Roman world was caught up in the discourse of *Romanitas*. The trick for local elites was to harness the power of this dialogue.

The result of the expansion of Roman identities is a gradual redefinition of various centres and peripheries. In republican Rome, the tension between centre and periphery was easily translated to geographical parameters – Rome the city versus her provinces and enemies. However, as the urban centres of the provinces began to assume their own idea of centredness, drawing on their own local stance and their participation in a wider empire, the idea of centre became more fragmented. Rome became an idea rather than a geographical location. At the same time, the peripheral was also undergoing redefinition. The provinces, as geographically remote as they were, had become, in some sense, centres. Consequently, the idea of the peripheral became equally as geographically dislodged and, following the fragmented centre, became a concept that could be relocated wherever necessary. Participation in empire, then, depended on each participant in empire, whether Roman or British, emperor or slave, struggling with his or her own sense of centre and periphery. Rome herself was equally a proud centre to aspire to and a luxurious pit to be avoided. Its emperor, as Hadrian had definitively demonstrated, was the human embodiment of both central and peripheral, a living empire.

7

The East Greek *Oikos*

n the last chapter we saw three different approaches to living in the empire. In all three examples, we witnessed local solutions to an empire-wide problem: how should a provincial live like a Roman, how could his home become a *domus*? This problem was exacerbated in the Hellenic and Hellenised Greek East, home to many of those cultural symbols that Rome had adopted as her own.[1] Some would argue that the houses of the Greek East were never Romanised but that the elites there remained detached from the rest of the empire.[2] Vitruvius, in defining the *domus* both in terms of architecture and social activity, had used the Greek *oikos* by way of contrast to Roman norms.[3] The Greek house was everything the Roman house was not; it did not have an *atrium* but was built around paved peristyles and divided into male and female space. The first part of the house, which Vitruvius labels the *gynaeconitis*, consisted of a peristyle as part of either a *prostas* or *pastas* arrangement and beyond, an *oecus*, the centre of domestic activity. The other rooms are identified as containing dining rooms and bedrooms for the family and household. The second part of the house is the main reception area, replete with dining rooms, *exedrae*, libraries, and guest suites. Vitruvius calls this the *andronitides*, the place for male, social activity. In essence, Vitruvius's description presents us with an amplification of the traditional Greek peristyle house with its *andron*, home to the *symposium*. In this ideal model, the *andron* becomes the only public area of a house design that seemed intended to protect rather than to expose family members. Vitruvius's *oikos* traces a similar division in the use of space, which seems to respect boundaries between public and private as much as, if not more than, those between the sexes. Lisa Nevett's recent work on the Greek house has proposed a similar conclusion; houses were organised to distinguish between intrusive, social activity and private life rather than between male and female activity.[4] Either way, Vitruvius's construction of Greek domestic arrangements set them squarely against his ideal Roman *domus* and its deliberately blurred boundaries. The Greek house was as fundamentally different from the Roman way of life as that of barbarians whose alien nature was generally understood through their not living in houses at all.[5]

On the other hand, of course, Greece provided the fantasies of Roman houses. Houses in Pompeii made the most of components that Romans attributed to the Greek world: witness the "Rhodian" peristyle of the House of the Gilded Cupids (Figure 45) or the "Corinthian" *oecus* of the House of the Labyrinth (Figure 40). An imagined Greece was reenacted in every home; providing a fantasy world where Romans could at last surrender themselves to their desires whilst also controlling them within the space syntax and viewing systems of a Roman house plan. Of course, the peristyles of Pompeii are no more than a loose recreation, an impression of the Classical Greek original. By the time the planted peristyle appeared in Italy, it had more in common with the peristyles of Hellenistic palaces. In these palaces, overt competition and the desire to demonstrate power through excessive display and inversion of domestic, civic, and natural norms fostered similar responses to those that would later appear in imperial architecture.[6] Roman villas also exploited Greek architectural terms, though they were often applied to new arrangements. So, for example, Vitruvius recognises the difference between the Roman use of the term *xystus* to describe an open promenade, and the Greek term, which denotes a colonnade where athletes undertake winter training.[7]

Of course, Italians were not the only people to appropriate Greek design. Often, the only recognisable features of the houses across the empire are those Hellenistic elements that had spread around the Mediterranean in the second century B.C. These elements of design had become major components of provincial homes; the houses of Volubilis and Vasio, for example, both owe a debt to the peristyle *oikos*. The peristyle, the portico, and decorative water feature are characteristics of houses across the empire. Decorational techniques such as mosaic and wall painting also had their roots in the Greek repertoire. The use of Greek art and architecture brought some common ground to many elites. As much as the Romans tried to distance them as evil luxuries, their proper management was a central part of the Roman experience across the empire.

Hadrian's Villa at Tivoli provided the ultimate impression of an empire accepting the hegemony of Greek culture. In his fantasy world, his concept of empire was essentially expressed by reference to Greece and, to a lesser extent, Egypt. His world conflated the mythic and geographical East into a fantasy empire over which Hadrian ruled. However, in the East itself that mythic and geographic conflation might be considered more than idle fantasy. Elites all over the East, particularly in the new foundations of the Hellenistic kingdoms, based their identities on the idea that they really did inhabit places beloved of the gods: Antioch's suburb Daphne really was the site where Daphne was changed into a bush, Ephesus was the home of Artemis. The clash between Rome and the Greek East, then, was predicated on a fundamental clash between reality and fantasy. For the Roman, his fantasies of divine presence allowed him to conserve his *Romanitas* by challenging it. For the Greeks, the idea of sharing divine presence was an important part of self-identity, confirming their geographical *locus* as well as their privileged relationship with the divine. This sense of confidence in their homeland is often taken as provoking a separatist feeling amongst the Greek elite, who refused to swap their identities for a Roman one. Equally, would Romans feel challenged by their superiority? How would Romans react when meeting Greek architecture at its source?

SYRIA

One of the greatest difficulties of examining acculturation across the whole empire is the tendency to understand the East as being uniformly Greek. But the East included not only the great mosaic peristyle houses of the seaboard cities but also the strange cultures of the interior.[8] The province of Syria was rural in the south and urbanised on her northern coast where stood the great city of Antioch. Away from the sea lay the desert, populated by nomadic tribes, and the caravan routes to the Far East.[9] This area of the empire saw the Roman world at its most vulnerable, exposed to attack by the Parthians. The presence of Iranian cultural influence, if not arms, in cities like Palmyra demonstrate that there were few absolute frontiers in the Roman world.[10]

As the empire progressed, its frontiers crept further East. The farther stretches of the eastern part of the empire were not even conquered until the second century A.D. by which time the rest of the empire was attaining new heights of prosperity and material elaboration. Many of these territories did not enjoy the long stretches of peace that afforded such opportunities for other provinces; frontier cities like Dura Europus passed in and out of Roman control with relative rapidity, such towns becoming places where different cultures clashed head on.[11] These distant cities, then, remained truly peripheral. One such city, Petra, did not come under Roman command until Trajan created the province of Arabia in A.D. 106. Petra was a city of the Nabataeans, a nomadic people originally from Arabia who arrived there in the fourth century B.C.[12] Before them, the area had fallen within the kingdoms of Assyria, Babylonia, and Persia and so was home to all types of foreign architectural influences, most noticeable today in the Assyrian crow steps on many of the city's tomb façades. The greatest of these façades, which have earned the city its modern fame, merge these eastern motifs with highly decorative Hellenistic architectural elements, broken pediments, and so on, which are often compared with Pompeian wall painting, the inspiration for both apparently stemming from Alexandria. The fame of these tombs reflects our modern European desire to seek out the familiar. They are far in the minority, perhaps commissioned by a royal elite who were eager to buy into the iconography of the Hellenistic kingdoms.

That the Nabataeans were felt to be strange foreigners is indicated by the writings of Diodorus Siculus, documenting the wars between Hellenistic Syria and the Nabataeans. Diodorus insists that the Nabataeans are so different that they do not even have houses, instead living as nomads.[13] In fact, the Nabataeans who settled at Petra lived in two types of housing, one cut into the rock and another free-standing. The rooms of these houses might be strung in a row, but one house built into the rock facing the theatre clearly shows that the interior had been arranged around a central court. The biggest rock house, the House of Dorotheos, had twenty rooms including what has been described as a huge *triclinium* opening onto a platform through a central door and five windows. Of the free-standing houses, the most defined was a pre-Roman example found in the Katute area. It was a row of square rooms bordering a courtyard, built of masonry faced with plaster and roofed in the traditional way with slabs of stone.

The resources and traditions of Petra rendered her very alien to a Roman visitor. In the centre of the city, however, the construction of a long colonnaded street leading up to the major Nabataean temple, known as the Qasr el Bint, offered some comfort. The colonnaded street had become a major part of city life in the eastern empire.[14] The adoption of the type by the people of Petra demonstrates an interest in adopting prestigious symbols used by the rich Hellenistic centres such as Antioch with which she had immediate contact. Similarly the tomb façades imply an enthusiasm for the demonstrably successful art of the Hellenistic *koine* amongst the ruling elite. A few features of the housing also seem to reflect influence from these cities; the painted plaster from the Painted House was decorated with a design of vines, unusual perhaps for a city whose alien character was reinforced by

Diodorus Siculus with the assertion that the inhabitants did not drink wine. However, the lack of obvious domestic building in the Roman era must presumably imply that earlier houses continued to be occupied with little change, just as funerary customs and religious cult seems to have gone on as before. The fact that Romans could cope with the Petran way of life and death is indicated by the occupation of one of the rock-cut tombs by Sextus Florentinus, *propraetor* of Arabia. Generally, however, it would appear that the sources of Petra's familiarity were influences from local contacts rather than inspiration from its relatively short-lived role as a component of the Roman empire.

The marginalisation of Petra, both in geographical terms as a city on the frontiers of empire and in the modern conception of the Roman empire, demonstrates the prevailing attitude towards the eastern empire as predominantly an "other" to the Latin West. On the other hand, most of the eastern empire was territory once covered by the kingdoms of the Diadochoi and their own successors. In many of these places, Romanisation was helped by the process of Hellenisation undertaken during the rule of the Hellenistic royal houses. In places like Egypt, the Ptolemies had already found ways of adapting the indigenous, pharoanic systems of bureaucracy. Rome was able to inherit these systems through the Hellenised centre of Alexandria. The rich epigraphic and archaeological sources for Egyptian housing show that most Egyptians organised their domestic lives very differently from the Romans.[15] Though integrated into the empire, they represent the essential localness of provincial culture. However, it was not the outlying towns but the presence of the rich, Hellenistic capitals that shaped the Roman experience of the eastern empire.

ANTIOCH

Antioch was a great flourishing city (Figure 88), the former capital of the Seleucid empire, which at one time stretched over Asia Minor as far as India.[16] As a new imperial dynasty, founded after the death of Alexander the Great, the Seleucids became major sponsors of Hellenistic art, architecture, and literature. By these means, they obtained legitimacy, demonstrating their direct link back to Alexander and through him to Classical Greece.[17] The first Roman aspects of the city were introduced by Antiochus IV, a childhood hostage of the Romans; he is said to have instigated both gladiatorial displays and the building of the *Capitolium*.[18] This anecdote demonstrates that the flow of cultural symbols in the Hellenistic world was not simply East to West but could also involve the input of all the elites in the Mediterranean

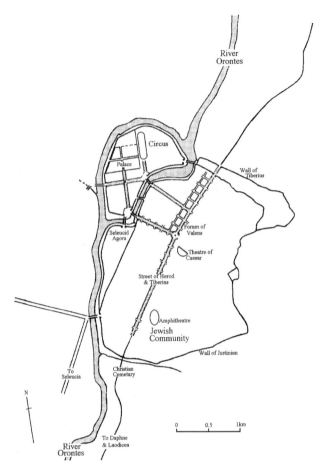

88. Antioch, plan.

basin. However, that this was not perceived as the norm might be illustrated by the tendency of later Greek and Roman audiences to view Antiochus as a lunatic and his innovations as further evidence of his madness.

Rome's close interest in Antioch was justified in terms of Rome's fear of Mithridates VI, king of Pontus, whose plans of expansion against the Roman world were dubbed as the liberation of the Greeks from Rome. In 64B.C., having beaten Mithridates, Pompey officially annexed Syria but granted *libertas* to Antioch. As the empire progressed, successive Roman building projects visually claimed the city for Rome. When Caesar oversaw the building of a *basilica*, theatre, amphitheatre, and baths at Antioch, he simultaneously renovated the city's *bouleuterion*. The restoration of this Greek building demonstrates the Roman regard for indigenous, Hellenistic architecture and recognition of order within its associated practises. It also implies disinterest in seeing a threat from local structures, which could be incorporated in the requirements of Roman culture. These civic centres were crucial in allowing Romans to cope and communicate with the countryside beyond their boundaries, in the case of Antioch with the alien, Syriac population of the hinterlands.

Antioch became an official capital and patriarchal seat of the late empire, abreast with Rome, Constantinople, and Alexandria. It had a palace for accommodating visiting emperors, and it was here that Julian planned his ill-fated Persian campaign, Jovian received omens of his impending death, and Valens held his notorious treason trials.[19] Perhaps befitting its status, Antioch was also famous for its wealth. In early accounts, Antioch represented all the evils of the East to visiting Romans like Cato the Younger, fulfilling expectations of cities given over to luxury and disinterested in Roman order.[20] Her reputation had not improved by the fourth century when both Julian and John Chrysostum, who preached here before becoming patriarch of Constantinople in 398, attacked the city's lascivious indulgences.[21] Despite Antioch's integral role in the empire, it was defined, even by her citizens, as a city peripheral to Roman expectations of behaviour.

Given that John Chrysostum specifically prepares us for houses sheathed in marbles, it is disappointing that not one full Roman house plan survives of the houses discovered in and around Antioch and the suburb of Daphne.[22] Instead, we find mosaics, dating from the second through to the fourth century, arranged in suites comprised of a large reception room overlooking a portico and an elaborate *nymphaeum*. Such arrangements indicate the presence of the House of the Calendar (Figure 89), the House of Cilicia, the Atrium House, and the House of the Triumph of Dionysus (Figure 90) amongst others. The houses appear to have been composed of typical Greek architectural elements; indeed, Stillwell comments that their asymmetrical disposition is similarly typically Greek.[23] Their arrangement, however, is ultimately a local design, evolved from Greek models over centuries of elite competition within Antioch. It is also imperative to point out that these are all elements of design associated with houses across the empire, easily detectable in many of those houses discussed in the previous chapter. However much the people of Antioch might like to claim a privileged connection to the Greek font of this architecture, they were working with a currency common across the entire empire.

The type of mosaics found in these rooms are, almost without exception, figured mosaics set in panels known as *emblemata*. In this, they might also be understood as specifically Greek, distinct from the mosaics of the western tradition which cover the whole floor in a carpet-like design.[24] In the House

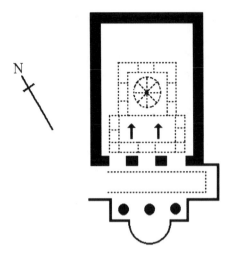

N

89. Antioch, House of the Calendar, sketch plan of surviving parts. After Stillwell.

90. Antioch, House of the Triumph of Dionysus, sketch plan of surviving parts. After Stillwell.

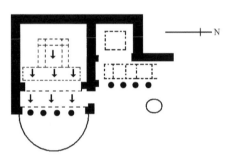

N

91. Antioch, House of the Triumph of Dionysus, mosaics. Photo: Princeton University.

92. Antioch, House of the Calendar, mosaics. Photo: Princeton University.

of the Calendar, the Atrium House, and the House of the Triumph of Dionysus, the floors of the principal room boast a T-shape design, which suggests that the room was intended to accommodate moveable *triclinia* couches. In order to make the T-shape, several panels have to be used together. In the House of the Triumph of Dionysus, built during the first century A.D. (though the mosaics might be slightly later), the body of mosaic under the bar of the T is broken up into seven smaller panels that border the central panel (Figure 91). The central panel of the abandoned Ariadne faces towards the back of the room, whilst the outer panels all face towards the walls in front of them, providing a viewpoint to the viewers along each wall. The mosaic decoration also works to combine the *triclinium* and *nymphaeum*. Across the portico, the mosaic of the *nymphaeum* also faces the *triclinium*, presenting a sea *thiasos* to the diners within and making the connection of the architecture explicit with iconography.[25]

The House of the Calendar, on the other hand, not only favours the viewer in the *triclinium* but also invites those in the portico. Its mosaics were laid shortly after a major earthquake in A.D.115 (Figure 92).[26] The bar of the T-shaped *triclinium* mosaic faces the entrant and presents the viewer with

Oceanus and Thetis surrounded by a sea of marine creatures. Behind that, the square panel is inscribed with a circle divided into twelve segments with personifications of the months, which radiate out to all angles of the room, allowing the diners equal vision. Once inside, the viewer looks out to find, facing him, a mosaic in the portico featuring a black macrophallic fisherman. The arrangement invites the entrant over a scene of Greek mythology/allegory to take a seat around the ordered world of the calendar. When he looks out, he can differentiate his own privileged position from that of the fisherman, whose race and professional status prevent his inclusion.

In these rooms, decoration often gives a deliberate impression of the use of space. The names given to several of these houses, the House of the Triumph of Dionysus or the House of the Drunken Dionysus, for example, reflect the fact that their *triclinium* panels all contain imagery associated with feasting and, more specifically, drinking. The iconography of Dionysus became a theme frequently associated with rooms used as *triclinia* all across the empire, lending an air of ritualisation and justification to the act of intoxication by linking it with the mysteries of Dionysus and the traditions of the *symposium*.[27] Of course, we should be wary of suggesting that such rooms were only (even, perhaps, if at all) used as dining rooms. Rather we should note that, whilst the room might have served multiple functions, the decoration always served to give the impression of Roman, social activity.

The initial popularity of Dionysus in the Hellenistic kingdoms was doubtlessly fuelled by Alexander's close association with the god and both their triumphs over the East.[28] Greek mythology offered more than dry allegory or idle romanticism to its Greek audience. The *emblemata* of the houses of Antioch make reference to their Greek cultural superiority through constant allusion to local myths. The *metamorphosis* of Daphne following her pursuit by Apollo, as represented in the House of Menander, took place in the eponymous suburb just outside Antioch, as did the Judgement of Paris, depicted in the Atrium House.[29] Similarly, the story of Pyramus and Thisbe, as featured in the House of Porticoes, had local connotations because the river Pyramus ran close by.[30] In the houses of Antioch, then, homeowners demonstrated local pride and Greek cultural superiority as a means of competing for social preeminence. Their images guaranteed their geographic and ethnic *locus*. The great Megalopsychia mosaic laid in the Yakto Complex during the fifth century boasts a topographic border that reveals a bird's-eye perspective of the suburbs of Antioch – there are no basilicas, no triumphal arches in this cityscape (Figure 93).[31] The homeowners of Antioch concentrated on the local, demonstrating Antioch and its immediate territory to be the centre of their world view. In reorienting

93. Antioch, Yakto Complex, Megalopsychia mosaic, topographic border.
Photo: Princeton University.

the world around themselves, they might equally be seen as peripheralising themselves within the empire. The appearance of a personification of Tryphe, Luxury, in the major reception room of the House of Menander reveals a city far from ashamed of its tendencies, which distanced it from the rhetorical norm of imperial behaviour.[32]

These mosaics would seem to justify the popular perception of the Greek refusal to join in with empire and the Roman inability to impose themselves on their eastern provinces. But is this a constructive way to understand a city with such a high profile in the empire, a city that in the fourth century produced not only the Greek rhetorician Libanius but also the Christian John Chrysostum and the last Latin historian Ammianus Marcellinus? By the time the mosaic in the Yakto Complex was laid, Antioch supported Greek, imperial, pagan, Christian, and Jewish, not forgetting Syriac, identities.[33] Many of these identities were overlapping rather than exclusive categories, so we must presume that these mosaics served a wider audience than simply resistant, pagan Greeks. In order to estimate how these other viewers might be accommodated, we should perhaps visit another great eastern city, Ephesus in Asia Minor.

EPHESUS

Ephesus, on the Aegean coast of Asia Minor, was a very rich harbour city (Figure 94), famous for the Temple of Artemis, one of the wonders of the ancient world. It was originally founded by Ionian Greeks following the advice of the Delphic oracle. It is, of course, worth remembering that these Greeks were building their city on a land with its own history. In the cult of Artemis herself, farther eastern traditions melded with the Greek; the symbolic image of Artemis (whose iconography is so alien to the Graeco-Roman repertoire that it is still not completely understood) and her eunuch priests,

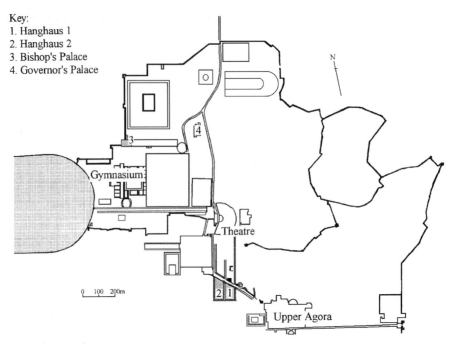

Key:
1. Hanghaus 1
2. Hanghaus 2
3. Bishop's Palace
4. Governor's Palace

94. Ephesus, plan.

the megabyzes, are just two elements of the alien embedded in Ephesus long before the Romans arrived.[34]

At the dawn of the Hellenistic era, after the death of Alexander, as his generals attempted to establish themselves throughout the eastern Mediterranean, Ephesus was refounded by Lysimachus. He moved the city, established it on a Hippodamian grid plan, and surrounded it with a wall. According to Strabo, this general's interest in Ephesus was intensely personal. In a desire to exert his personal control over the city, he renamed the city Arsinoe after his wife and meddled with the structure of the Artemis cult.[35] This megalomanic coercion of one family's private life onto the public arena provided a model for the later antics of Roman emperors, most obviously Nero and his suspected plan of rebuilding Rome as Neropolis. Here at Ephesus, the moves can be read as a direct challenge to the overtly public, power-sharing order of the Greek city, ruled by the *boule*. Lysimachus's plans, however, were not realised, and the city became part of the Attalid empire, ruled from Pergamum, which was bequeathed to the Romans in 133 B.C. by its last king, Attalus III. Ephesus remained a free city, and her record of allegiance to Rome during the republican period was not good, apparently gladly answering the call to arms from Mithridates VI. Later, in the Roman civil wars, Ephesus again became associated with the struggle of the East by becoming the temporary residence of Antony and Cleopatra. Under the empire, however, Ephesus became an important city in the province of Asia; the home of both the *proconsul* governor and the *koinon Asias*, the collection of Asian towns that met to carry out imperial cult. The wealth generated by this high-profile and harbour trade is shown by the excavations of the city.[36]

During the high empire of the second century A.D., Ephesus featured not only a grand combination of Hellenistic Greek civic structures – a theatre, library, *gymnasia* and an *agora* – but also buildings that signified the city's inclusion in the Roman empire, most obviously the temples to deified emperors but also a *basilica*. The city continued to be run from the *bouleuterion*. However, although the architecture and the labels of many buildings refer to classical Greek prototypes, these cities had progressed far from that ideal. This is particularly clear in the layout of the *gymnasia* dedicated during the Roman period, which borrow the symmetrical, vaulted layout of Roman *thermae*. The Vedius gymnasium, founded by Publius Vedius Antoninus in the mid-second century A.D. is a Roman bath and *palaestra* by any other name. What it was to be Greek was changing as much as what it was to be Roman.

As with the cities of the western provinces, the variety of local cults reflects the international influences acting on the populace of any city. The frieze of the Temple of Hadrian, just across the way from the surviving terraced houses, features a lineup of all the major gods of Ephesus – Artemis, the city's founder Androclus, the gods of the traditional Greek pantheon, and foreign deities such as Cybele. The reliefs show the complexities of local influences. In attempting to reconcile these figures with the Roman emperor, it is irrelevant to question whether Hadrian is in charge of them of all or whether the presence of the local is a blow against imperial cult. Rather, the relief shows how all had become part of the Ephesian makeup. There were more than likely tensions between the different manifestations, but they would have pulled in all different directions. Mediating them was part of being an Ephesian. In fact, this frieze was only translated to the temple in the fourth century, so it also adds the complexity of an emergent Christian identity. The frieze offers a hint at how successive influences did not supplant each other but all became part of the city's complex identity.[37]

PLACE OF INDIVIDUALS IN THE CITY

One of the principal differences between a Greek and Roman town was the Greek city's public emphasis of the stages of a man's life at the expense of interest in his domestic arrangements. Young men should join the ephebes to train in ways of adult life from where they might eventually take their place within the *boule*. For the old men, the *gerousia* provided a public *locus*. In Roman Ephesus, the city seems to have continued a long tradition of paying both sophists and medical doctors to set up schools and practices within the city with a view both to provide for the local citizenry but also to enhance the city's reputation. The role of intellectual pursuit as a means of reputation and competition between the cities of the Greek East was deep-seated and long-lasting. In the fourth century, Julian the future Apostate emperor was lured away from his studies in Pergamum to study at Ephesus under Maximus. The presence of members of the imperial family in these schools may well have intensified competition, but it also had the effect of raising the stakes. As Julian's tutor, Maximus of Ephesus became an imperial advisor known throughout the empire.[38] Indeed, it was presumably a further sign of condemnation that, when he fell into disfavour, he lost not only his life but also his place on that imperial stage as he was sent to be executed back in his home city.[39] Nevertheless, his example demonstrates how competition for intellectual superiority amongst the cities of the East was brought into imperial focus. The most famous privately funded public monument in Ephesus is the Library of Celsus built by Ti. Julius Celsus Polemaenus, *proconsul* of Asia, at the very beginning of the second century. The libraries of great eastern cities such as Pergamum and Alexandria had been founded as a means of asserting their cultural prowess over other Hellenistic centres. But the library also served as Celsus's tomb, so the edifice works both to commemorate man to city and to commend city to empire.

All over Roman Ephesus there are signs of the euergetism with which prominent locals reflected their pride and their place in the city. This euergetism had a second advantage of providing an excellent opportunity for individuals to synthesise local and imperial identities. The dedicatees of the imperial period are invariably Roman citizens as well as local council members. Early examples include C. Sextius Pollio and his wife, Ofillia Bassa, who built the Basilica on the northern edge of the Upper Agora. The dedication of the Basilica, to Artemis, Augustus, Tiberius, and the people of Ephesus perhaps demonstrates an early attempt to reconcile Ephesus with her place in the empire. From the second century come several examples of citizen builders; the names of Vedius and P. Quintilius Valens Varius, who was responsible for both the Temple of Hadrian and the baths next door, are recurrent. The active nature of these leading men would imply that at least this class of society was eager to take advantage of the possibilities afforded by their new dual identities.

One of the most important factors of these dedications is the recurrent appearance of husband and wife teams. Pollio and Ofillia are an obvious example, but Vedius and Varius both worked with their wives on various projects. The inclusion of the wife reveals an emphasis on the individual family unit as families attempt to project themselves onto, rather than be swamped by, the public sphere. For Van Bremen, the increased role of couples in dedications and the growing emphasis the elite placed on their family, over their civic, relations demonstrates the gradual "domesticisation of public life," a trend that begins in the Hellenistic era but reaches its height under Roman rule as the elite compete to assert their domination over the city.[40]

These practices have important repercussions for the domestic arrangements of the inhabitants of Ephesus. Changes in civic power, which have their roots in the Hellenistic period, had completely altered the balance between public and private. As the family became a public tool, it would seem unlikely that they should be divided from the man of the house at home. Similarly, as civic leaders continued to promote themselves in the context of their noble families, it would be appropriate that they might be sought in their homes as much as in the *bouleuterion*. Whilst the Vitruvian description of elaborate guest wings might be taken to reflect the opening-up of the *oikos* in the Hellenistic era, the contemporary provision of many houses throughout the Greek East with richly decorated second peristyles would seem to tell a similar story.[41] The extra space is often understood as enabling the house to accommodate the new influx in the house without compromising the original, private retreat. Hellenistic culture had already begun to impose a wide-reaching cultural standard that was adopted across the Mediterranean for reasons other than political necessity and before Roman conquest. Aspects of behaviour that seem so familiar to us as Romanists do not, therefore, necessarily indicate active self-Romanisation, but they do allow us to observe how those elites might engage in and be engaged by the empire without much change.

HOUSES IN THE CITY

Like the public architecture of Ephesus, the houses of the block across from the Varius baths appear to reflect the essential Greekness of the city. The excavated homes are all in two adjoining blocks constructed on terraces that descend the hill on which the houses are built (Figure 95).[42] The blocks were built in the first century A.D. but were inhabited into the seventh century. The presence of the peristyle house under the so-called *domus* of Hanghaus 1 demonstrates that the site was already used for domestic life in the

95. Ephesus, terraced houses, general view. Photo: Nicolas Gail, Österreichisches Arhäologisches Institut.

Hellenistic era. The road was a major route through the city, and the houses situated on the bend, and overlooking it from their high position, could take advantage of being on both streets: the Embolos or Kuretenstrasse leading out to the Upper Agora and the Marmorstrasse arriving at the terraces from the theatre. Occupying a corner plot on a major through way, the area immediately in front of the houses would have been full of people, providing a potential audience. By the second century A.D., the *floruit* of much of the Roman empire, the area was important both as a secular thoroughfare leading to the main administrative *agora* and out through the Magnesian Gate and as a processional route for Artemis ritual. Rogers shows how this route was designed so as to bring together all elements of Ephesus's civic identity, bearing on her sacred story of Artemis, mythological foundation by Androclus, and the historical foundations of Lysimachus and the Romans.[43] All these elements were visually prominent in the street outside the houses. Hanghaus 2 lay behind a series of Hellenistic and Roman tombs (Figure 96). A statue of Artemis stood nearby. Opposite were the Varius baths and the Temple of Hadrian. To their left stood the library and the gate, dedicated to the family of Augustus, which led to the commercial *agora*.

Because of the steep terracing of the houseblocks, access to the houses themselves was up the stepped streets that ran up the sides of the blocks. In most cases, the entrance is treated as of marginal importance, giving

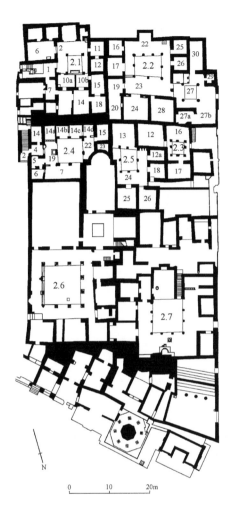

96. Ephesus, Hanghaus 2, plan.
After Hueber.

nothing away of the interior. In House 2.1, the entrance leads only to a
flight of stairs. On reaching the landing, a fountain greets the visitor before
he descends further into the peristyle. The fountain was lined with marble,
a pleasing sight but only for those who had already gained entrance and
not for those passing.[44] Other suggestions that the fountain served to cut
down on noise and dust entering (or leaving?) the house emphasise the
idea of seclusion. Similar entrances can be observed throughout the block.
When the visitor does reach the peristyle, he is generally let out onto an
insignificant angle, afforded none of the importance that he can imagine
himself to enjoy in the Pompeian *domus*. The visitor, at least at the point of
his entry into the house, was therefore not at the forefront of the designer's
mind, and many of the vestibules, lacking the impressive size of those at
Volubilis, could not hold a huge crowd of people.

97. Ephesus, Haus 2.2, peristyle, glass mosaic from niche.
Photo: Österreichisches Archäologisches Institut.

The interior is not governed by much regard for symmetry. The basic plan
of the apartments in block 2, however, is fairly standard, based around a central, paved peristyle. The peristyle is surrounded by the rooms of the house,
generally only one room deep, on one side dominated by a larger room.
There is no concept of long-ranging viewing systems within the house. The
neglect of such views is most clearly shown in Hanghaus 2.2 where the south
side of the peristyle features a niche with a beautiful glass mosaic of vines
and birds surrounding a medallion of Dionysus and Ariadne (Figure 97).
The area of the colonnade immediately in front of the niche is signalled by
a break in the geometric mosaic floor pattern. This part of the floor is laid
with a mosaic of Amphitrite and a triton riding on a hippocamp.[45] The
decoration in this small area is by far the most sumptuous of the house,
but from the other side of the peristyle it is obscured by columns, and none
of the doorways opening onto the peristyle are directly lined up with it
(Figure 98). The views are only for those in the immediate environment.

The arrangement of the interior of the terrace houses implies a deliberate
continuation of Hellenistic tradition. The Hellenistic peristyle house under
the Roman units was also arranged around a peristyle and had an upper
level. Again, however, we must remind ourselves that, in continuing a local
housing type, Ephesians were hardly alone in the empire. Nor were they
alone in adopting Greek domestic arrangements in an attempt to assert
cultural superiority.

The exception to the peristyle unit is observable in the much grander
"*domus*," the biggest unit in Hanghaus 1 (Figure 99).[46] Far from reflecting
Greek domestic traditions, this unit had an *atrium* and several vaulted

98. Ephesus, Haus 2.2, view over peristyle and niche. Photo: Österreichisches
Archäologisches Institut.

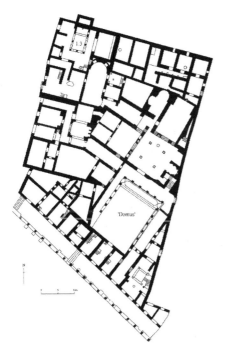

99. Ephesus, Hanghaus 1, plan of block in
late Antiquity. After Lang.

100. Ephesus, Hanghaus 1, *domus*, reconstruction of *atrium*. Gerhard Lang.

rooms. In the second century, when the unit was remodelled to reach its most excessive phase, the *atrium* was given a grand fountain, lined with marble and featuring appropriate statuary such as the figure of Poseidon. The peristyle was a two-storey colonnade, again punctuated by statues and with a water basin. The barrel vaulted room SR1 was also given a fountain at the end and was lined with marble. These refinements added grandeur to a room whose vaulting, unusual in urban domestic architecture of this date already prompted association with the public or palatial sphere. The *atrium* served as a link between all these elements and was punctuated with doors and windows to each room (Figure 100). The door from the *cenatorium* was almost on line with the *atrium nymphaeum*, certainly allowing a continuous view between the two. Similarly, although on slightly different axes, the doors between SR1 and the peristyle lay almost exactly opposite each other.

In keeping with this "Romanised" plan, attempts have been made to restore an axial entrance on the Embolos. We must be careful, however, in overestimating the "Roman" nature of this house. Although dubbed the *domus*, the arrangement of rooms bears little resemblance to a Roman layout. The *atrium* only got its *impluvium* and *compluvium* at the time when the entrance was removed to the peristyle. If it is possible to dub this hall and the others of the terrace houses *atria* (the forehall of the *basilica* in 2.6 is also sometimes labelled an *atrium*), then they certainly do not recreate Italian examples. Instead, they are used in a new manner, a fantasy of what an *atrium* might be, just as the planted peristyle represented a Roman take on the Greek colonnaded court.

However, although the *atrium* cannot have fulfilled its Roman function, other spaces associated with Roman tradition can be observed within the peristyle houses of the terraces (Figure 96). In most of the houses, one large room, opening directly onto the peristyle, has been signalled out as a focus for attention. In House 2.5, the large room at the south of the peristyle is covered in *opus sectile*.[47] In House 2.2 room 24 and in House 2.1 room 6, the decoration of these large rooms have not only excessive decoration but also a mosaic design that appears to allow the accommodation of a U-shaped space for dining couches. A T-shaped mosaic design in House 2.2 room 24 looking onto the wide portico north of the peristyle also denotes space for *triclinia* couches. In this case, the room is further marked out by the two fountain niches with glass mosaic that flank the door. All these rooms, even when bereft of furniture or diners, gave the impression of accommodating social intrusion through the tradition of the *cena*.

In the Classical Greek house plan, the largest room served as the *oecus* or family room of the house. The evolution necessitated by social change in the Hellenistic and Roman periods is demonstrated by the transition of the function of that large room from living to display area. In Houses 2.1 and 2.2, the room purports, through its mosaic arrangement, to serve, amongst other functions, as a *triclinium*. In House 2.5, room 13 is decorated with *opus sectile*, and in House 2.3 room 12, known as the Muses Room because of the figures of the Muses who float in the painted panels, the space is further gentrified with the addition of two columns at the far end (Figure 101).[48] For Romans, the term *oecus* implied an architectural type rather than denoted a specific function. The *oecus*, once provided with a hearth to facilitate family life, is now most likely to suggest, if not actually deliver, social functions. The intrusion has two results, also evident in Pompeian houses: first, private, family life is ostensibly pushed into second place. Conversely, the whole family is put on show – there is no room for separating family members off here and certainly no evidence of Vitruvius's women quarters. Similarly, in common with most other houses in the Roman empire, there is very little observable space specifically for slaves or domestic occupation. House 2.2

101. Ephesus, Haus 2.5, Muses Room. Photo: Nicolas Gail, Österreichisches Archäologisches Institut.

102. Ephesus, Haus 2.6, *basilica.* Photo: SJH.

does have a kitchen, House 2.1 had its own private baths as did House 1.3. Whilst the bathroom of House 2.1 is not very like its Roman counterparts, the role of private baths implies that these elites did like to assert their power by removing themselves from the public baths/gymnasium and perhaps orientate others around their private suites. As in the Maison aux Travaux d'Hercule at Volubilis (Figure 84), both of these bathrooms could be accessed by secondary entrances into the house. These houses, then, had much in common with houses across the empire, not least in their blurred boundaries between public and private space.

That these householders were aware of the interaction between private and civic architecture is reflected in the vaults and columns of peristyles and reception rooms. However, the intrusion of public architectural types becomes clear on a grand scale in late Antiquity when House 2.6 was converted into a huge "palace." A huge barrel-vaulted *basilica* took up a large part of the extended space (Figure 102), fronted by an ante room with fountain pool. Like the *domus*, House 2.6 was entered from the main street via a sizeable vestibule. The south side of the peristyle led to the "*atrium*" of the *basilica* as well as a gigantic marble-lined chamber to its left, which was accessed by a tripartite entrance. The huge size of these rooms outstrips anything else in the block. They impress both by their height and the extent of their marble cladding. The great hall was lined with marble panels arranged between flat pilasters. A barrel-vaulted *exedra* opening off the ante room to the *basilica* was decorated with painted marble and stucco. It has been suggested that the owner was using some of these rooms to celebrate Dionysiac cult.

However, a similar room appeared in the only recognisable peristyle house of Hanghaus 1, 1.3, during refurbishment dating perhaps to the fifth century. It, too, was barrel vaulted, had an apse, and was paved in *opus sectile*. The apse was decorated with two niches and marked off from the rest of the room by pilasters. There is no evidence to suggest that this house had become anything more than a domestic unit, so it appears that these two later examples represent a new trend in public display within the house.[49] A similar hall appeared in the House of the Hunt at Bulla Regia in North Africa during the fourth century, and the type is well attested across the empire.[50] Already in the first century back at Rome, Domitian had chosen the apse as the best means in which to reveal himself to his audience in his palace, and the form became increasingly popular for imperial presentation throughout late Antiquity.

The creation of the basilical space in House 1.3 and 2.6, as with the creation of the *domus* in the neighbouring block three centuries earlier, demonstrates the competitive use of space within the terraces. The high vault of the *basilica* ate into the northwest corner of House 2.4 just as the creation of the heightened rooms of the *domus* of Hanghaus 1 forced the closure of rooms on the level above it. On a smaller scale, House 2.2 took several rooms from 2.1, enlargening its own space whilst forcing the contraction of House 2.1 whose peristyle became smaller. At the same time, Hanghaus 1 was being broken down into tiny, though well-decorated, apartments throughout late Antiquity.[51]

The current state of these blocks shows to what extent constant competition had altered the houses from the almost equal parcels in which the blocks seem to have been divided on their conception. The more successful houses win for themselves more display capacity and a heightened impression of authority. The size and quality of the decoration of the house was vital to the patron as a means of expressing his success in social competition. To trace such competition in the West is often to trace the spread of Romanisation as elites learned to compete for local authority and to express their intent in the aspirative decor of their homes.[52] Here, perhaps, the origins of the competitive display lie in the Hellenistic era when both Roman and eastern Mediterranean elites were formulating codes by which they might vie for social success. This possibility serves as a warning in interpreting the rhetorical distance between Greeks and Romans. The real gulf between them reflects their self-perceptions and eagerness to express difference rather than the similarities forged in domestic display and function in the pre-imperial period.

DECORATION IN HOUSES

Almost all the rooms of the terrace blocks had mosaic and wall painting decoration. Of course, since both forms of decoration appear to have originated from the Greek East, this may seem to be of little surprise. It is more interesting, perhaps, that Dunbabin remarks on the western character of many of the Ephesus mosaics, particularly those black-and-white carpet designs usually thought to have originated in Italy.[53] The use of these mosaics in a city with such a proud Graecoised history as Ephesus demonstrates the widespread cross-pollination of design ideas across the Mediterranean. Those who preferred to see themselves as Greeks were not necessarily immune from other ideas and fashions besides their own. Their choice of mosaics provides another hint that Ephesians were open to the possibilities of empire and ready to engage in negotiation between their own and Rome's sense of centre and periphery.

During later reconstruction within the house block, House 2.2 extended itself by buying a suite of rooms from House 1 (11, 12, 14, 15, and 18). In the construction mess was found a small ivory frieze that had once decorated the wall or an item of furniture in room 18 (Figure 103). It features a Roman military procession, clearly aping the sculpture on public buildings and featuring the emperor Trajan, Hadrian's expansionist predecessor. Direct reference to Roman power is not lacking elsewhere in the houses. Several busts of emperors were also recovered, implying that the homeowners were not averse to linking themselves to the ultimate power or to mediating their local identities with that of the empire.[54]

Challenges to the boundaries between public and private, inside and outside are also found in the wall painting. In House 2.4, the marble dado and painted white fields of the walls around the peristyle court, painted in late Antiquity, opens in the corners to reveal a much earlier painting of a garden beyond, inevitably recalling the popular garden paintings of Italy (Figure 104). The peristyle in House 2.2 also offers some glimpse of an open sky, populated by erotes, beyond the marble panelling of the wall. Elsewhere, birds and flowers are very popular but are never depicted in a cohesive scene, rather appearing as floating motifs, evoking the natural world in an abstract manner.

If the tensions between inside and outside seem less emphasised and less fully expressed in Ephesus than Pompeii, they are still popular and evocative. However, the Ephesians seemed to have a different fantasy world they wanted to visit. In almost every house, there is a representation of intellectual pursuits, portrayed in the so-called theatre room of House 2.1 by the depictions of scenes of the tragedies of Euripides and the comedies of Menander. More often, however, the intellectual sphere will either be represented by the depiction of famous philosophers or by the Muses. It is also, presumably, significant that they are portrayed in the grandest rooms of the house: the Socrates Room in House 2.4 and the Muses Rooms of Houses 2.2 and 2.3 (Figure 101), which is further dignified by the columns at the far end. Muses can be found in Pompeii – often as in Ephesus – as figures floating in panels. The decoration of the peristyle of the House of the Vettii with such figures provides a reference point (Figure 52).[55] However, they are by no means omnipresent, overshadowed by the more familiar themes of animal hunts, divinities, Egyptian scenes, and landscapes. At Ephesus, these worlds are occasionally toyed with; motifs associated with an animal hunt are painted over the original bird motifs of 2.4.22. Certainly, the exotic exercised a pull on Ephesians as on other provincial homeowners. An African head from House 2.1 and images of Isis and Serapis from House 2.2 pick

103. Ephesus, Haus 2.1, room 18, ivory frieze. Photo: Österreichisches Archäologisches Institut.

104. Ephesus, Haus 2.4, peristyle, garden painting. Photo: Österreichisches Archäologisches Institut.

105. Ephesus, Haus 2.4, Socrates Room, Artemis niche. Photo: Österreichisches
Archäologisches Institut.

up on themes shown elsewhere in the empire.[56] An interest in Egyptian
cult (though, as all over the empire, in a safely Hellenised version) was
also provided on a civic level by the Temple of Serapis, demonstrating that
Ephesians, like other provincials, were aware of a larger world beyond their
immediate Greek environment.

However, the overriding dynamics of Ephesian life were clearly organised around giving an impression of Greek, intellectual capacity. They lived
surrounded by the muses. The decoration of Ephesus reminds us of the
different bases on which local elites assumed power and respect in their
communities. Their interest in linking themselves to a wider local culture
is emphasised by the depiction of Artemis in House 2.4. At a late stage in
the apartment's development, a decorated niche in the Socrates Room was
filled with a statue of Artemis (Figure 105). Rather than being a reflection
of the public icon of the Ephesian Artemis, this private take on the goddess
adopted traditional Graeco-Roman iconography of the striding goddess
dressed in hunting boots and a short hunting dress.[57] A second Artemis
was found in House 2.1, this time rendered in Archaising style.[58] The point
of the sculpture's presence appears to be to demonstrate conformity to a
Greek aesthetic rather than local pride. Given the peculiar iconography

of the Ephesian Artemis and her profile as icon of the city's identity, promulgated on coins and in souvenirs, the homeowners' choice of Artemis is clearly important.[59] The Artemis statues provide an expression of local identity, but only as it might be understood when filtered through a wider Greek culture. As such, they are inclusive rather than exclusive, acknowledging and appealing to a wider audience than the immediate population of Ephesus.

Based on this similarity between the domestic iconography of the Greek East and that of the rest of the Mediterranean, we must question the role of iconography as simply Greek resistance to Roman conformity. The case of Antiochene preoccupation with the immediate geographical context appears to be more exclusive than that practised by Ephesian homeowners. But even those images of local myths and personifications might not be read as alien or aggressive by the Roman visitor. The Roman elite's *urbanitas* partly rested on their literary knowledge and classical education or *paideia*. Roman poets, such as Ovid, paraded such knowledge in their work: his *Metamorphoses* relates the transformation of Daphne.[60] Italian craftsmen depicted episodes from Greek myth and literature on floors and walls. However unintentionally, the Antiochene's symbols of local pride guaranteed him a twofold place in Roman culture: as part of a centrally practised education and as a stock periphery. The point must be made again, then, that the difference between Greek and Roman houses was not so much, as Vitruvius might assert, in terms of space or decoration but rather in the self-perception that lies behind these choices. Most importantly, Greeks as much as Italians worked to promote themselves within the arena of empire. They negotiated with the centre by simultaneously communicating with and distancing themselves from Rome. In other words, their defiance as much as their co-operation bound them to the rhetoric of empire.

The use of favoured motifs by which Ephesians strove to assess their central role in the life of their city, and beyond that the empire, continued for centuries. The houses underwent successive redecoration, particularly in terms of painting, the most easily altered medium. Most of the decoration, however, appears to fall into two main phases. The first dates to the second century when Ephesus and the empire were in boom and the houses were reaching their fullest expression. Many of the walls were then redecorated in the fifth century to spruce up apartments much damaged and altered by earthquakes and economic change. What is immediately striking is how little fashions changed in three hundred years. The later walls follow much the same pattern of panels with floating figures and large quantities of imitation marble. If it seems tempting to suggest that such intense conservatism might simply demonstrate the cultural irrelevancy of domestic decoration, it is as wise to bear in mind the strength of tradition in the ancient world. The homeowners of the terraces, even if they now only own one or two rooms of an original houses, appear eager to preserve the correct impression within their homes.

THE EAST IN LATE ANTIQUITY

Developments inside the terrace block over the course of the city's history should, of course, be related to changes without it. By the fifth century, even familiar landmarks had changed. The library adjacent to the blocks had been resurrected as a fountain façade, and the Baths of Varius had been renovated by a Christian woman, Scholasticia, whose statue stood in the entrance hall. Next door, images of the Tetrarchs flanked the Temple of Hadrian. An inscription of an edict of the emperor Valens had been set up on the Octagon, one of the tombs outside Hanghaus 2. As for the outward appearance of the houses themselves, the whole front of Hanghaus 1 was dignified by a colonnade that ran along the whole block, carpeted in mosaic and inviting people into the shops that had opened up in the front of the house. The street was paved with marble as it became a place to stop as well as to pass. With the shops in the terraces, both in front and at the rear of Hanghaus 1, the houses were increasingly caught in the public world. The other side of the street also received a colonnade, made from columns bearing the lists of the Kuretes, the priests of Artemis. They had been robbed from the Prytaneum which, in a Christian society, had lost its function as a civic shrine. The decontextualised columns, put to new use, became souvenirs of the past, symbols of Christian victory. At the same time, the statue of Artemis was replaced with a cross.[61]

Christianity added a new dimension to identity in Ephesus. The immediate context of the house blocks was changed forever. The pagan traditions of the city had to contend with yet another new centre, the church. The most obvious intrusion of Christianity occurred with the insertion of a chapel into two rooms towards the rear of Hanghaus 1 (Figure 99) during the sixth century.[62] Elsewhere in the block one of the peristyle columns of House 1.3 was inscribed with a plea to Christ – "Save your servant." In a house built in the new residential area once covered by the Harbour Gymnasium, Christian presence is again attested by an inscription of letters between Abgar of Edessa and Christ.[63] However, whilst the use of overt Christian symbols and words identify Christian presence elsewhere, it is hard to observe the rise of Christianity in the decoration of Hanghaus 2.

The impression of restoration in the fifth century included the reuse of pagan imagery; Cupids graced the walls of 18 in House 2.5; Dionysus, the floor of 16a next door in House 2.3. Perhaps the eagerness of a Christian elite to preserve pagan symbols, both on wall paintings and other luxury objects, might indicate their reluctance to surrender the use of such socially potent iconography. The preservation of decorational schemes and architectural layouts in their essence proves their importance in preserving a *memoria* of the past and of affirming an acceptable *locus* for imperial life.[64] The choice of iconography for these late wall paintings might well reflect that, as elsewhere, Ephesians built their identities with a process of mediation rather than relying on absolutes. Christianity was dragged into that negotiation rather than superceded it. That many favourite domestic iconographies, for example vine motifs long associated with Dionysus, were given new Christian meanings might be understood as part of this process of renegotiation. The opposition between Christian and pagan was only one of the tensions within a homeowner's life and not necessarily, as we might be tempted to think, the most important.

Just as the local Greek elite were also the Romans, similarly Christians were not invasive outsiders but these very same men. It is unlikely, then, that the terraced houses all belonged to deliberately resistant pagans. The house of the bishop in Ephesus was clad in marble no less than that of his secular contemporaries.[65] In Antioch, although John Chrysostum's sermons represented an attempt to distance his congregations from Hellenes who clung to pagan philosophy, his split is largely artificial.[66] Chrysostum himself was a product of a classical, rhetorical education, taught by Libanius whose pupils included pagans, Christians, and Jews. Antioch remained notorious as domestic display continued to predicate social success. Whilst, from the distance of the pulpit, Chrysostum can reinvent a past for Antioch that revolves around her Christian pedigree, the mosaics from domestic space continue to draw on the old traditions of the city's foundation and location.[67]

Whilst decoration might be little affected, the housing situation of Ephesus in the Christian era does show a remarkable change in the disposition of houses within the city. The houses on the Embolos were still essentially peristyle houses, even though industry had penetrated even block 2 – a water mill there was fed by a canal running down the stepped street alongside its east side. But the most remarkable changes are the changing use of the landscape throughout the city. Houses appeared in the Upper Agora and in what had been the Harbour Gymnasium. Even the Library of Celsus, before its renovation as a fountain, may have been taken over by a neighbouring house. As certain public buildings fell into disuse, housing moved in, crowding the streets and upsetting the previously inviolate grid plan. An entry in the Theodosian code dated to 398, banning the extension of houses over public space, suggests that this was an empire-wide phenomenon.[68] As private space changed, so did the public; the whole shape of the town was changed as the streets of the Embolos and the Arcadiane took over the function of the *agoras* as commemorative, commercial, and social centres.[69] It would be wrong to assign these changes to the death of the pagan city; whilst the Harbour Gymnasium may have come to its end, Scholasticia breathed new life into the bath house on the Embolos. Back in Antioch, both Libanius and Chrysostum refer to bathing as an integral part of civic life.[70]

An increased difference is noticeable between the shrinking and increasingly commercialised units of the Ephesian terraces and the new, luxurious free-standing houses. Two of the most extensive houses from this period are today attributed to the homes of public officials. The first, the "bishop's palace," was attached to the Church of St Mary, the main church of Ephesus. This long *basilica* and *atrium* church had once been a hall of the gymnasium complex, and the area unused by the church became a domestic residence, arranged around a peristyle court with its own bathsuite.[71] In 400, the bishop Antoninus was denounced, accused of taking columns and marble from the church and its baptistery to adorn his home.[72] Several stories, related by Foss, surrounding the controverises of the church councils held in Ephesus during the fifth century show that the link between public and private was relevant to ecclesiastical circles. During the council of 431, the people's riots were recorded as centring not on the church but on the houses where the visiting bishops were staying.[73] A procession accompanying Cyril of Alexandria from the church to his house revived the link between the private and public life of civic leaders.[74] These stories reflect a growing change in society whereby the *demos* begin to look to bishops as patrons but take with them their traditional methods of relating to their leaders. More generally, the stories of riots turned against private property, which can be echoed in Ammianus's and Libanius's accounts of life in Antioch, demonstrate that the Romanised pattern of domestic life was not simply an elite affectation.[75] The public role of the house was understood by the populace at large and fully integrated into local, civic life presumably through patronage networks.

The so-called Governor's Palace reveals architectural features familiar from long-term developments within *villa* architecture in the West (Figure 106).[76] The house is laid out on several axes, held together by a long corridor. This transverse hall, apsed at either end, offers comparison

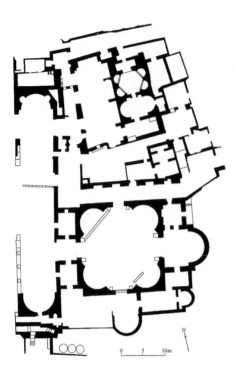

106. Ephesus, Governor's Palace, plan.

with the corridor of the Great Hunt in the Villa at Piazza Armerina in Sicily, itself arranged around several axes and usually dated to the Tetrarchic period (Figure 7).[77] The northern half of the corridor runs alongside a bath-suite; the southern half gives onto an octagonal hall with four semicircular niches that open off alternate sides. One of the flat, short sides forms the entrance to the corridor, and its opposite side leads to an apsed room, presumably the place of the owner. The apse we have met before; the niched hall is reminiscent of the Piazza d'Oro at Hadrian's Villa (Figure 18).[78] Similar, globular shapes become increasingly popular in western *villas*. In Italy, *villas* such as that at Desenzano feature apses and octagons. The fourth-century *villa* at Valentine in Gaul had a semicircular court entered via just such an octagonal, niched room as that in Ephesus.[79] The embrace of these forms in city houses truly remove us to the realm of the *palatium*. In the first-century A.D., only Domitian could live like this: now the provincial elite claimed this right for themselves. Christian controversies may have divided East and West more than ever before, but clearly a class of people who transcended the local to embrace the imperial remained.

In fact, the domestic remains across the empire attest to growing similarities between provincial, elite cultures at this time. Lavin notes the increasing tendency for the mosaics of Antioch to incorporate designs and iconographies generally associated with western mosaicists.[80] He gives the example of the increasing use of the all-over carpet design and the popularity of scenes from everyday life, particularly hunting mosaics that recall a theme popular in North Africa. The topographical border of the Yakto Complex (Figure 93) surrounded a hunt, albeit with mythological protoganists (Figure 107). The hunt scenes from Room 1 of the Constantinian Villa featured both the mythological and the human realm and were surrounded by panels of rural, *villa* life (Figure 108). The mosaics show a predominantly (sub)urban elite taking an interest in the rhetoric of town and country and inviting that countryside into their homes. The parade of animal species associated with hunt mosaics was, like other "pagan" motifs, adopted into Christian iconography. The ambulatory of the Martyrion of Seleucia provides an example of renegotiation of the meaning and function of favourite motifs.[81]

On a small scale, such interests might be found creeping into the homes of Ephesus; the hunting motifs from House 2.4 are a late addition. Similarly, in the West, the elite of Britain in late Antiquity were surrounded by goods and motifs identified with the Greek East. Villa mosaics featured mythological subjects as did silverware. The Bacchic Plate from the Mildenhall Treasure mentioned previously is a famous example of the survival of Hellenistic style and content. All over the empire, then, late Antiquity appears to have represented a high point in the process of material acculturation. This era also saw the increasing testing of boundaries inherent in Roman domestic space since the late Republic: the triumph of architectural elements associated with the *villa* and the *palatium* in the urban landscape and the growing integration of motifs and themes. At the same time, a more complete re-creation of public space was evident within the house in the form of apsed basilicas, often provided with separate entrances from the rest of the house.[82] These phenomena show the elite house becoming simultaneously both more public and more private, finding new ways of both reconciling and respecting the boundaries between the two poles.

However, it is important to place this apparent homogeneity of an imperial super-elite into perspective. The domestic art and architecture of this elite would serve to show a certain amount of uniformity, but the impulse for elites to adopt these techniques was local as well as imperial. For a limited elite, truly imperial competition was a real prospect but for the majority, their sphere of influence remained on a more parochial level. They used their domestic space and decoration to create an impression of themselves that would encourage their socio-political success. As such, the choice of decoration also had to meet the demands of those who would be called

107. Antioch, Yakto Complex, Megalopsychia mosaic, mythological hunt. Photo: Princeton University.

108. Antioch, Constantinian Villa, room 1, mosaic. Photo: Princeton University.

on to view that impression. Those clients and locals who viewed that decor chose to believe in the power of their patron. Acculturation was not simply a conceit of the elite. Its success depended on the reaction of the populace and what they regarded as potent display. The real test of elite culture, then, was on the local level. We come back to the notion of an empire that was multilocal, a model that allows for the variety of provincial houses as well as the similarities. This model also allows us to begin to understand how domestic culture might appear to be at its most homogenous when the empire was at its most strained politically and militarily and divided in terms of both secular and religious leadership. The real fabric of the empire lay in each province recognising itself and its own cultural amalgamation as the centre of empire, in effect as "Rome."

CENTRES AND PERIPHERIES

The complexities of the Greek East, which could only be hinted at here, show the variety of centres and peripheries that were continually being built up and broken down within the empire. The fetishised appeal of the East in itself peripheralised the eastern Mediterranean whilst also making it more recognisable to Romans and so closer to the centre than incomprehensible barbarians. This apparently incompatible stance is utterly typical of Roman attitudes to identity. Despite seeing Greece as utterably alien, Greece was indispensable to Roman culture. Roman houses across the empire were predicated on Greek design. Meanwhile Greek homeowners were eager to demonstrate their cultural superiority within a social system that, along with that of Rome, was developed across the Mediterranean during the Hellenistic period.

The retention of such a strong cultural identity by the Greek elites was not necessarily an anti-Roman act though it sometimes might have been deliberately intended as such. Although, undoubtedly, the Mediterranean's familiarity with, and dependence on, Greek culture allowed Greeks to "get away with it" to an extent perhaps denied Britons, local culture was a crucial part of the Roman experience. Multilayered identities come to play an increasingly important factor in imperial self-expression. Libanius calls himself and his colleagues *Romaoi* but fiercely rejects the suggestion that his grandfather was Italian and deplores the growing popularity of Latin, the language of a naturally inferior culture.[83] Other Greeks seem to have embraced a concept that divorced Romanness from Rome the city at an earlier stage. Aelius Aristides, in a panegyric to that great city delivered to the imperial court in A.D. 155, affirms that everywhere in the empire is equally Rome.[84] Whereas the city-state was once compared with a private household, now the whole empire is one house.[85] Divorce between notions of an ideal Rome and the geographical location of the real city enabled locals to embrace the term and make it theirs. Ammianus seems to consider Rome to be the natural centre of empire, but he can also champion the parsimonious behaviour of the provinces over the depraved and thus peripheralised Roman, senatorial elite.[86] His assessment squarely throws back long-held views on the vices of Antioch to the one-time centre. The condemnation should not necessarily be viewed in terms of the triumph of the East, however, but a reiteration of the view already expressed over two centuries earlier by Tacitus concerning the moral superiority of the Britons. Instead, Ammianus's views demonstrate the continued reliance of the empire on rhetorical tensions as a means of defining itself and the flexibility of a rhetoric that could encourage participation by casting any player as the centre.

Confidence in the superiority of Greece did not preclude her elites from participation in the empire. The dislocation of Roman elites from their immediate surroundings did not occur in the West only. Swain's investigation of Hellenism implies that the pursuit of Greek literature and culture increasingly became an elite pastime rather than specifically a Greek one.[87] Just as with Rome, a divorce between concepts of Greekness and Greece as a geographical location was becoming increasingly apparent. Whilst the eastern elite were still eager to champion their heritage and culture, they were looking for a bigger arena in which to compete – the Roman empire. The tendency can be seen in the choice of Artemis figures in the hanghäuser of Ephesus. In public, the elite might wheel behind the civic identity of Ephesus; as individuals at home they seem to have been eager to buy into a system that might allow wider communication.

At the same time as concepts of centre and periphery changed, Greek intellectual culture became major currency throughout the empire. Hellenistic culture gradually became a major source of competition and communication between educated elites across the entire empire. In the second century A.D., the arguments between Polemo and Favorinus, a Gaul, saw a philosophical discourse that broke the barrier of distance.[88] Inevitably, the adoption of an imperial culture based on Greek learning set the traditional Roman rhetoric, which contrasted Greek and Roman, under great strain. To embrace Greek intellectual culture was now to be Roman. This was all part of a more general phenomenon, witnessed in the West in Chapter 6, which saw the boundaries shift between various centres and peripheries. In some sense, such a reappraisal was necessitated by the redefinition of the ultimate centre, Rome. Once the idea of Rome was freed from its connection with the city, adoption was open to anybody. This left the traditional peripheries, such as Greece, to be accommodated within the centre. Adopted as a crucial counterpoint to *Romanitas* in republican Rome and exported to the provinces as such, these peripheries came to be regarded as an essential part of the Roman package. The exploitation of differences between Greek and Roman remained an important rhetorical tool but one increasingly bereft of any single direction. The versatility of the terms would explain how John Chrysostum could dismiss his pagan adversaries as Hellenes without compromising the ethnic identity of his congregation. The ongoing tensions between East and West, each continually competing for the right to be perceived as centre by peripheralising the other, should not necessarily be thought of as destructive of imperial unity. Instead, they reflect an empire brought together by competition and negotiation rather than by uniformity. The ongoing mediation between and creation and redefinition of centres and peripheries saw the Roman empire survive the loss of the West and reconvene in the East around Constantinople.

As the empire progressed, some domestic tensions were reconciled, whilst new ones were introduced, such as the need to accommodate Christianity. In terms of architecture, distances between the traditional categories of *domus* and *villa*, *domus* and *palatium*, *domus* and *oikos* further collapsed until the later elites of Ephesus were able to live like the emperors of the first and second century A.D. These houses express the distance between public and private more starkly than had the houses of Pompeii. They express the ongoing evolution of the empire. They provide a means of observing the reconciliation of old crises in order to make way for more pressing struggles to be played out within the domestic sphere.

In this final chapter, we have travelled both chronologically and geographically far from the *domus* of Rome with which we began. The houses here are very different from those described in the texts of republican Rome or the houses of Pompeii or Verulamium. However, we could not say that the houses we have found here are peripheral to those of the centre, that they demonstrate an opposite to the Roman home. Instead, we find that all homes in the empire are joined by their participation in the battle between the extremes of belonging and of transgression. Although they might express their participation in very different ways or even with varying degrees of enthusiasm, it is through this participation that they earn the title Roman. Even the *oikos*, which was then, and is now, seen as the most resistant house type to the Roman *domus*, is found to be thoroughly implicated in the rhetoric of empire.

Epilogue

The preceding chapters of this book surveyed homes across the Roman empire: from the palaces of Rome and familiar homes of Pompeii to the houses of Britain, Gaul, North Africa, and the Greek East. They do not, however, survey the mechanics of the domestic life of the empire. We have learned more about social acculturation than private domesticity, have considered at greater length how a *paterfamilias* related with his clients and fellow citizens than his offspring. This approach was not entirely an oversight but a conscious decision to respect the wishes of the homeowners whose domestic space we have been investigating. The houses of Pompeii, it seemed, wanted to hide rather than flaunt the mechanics by which the living family provided for themselves. Instead of introducing his family, the *paterfamilias* thrust forward his ancestors, and his guests were the gods. Rather than reclining in a cosy lounge, modern trespassers find themselves in temple precincts, at the theatre, in the wilderness.

It is precisely these attempts to override the realities of domestic life with painted fantasies of other worlds and to allow real guests to mingle with the occupants of those worlds that makes the Roman house such a rewarding study. There are conceptual and physical boundaries within any house, based on the layout of the house itself – inside, outside – or on the people using the house – male, female or elite, common. All these thresholds are dangerous; they are the places where pollution can most easily occur, where one category can seep into another. As such, these areas are often strongly demarcated and made visible by elaborate decoration. All areas of the Pompeian *domus*, with the exception of invisible service areas, are highly decorated. The whole house acted as a threshold between different rhetorical *topoi*: public and private, town and country, mortal and divine, Roman and alien. Investigations that only compare and contrast space on either side of the threshold of the front entrance to the *domus* fail to realise the extent to which other boundaries operate on either side of the door. The outside world seeped into every area of the *domus*. Similarly, the Roman family's domestic domain reached out over the city, beyond the walls to family tombs and country *villa*s.

The inability of the *domus* to provide any unequivocal, or pure, statement of domestic life is an indication of how these houses took their place in the Roman empire. The numerous thresholds within the Roman house seemed positively to invite pollution. If "purity is the enemy of change, of ambiguity and compromise" then Romans too seem to have shunned the stultifying safety of purity.[1] In seemingly inviting potential chaos across its parameters, the threshold of the house resembles the borders of empire. The Roman empire was not a place for purity. Its success depended on finding a place for everybody as it expanded over the world and through time. The very idea of being Roman and living like a Roman must similarly accommodate pollution.

The ambiguity of being Roman is played out in the decoration and architecture of all the houses within the Roman empire. In the houses of the provinces, the clash of worlds was made most urgent as Roman met local. The whole house became a threshold of communication between the local traditions of the elite and the new Roman practises that they must assume to function successfully within the empire. This negotiation was played out all over the Roman world, resulting in a myriad of architectural manifestations. The extent to which there was no conception of a "pure" Roman house is demonstrated by the relations between the houses of the peripheries and of the centre. The imperial palaces offered no straightforward Roman archetype to which those houses on the edge of empire might aspire. Quite the opposite, their owners indulged in the most extreme fantasies of other worlds, whether foreign, divine, or wild, looking desirously out to those very peripheries.

These fantasies of conformity and transgression contained within the palaces and houses of the empire are an invaluable tool for investigating *Romanitas*. The Roman perception that the house was literally answerable for its human inhabitants enables us to use the art and architecture of the *domus* as a manifestation of how owners chose to project themselves into Roman society. To this extent, the decoration of the Roman house not only provides insights into how Romans lived at home but, more importantly, how they imagined their role and place in the Roman empire.

The Romanisation of the house is a direct indicator of the Romanisation of its owners.

To be Roman was to learn how to manipulate Roman rhetoric, to avoid alienating oneself by coming down too hard on any one side of any rhetorical *topos*. Latin literature attacked as enemies of the state those who lost balance, like Antony who became enslaved to a foreign queen. They could equally attack the man through his houses, men like Lucullus who turned their backs on civic Rome to live a life of eastern luxury in the countryside. They attacked neither man simply because they had indulged in the foreign and exotic but because, in doing so, they had neglected the other side of the *topos*. It was not so much loving Cleopatra that earned Antony such opprobrium as the idea that he had turned his back on Rome. Similarly, Lucullus was not under attack simply for owning these *villa*s but because he was seen to reject civic life at Rome. Succeeding where Lucullus failed would not entail securing a *domus* on the Palatine and refusing to buy property beyond the city walls, it would rather involve balancing the demands of both *domus* and *villa* life. As the empire progressed, these rhetorics became increasingly flexible as they were adopted by the peripheries. Provincial communities used them to attack the traditional centre of Rome as a means of asserting themselves as centres. Some tensions were reconciled and new ones were developed to maintain the negotiation inherent in imperial life. That the emperors were literally kings of the balancing act of conflicting rhetoric merely shows that this is what being Roman entailed. Hadrian, as emperor of the Roman empire at its apex, conceived a whole fantasy world within his *villa* at Tivoli. He demonstrated his fitness for leadership by the extremity of his fantasy, by his ability to go furthest in materialising the opposing extremes of popular *topoi*.

The houses of the Roman empire shed more light on the acculturation of the provinces than any text has managed to convey. They demonstrate that it is impossible to trace an archetypal Roman house, an archetypal Roman identity. Instead, the empire was multilocal – an infinite combination of negotiation between local and Roman. Even at Rome, citizens had to craft such an identity. Even in Greece, proud local identities were brought into the wider arena of empire. It is redundant to think of Romanisation in terms of success and failure demonstrated by conformity, either forced or voluntary, and resistance, since *Romanitas* itself was constructed as a mixture of these reactions. The senatorial elite of Rome were just as disinclined to live trapped within a strict definition of pure Romanness as we might expect a disgruntled, conquered local elite to be. *Romanitas* itself, therefore, was an identity based on negotiation and compromise rather than purity. To be seen to be entering, or indeed to find yourself entered, into this debate was to become Roman.

Art, and the fantasies it created, played an integral part in realising this debate. Whilst much Roman literature remained driven by the attack or rehabilitation of rhetorical dichotomies, art was able to contract those differences and throw all of them together in the one house. The homeowner, whether he was a Verulamium shop owner or a Roman emperor, was able to challenge all these different worlds and show his *Romanitas* by his ability both to explore and conquer them. The art of Roman houses across the empire, through the impressions it created for visitors, leaves us today our most succinct expressions of being Roman. It shows us a system of fantasising that encompassed all races and all ranks. The acceptance of these painted fantasies as valid manifestations of *Romanitas* is, in itself, a demonstration of the ambiguous tenets on which Rome was based.

This book has purported to be about houses, about the art and architecture that shapes domestic space in the Roman world. In fact, any investigation into the Roman *domus* is about more than simply private life. The remains of houses across the empire are our biggest resource for investigating how people living within the Roman world thought of themselves and how they communicated this self-image to the world. Their houses could be read by contemporaries as a dialogue between the individual and his environment and today provide us with a rich data for exploring Roman self-image at both a communal and individual level. In constructing his house, the homeowner was quite literally building an identity.

Notes

INTRODUCTION

1 August Mau notes this link in passing. He writes that the *forum* is the *atrium* of the city. Mau 1899 p. 61.
2 The makeup of the Roman family is discussed in Saller 1984 and Dixon 1992. Hope 1997 discusses the continuation of this association after death.
3 For a general account of daily life, see Balsdon 1969 pp. 17–55, 82–129. For an account of ritual activity in the house, see Clarke 1991 pp. 1–29.
4 For the rituals of dining, see the collected essays in Slater 1991. The low status of public drinking establishments is discussed in Laurence 1994 pp. 78ff.
5 For the *atrium* as centre for birth, marriage, and funerary rituals, see Flower 1996 pp. 200ff.
6 Mazzoleni 1993 p. 292.
7 The setting up of special altars to mark births is recorded at Macrob. *Sat.* 1.16.36. For the decoration of the threshold, see Statius *Silvae* 4.8.37–41. For a brief overview of the rituals associated with a family birth, see Dixon 1992 p. 134.
8 Dixon 1992 pp. 61–97.
9 The fullest description of the Roman funeral is preserved in Polybios 6.53–5. Dixon 1992 pp. 135–6.
10 Wilkins 1996 p. 123 argues that what is regarded as civic or municipal can be a form of ritual. Turner 1984 p. 21 understands culture's role to be to bring the individual into a collective body and to restrain them with their collective obligations.
11 Bell 1992 pp. 118–41 discusses the use of ritual in justifying power relationships by appealing to tradition. Hobsbawm & Ranger 1983 pp. 1–14 deal specifically with inventing tradition as does Wilkins 1996 p. 3. Bloch 1989 pp. 1–18 discusses how apparently timeless ritual systems are affected by social change, whilst Hobsbawm & Ranger 1983 p. 4 propose the link between rapid social change and an increased invention of tradition.
12 Bell 1992 p. 107. At pp. 88–9, ritualisation is specifically understood as a process designed both to escalate and resolve threatening conflicts within society.
13 Cicero, for example, blasts the bad taste of a friend he has charged with procuring statues for his villas. Cicero *Ad Fam.* 7.23.

14 Vitruvius's advice for the layout of the elite *domus* can be found in *De Arch.* 6.5.1–3. See Nappo and Wallace-Hadrill, both in Laurence & Wallace-Hadrill 1997, for new thoughts on the development of the *atrium* house in Pompeii.

15 Spinazzola 1953 pp. 297–314.

16 A traditional explanation for the uses of rooms in the Pompeian house can be found in Mau 1899 pp. 239–73.

17 Allison 1993 pp. 1–8 and Berry in Laurence & Wallace-Hadrill 1997 pp. 183–95.

18 Bell 1992 p. 33 from Geertz 1973 p. 144 defines culture as an ordered system of meaning and symbols in which social interaction takes place. Laurence 1993 p. 79, with direct reference to Rome, speaks of a cultural meaning enshrined in a series of symbols and monuments and made explicit through ritual and mythology. Hobsbawm & Ranger 1983 p. 10 recognise the power of symbols to trigger a sense of collective citizenship. Rapaport in Kent 1990 p. 11 raises the possibility that architecture influences behaviour, whilst Donley-Reid in Kent 1990 p. 114 recognises the cyclical relationship between culture and architecture.

19 The nature of imperial divinity is most succinctly discussed in Hopkins 1978. The entrance to the underworld is described in Virgil *Aen.* 6.237–63.

20 The *suburbia* are best described in Purcell 1987. The interdependence of town and country in the ancient world is discussed in Rich & Wallace-Hadrill 1991. For bathing and sanitary arrangements, see Robinson 1992 pp. 113–16 and 119–22.

21 These representations are recognised as crucial to Roman historiography by Woodman 1988 esp. pp. 88ff. Edwards 1993 pp. 137–73 gives an important account of the accusations of immorality in the Roman texts, observing the role of familiar rhetorical *topoi* in framing or, indeed, in fending off such attacks.

22 Laurence in Laurence & Wallace-Hadrill 1997 pp. 9ff. For a more general understanding of the capacity of art to serve rhetorical purpose, see Leach 1988 and Bergmann 1994.

23 A catalogue of imperial house types can be found in McKay 1975 and Ellis 2000. Percival 1976 discussed the functions of the Roman *villa* in terms of an empire-wide phenomenon. Neudecker 1988, in researching the sculptural arrangements of villas, used a similarly wide geographical basis for his investigation.

24 Thébert 1987.

25 Wallace-Hadrill 1994.

26 Mielsch 1987 discusses the architecture and lifestyle associated with the *villa*.

27 The dissemination of luxuries from the rich to the poor is generally seen as imitative. See Wallace-Hadrill 1994 pp. 43–74 and Zanker 1998 pp. 19–20. Packer in Andreae & Kyrieleis 1975 remains isolated in its attempt to discuss the poorer housing of the Campanian cities.

CHAPTER 1

1 Cicero *Ad Fam.* 5.12.

2 See Woodman 1988 pp. 88ff.

3 Livy's account of Camillus contrasts his moment of glory, the Fall of Veii, at 5.21–2 with his subsequent disgrace, 5.32, and then recall from exile to save Rome from the Gaulish sack and become, as did Cicero, *pater patriae*, 5.48–9.

4 Virgil. *Aen.* 6.851–853.

5 Livy 2.10.

6 Mattingly 1937 pp.103ff. discusses the canonisation of these virtues through their worship as cult personifications.

7 Livy 1.57.
8 For this aspect of the funerary rite see Toynbee 1971 pp. 43–4 and Seneca *Ad Marciam* 3.2. A full discussion of Roman names can be found in Kajanto 1965. A helpful summary can be found in Gordon 1983 pp. 17–30.
9 Pliny *Eps.* 3.10. A discussion of artistic and literary patronage can be found in Gold 1982. See also Leach 1990. For the elite's creation of a tradition of *Romanitas*, see Gruen 1992 pp. 6–51 (literature) and pp. 131–82 (art).
10 Pliny *N.H.* 34.10.19.
11 Kleiner 1992 pp. 31–47 and Gruen 1992 pp. 152–82.
12 Elsner 1995 p. 55 discusses the loaded use of the term *veritas*; Tacitus *Ann.* 1.1.
13 Douglas & Isherwood 1979 p.145 understand standardisation as a sign of increasing competition.
14 Contrast Cicero *Pro Rosc.* 75, which attacks the luxury of Rome and the eulogy of country life in Tibullus 1.1, with the praise of the urbane man in Quint. *Inst.Or.* 6.3.108 and of the splendours of the city of Rome in Ovid *Ars Am.* 3.113–28.
15 This tactic is discussed in Edwards 1993 and Miles 1987 pp. 260–8. Edwards is particularly concerned with the framing of such accusations in moral terms.
16 For a general overview of rhetoric, see Clarke 1996. For ancient education, see Marrou 1956.
17 Pliny *N.H.* 36.7.48–49.50 records the race amongst the elite to utilise marble, symptomatic of a spiralling competition expressed in lavish domestic display.
18 Cicero *De Off.* 1.54.
19 Clarke 1991 opens his discussion of the art and architecture of the Roman house with a resumé of the rituals played out within the domestic sphere. pp.1–29. For an account of the *salutatio* in its domestic setting, see Wallace-Hadrill 1989a pp. 63–88.
20 Cicero *De Harus. Resp.* 17.37.
21 Vasaly 1993 discusses the relationship of *ethos* and *locus* as portrayed in the works of Cicero.
22 Cicero *De Rep.* 2.4.10 discusses how Rome's geographical location and climate fit her for world rule.
23 The tirade stretches from Cicero *Phil.* 2.27.67 to 2.28.70. He goes on to accuse Antony of similar behaviour in the former house of Varro at *Phil.* 2.40.103–41.105. These activities are also recorded in Plut. *Ant.* 21.2–3.
24 Cicero *Post Red. in Sen.* 5.11.
25 Cicero *In Verr.* 2.1.52 and 2.5.15.
26 Whitehorn 1969 compiles a list and the nature of ambitious building in Rome. Tert. *Apol.* 11.8; Amm. Mar. 22.8.16 and 23.5.16.
27 The senator's career is set out in Keaveney 1992.
28 See Plutarch *Luc.* 39.1 for the division.
29 Blame is laid clearly on Asia in Sallust *Bell. Cat.* 11.4–7 and Vell. Pat. 2.1.1–2.
30 Varro *De Re Rust.* 3.4.2–3.
31 See Pliny *N.H.* 9.170 and Vell. Pat. 2.33.4. On the nature of Plutarch's apparent defence of Rome, drawing accusations of luxury to eastern origins, see Swain 1996 pp. 135–86, which discusses the biographer's attitude to Rome.
32 Cicero *De Off.* 1.39.140.
33 Cicero *De Leg.* 3.13.30.
34 Suet. *Aug.* 73.1.
35 Suet. *Aug.* 72.1.
36 Suet. *Aug.* 72.2–3.

37 The canonical account of the endeavours of Augustus, or Augustan architects, to build a new Rome is Zanker 1988. See esp. pp. 239–63 on the moralistic rhetoric of Augustan art and architecture. See, more recently, Favro 1996 and Galinsky 1996 pp. 141–224.

38 Suet. *Aug.* 2.28.

39 Elsner 1996 discusses the implications of the *Res Gestae* in redefining the city of Rome. See also Sablayrolles 1981 and Yavetz in Millar & Segal 1984.

40 Most writing on Vitruvius concentrates on extracting "facts" concerning building and machinery such as is found in McKay 1978. For the most recent edition of his work, see Rowland & Howe 1999.

41 Wilkinson 1969 dismisses the idea that the *Georgics* could be of practical use.

42 Varro *De Re Rust.* 3.3.10.

43 The ease with which Ovid shattered the appearance of the new moral reawakening is dicussed by Wallace-Hadrill 1989b.

44 Ovid records his banishment in the *Tristia* and *Ex Ponto*. Recently, Williams 1994 esp. pp. 3–49 has doubted that the exile ever happened. Nevertheless, Ovid's presentation of himself as punished exile indicates that he and his readers were well aware of the subversive character of the *Ars Amatoria*.

45 Elsner 1995 p. 56 issues a clear warning that Vitruvius cannot be regarded as "ideologically" innocent.

46 Elsner 1995 p. 59.

47 Vitr. *De Arch.* 9.

48 Wallace-Hadrill 1994, for example, takes the various levels of accessibility as a guideline to the function of and flow around the house. Elsner 1995 pp. 59ff. also takes the Vitruvian presentation of public and private as a prescription for spatial organisation. See esp. p. 61. Leach 1988 pp. 199ff. discusses the same theme as it appears in literature and art. See also Zaccaria Ruggiu 1995 pp. 121–80.

49 Carettoni 1960.

50 Pliny *N.H.* 36.24.109. A similar story unfolds in Vell. Pat. 2.10.1.

51 Pliny *N. H.* 33.18.57, 34.7.13–8.14, and 36.7.48–50. Seneca passes moral comment in *Ep.* 90.38–43 and *Ep.* 94.9.

52 The Saecular Games were commemorated by Horace in verse and are briefly mentioned in Suet. *Aug.* 31. Zanker 1988 pp. 167ff. discusses their role in heralding a new age.

53 See also Juv. *Sat.* 6.2–7, Seneca *Ep.* 90.7–10, and Plut. *Numa* 5–6.

54 Plutarch mentions the hut at *Rom.* 20.4. For the ongoing importance of the hut in defining Rome, see Rykwert 1988 pp. 28–40.

55 For a discussion of Pliny's attitudes to nature and luxury see Wallace-Hadrill 1990. Beagon 1992 pp. 55–91 investigates the author's opinions on man's relationship with nature. See esp. pp. 75–9 for luxury as exploitation of nature. This theme is also explored in Isager 1991 esp. pp. 52–6. For the morality of building, see Edwards 1993 pp. 137–73.

56 Other complaints concerning the growth of luxury include Sallust *Bell. Cat.* 13.1–2 and 20.11, Seneca the Elder *Cont.* 2.1.11–13, and, later, Juv. *Sat.* 7.178–88.

57 See, for example, Seneca the Younger *Eps.* 86.6, 89.201, 95.8–9, and 122.5–8.

58 Suet. *Nero* 120.1.

59 Iacopi 1963 provides a description.

60 Vitr. *De Arch.* 7.5.3–4. Elsner 1995 discusses the possible agenda behind the author's attack pp. 51–8.

61 Horace *Ars Poetica* 1–5.

62 Elsner 1995 p. 57.
63 Both Lucr. *De Re Nat.* 2.20–36 and Cicero *Laws.* 1.15 see Nature as the harbour of justice and morality.
64 Griffin 1990 considers the relevance of the *Georgics* to Augustan Rome. The episode of the garden at Tarentum, 4.116–48, stresses both the adversities and rewards of nature.
65 For example, Tib. 1.1.11–14.
66 See Horace *Ep.* 10.1–33, Juv. *Sat.* 3.190–202, and Pliny *Ep.* 1.3.3.
67 These paintings are published in Gabriel 1955.
68 Horace praises his *villa* in the Sabine Hills in *Sat.* 2.6.1–4. He sets it off against both city politics and huge country estates in *Odes.* 2.16.
69 Juvenal *Sat.* 3, for example, is written on the premise of bidding farewell to a friend who is leaving for Cumae. How much better Cumae than Rome where, within the first fifty lines of the satire, Juvenal has located fraud and conspiracy (ll. 41–50) before panning onto streets filled with prostitutes (l.65) and brawlers (ll. 278–82)?
70 Tibullus opens his books of elegy with a eulogy to the country at 1.1. Also contrast his desperate love of 1.2 with the loving ideal of 1.5.19–34.
71 Anderson 1985. See esp. pp. 87–100 for the interest in hunting fostered under the Principate. Compare this with moralistic criticism of the sport in the late Republic. Sallust *Bell. Cat.* 4.1.
72 Carandini 1982.
73 Cicero *Pro Sulla* 17.
74 Vitr. *De Arch.* 6.5.3.
75 The elite's ongoing relationship with the country is considered by Wallace-Hadrill in Rich & Wallace-Hadrill 1991 pp. 241–272.
76 An excellent account of the *horti* is given by Purcell in MacDougall 1987. He specifically sees the *horti* as being both town and country residences at p. 195.
77 Purcell in MacDougall 1987 p. 303 records the passing of the *horti* to the hands of the emperors.
78 Cima & La Rocca 1986.
79 Dio 43.44.6 records that Caesar lived on state property, built for him by the public.
80 Such rewards as those granted to Poplicola (Plut. *Popl.* 20.2 and Pliny *N.H.* 36.42.112) to have his doors open outwards imply that the doors would have been often open in order to show their uniqueness.
81 Ovid *Am.* 1.6 is written as a lament to the doorkeeper blocking his way to his mistress. Tib. 1.2.7–14 pleads with the locked door before him, whilst the door gets a chance to air its views in Prop. 1.16.
82 Pliny *Pan.* 47.5–48.4.
83 See Sallust *Bell. Cat.* 2.13 and Livy 6.22.8–14. Such suspicion is also expressed in Livy 24.16–17 where the people of Beneventum greet the forces of Gracchus by arranging meals in their *atria*. Tellingly, the soldiers are allowed to partake of these meals only if the doors of each house are kept open.
84 Cicero *In Cat.* 2.13.
85 Tacitus *Ann.* 15.51.

CHAPTER 2

1 Rawson 1975 (new ed. 1994). An account of Cicero's attitudes to the public life of his time can be found in Wood 1988 and Mitchell 1991 esp. pp. 9–62.

2 See Rawson 1975 (new ed. 1994) pp. 60–88 and Sallust *Bell. Cat.* for Cicero's involvement in the incident. Cicero's own perception of his contribution is made in *Pro Sulla* 33.

3 Cicero *Ad Fam.* 5.6.2; Aulus Gellius 12.12; Richardson 1992 p. 123. For an economic assessment of Cicero's investment in both this *domus* and the villas he owned throughout Italy, see Shatzman 1975 pp. 403–25. For the results of recent excavations on the Palatine see Steinby 1993– vol. II pp. 202–4.

4 Vell. Pat. 2.14.

5 Wood 1988 pp. 105–19 deals specifically with Cicero's views on the ownership and accumulation of private property.

6 For an ancient account, see Plut. *Cicero* 31.1–33.5. For a modern perspective, see Rawson 1975 (new ed. 1994) pp. 106–21 and Allen 1944.

7 These sentiments are repeated to Atticus at *Ad Att.* 3.15 and 3.20 as well as to his wife at *Ad Fam.* 14.2.3.

8 Cicero *Phil.* 1.5.12 and 5.7.18–19.

9 See Hales 2000.

10 Livy 5.41.1–8.

11 Plut. *Caes.* 68.6.

12 Vell. Pat. 2.14.

13 Dio 53.27.5; Cicero *Pro Cael.* 18; Cicero *Pro Cael.* 59; Plut. *Crassus* 2.4–5; Suet. *Aug.* 72. For a review of the archaeological remains, see Steinby 1993– IV pp. 22–28. Also Royo 1999 pp. 9–117.

14 Plut. *Marius* 32; Plut. *G. Gracc.* 12.1.

15 Suet. *Jul.* 46.

16 Livy 2.7.5–12.

17 Plut. *Cicero.* 8.3. Cicero is here seen following in the footsteps of Marius. Plut. *Marius* 32.1.

18 Cicero *Pro Cael.* 7.18.

19 For examples of arguments initiated by views, see Cicero *De Or.* 1.39.179 and Seneca *Cont.* 5.5. A good discussion of the function of the view in the house can be read in Bek 1980.

20 Cicero *Ad Fam.* 7.1.1.

21 Drerup 1959 pp. 147ff. set out the distinction between *bildraum* and *realraum* in the understanding of views. Whereas the latter revealed a view of real space, *bildraum* is a contrived view of which it is the aim to provide an impression of the interior space rather than reflect its reality.

22 The perceived power of the view in implying senatorial authority is suggested by Cicero's sensitivity in his letter *Ad Att.* 2.3. In replying to criticism of the small size of his windows, Cicero is forced to call upon some fairly improbable physics in order to defend his property.

23 Cicero *Phil.* 2.28.68.

24 Plut. *Gracc.* 15.1.

25 For the *atrium* as centre of family death, see Flower 1996 pp. 93–7.

26 *Invective Against Sallust* 14; Cicero *De Or.* 2.55.

27 Plut. *Popl.* 20.2 and Pliny *N.H.* 36.24.112; Plut. *Caes.* 68.6; Dio 55.12.4–5. Suet. *Claud.* 17.3 presents Claudius with a naval crown. Martial *Epig.* 12.2.10–2 mentions laurels on the posts of a private citizen. For a modern consideration of such display, see Wiseman 1987.

28 Cicero *Pro Planc.* 64–6. See also Rawson 1975 (new ed. 1994) pp. 35–6.

29 Quintilian *Inst. Or.* 11.2.17–22. *Ad Herennium* 3.16.29. The technique is discussed in Yates 1966 pp. 1–26.

30 Bergmann 1994 experiments with applying these techniques of memory to real ancient houses, using the House of the Tragic Poet in Pompeii.

31 Belting 1994 pp. 9–13 distinguishes between image and narrative. Narrative remains rooted in the past but the image can bring its *memoria* to the present time by giving an impression of its subject and providing the viewer with the experience of a personal encounter. For the *memoria* associated with portraiture, see Vitr. *De Arch.* 9, Praef. 16.

32 Cicero *Phil.* 2.28.68 and Plut. *G. Gracc.* 15.1 record the decoration of *atria* with memorabilia of the family's achievements. For a discussion of ancestral masks, see Flower 1996 pp. 185–222.

33 Cicero *Ad Fam.* 5.1.

34 Cicero *Ad Quint. Frat.* 2.12.5.

35 Cicero *De Or.* 2.48.275–6.

36 Cicero *De Harus. Resp.* 13.30–14.32.

37 Dion Hal. 12.1.1–4.6; Cicero *De Dom. Sua* 101. Richardson 1992 p. 3.

38 Livy 2.41.11; Cicero *De Dom. Sua* 101. Richardson 1992 p. 123.

39 Aulus Gellius 13.24 sees Cato the Younger consciously emulating his ancestor. Comparing Plutarch's *Cato* 2.1–2 with *Cato the Younger* 3.5–4.1 shows that his attempt was largely successful.

40 Cicero *Ad Fam.* 13.1.3–4.

41 Martial *Epig.* 8.61.

42 Suet. *Nero* 38.2.

43 Richardson 1992 pp. 44–5.

44 Cicero *Ad Att.* 12.21.2.

45 Suet. *Jul.* 83.2.

46 Appian *Bell. Civ.* 3.14; Asconius *Ad Cic. Milon.* 32. Richardson 1992 p. 201.

47 A discussion of the economy of *villa* life can be found in Percival 1976 pp.145–65. For the decoration of villas, see Mielsch 1987 and Neudecker 1988.

48 Mielsch 1987 pp. 45–9. Pliny *N.H.* 22.6.12.

49 Cicero *Ad Att.* 8.9.1, 9.15.2, and 9.18. See Mitchell 1991 p. 258.

50 Plut. *Cicero* 7.2.

51 Laurence 1993 esp. p. 79 understands the conception of Rome as defined specifically through ritual. Architecture contains meaning, but this is made explicit through the ritual enacted around it.

52 Laurence 1993 p. 81.

53 Cicero *Phil.* 2.69.

54 Geertz 1973 pp. 21–2 dismisses the microcosmic model as a means of interpreting cultures. Contrast this with Hingley in Samson 1990 pp. 125–48.

55 See Bradley 1984 pp. 87–99.

56 Vitr. *De Arch.* 5. Preface. 5.

57 For Circus Flaminius, see Richardson 1992 p. 83. For Porticus Metelli, see Richardson 1992 p. 315.

58 Livy 44.16.10–11. Richardson 1992 p. 134.

59 Val. Max. 8.15.1. See also Walbank 1967.

60 Richardson 1992 pp. 359–60.

61 Cicero *De Nat. Deo.* 2.4.11.

62 For example, the Senate of imperial times met in the Temple of Mars Ultor if discussing war. Suet. *Aug.* 29.2.

63 Cicero *Ad Att.* 1.1, 1.4, 1.6, 1.8, 1.9, and 1.10. For the *xystus*, see Vitr. *De Arch.* 6.7.5.

64 During this time, Rome became notorious for extravagent house building. See Pliny *N.H.* 36.110. Also see Strabo *Geog.* 5.3.7. Zaccaria Ruggiu 1995 pp. 181–228 discusses the legal attempts to deal with this phenomenon.

65 That the two should be kept separate is implied by Cicero *Pro Mur.* 76.

66 Pliny *N.H.* 34.36, 36.113–15. Pliny *N.H.* 36.24.115.

67 Plut. *Pomp.* 5; 40.

68 Cicero *Ad Quint. Frat.* 3.1 and 3.9 are largely reports on the progress of home extensions and renovations at multifarious *villas* belonging to Quintus.

69 See Vasaly 1993 pp. 104–24. The sentiment that such greed is the result of public expenditure is expressed in Vell. Pat. 2.1.1–2. The collecting of sculpture by individuals for their homes is discussed by Bartmann in Gazda 1991.

70 The houses of Athens are investigated from the viewpoint of interpreting the social use of space by Jameson in Kent 1990.

CHAPTER 3

1 The development of the palatial tradition is discussed in Wiseman 1987, Tamm 1963, and Frézouls in Lévy 1987.

2 Nicolet 1991 pp. 98–111.

3 Kleiner 1992 pp. 283–5. For the reliefs from the Sebasteion at Aphrodisias, see Erim 1986 pp. 106–23.

4 Zanker 1988 pp. 188–92, Elsner 1995 pp. 159–89, and Galinsky 1996 pp. 155–64. Galinsky pp. 24–8 deals with the implications of *auctoritas* purveyed in the piece. Pollini 1987 discusses the excavation of the statue from the *villa* at Prima Porta.

5 For comparison, see the bust of Hercules-Commodus found in the Horti Lamiani. Cima & La Rocca 1986, pp. 88–91.

6 Suet. *Aug.* 72–3.

7 Pliny *N.H.* 36.7.48–8.50. The lavishness of imperial domestic luxury is mentioned in *N.H.* 36.24.111–2.

8 Suet. *Aug.* 29.3. Ovid *Fasti* 4.951–4 shows Apollo, Vesta, and Augustus housed side by side. For the domestic role of Vesta, see Foss in Laurence & Wallace-Hadrill 1997 pp. 198–9.

9 Plut. *Pomp.* 40.5.

10 Suet. *Aug.* 29.3.

11 Dio 55.12.5. Dio 43.44.6 and Suet *Jul.* 46 mention that Caesar as *pontifex maximus* had a public house. This provided a model for imperial housing.

12 Dion. Hal. 1.79.11 and Plut. *Rom.* 20.4 reflect the importance of the site to contemporary Romans. Rykwert 1988 pp. 28–40 discusses the centrality of Romulus to the foundation of Rome. See also Wiseman 1987 pp. 401–3.

13 Suet. *Aug.* 72.1 records the house as having belonged to Hortensius.

14 Dio 53.16 explains the beginnings of *palatium*. Viarre 1961 traces the meaning of the word. The process by which Augustus reorientated the Palatine around the Principate is best discussed in Wiseman 1987 pp. 398–406. See, more recently, Royo 1999 pp. 119–207.

15 For the plan of the House of Augustus and a description of its decoration, see Carettoni 1983.

16 These honours are recorded by Dio 55.12.4–5 and by Augustus himself in the *R.G.* 34.2 and 35.1. See Wiseman 1987 pp. 398–9.

17 Pliny *N.H.* 35.37.118 attributes the decline of the standing of painters to their habit of painting private walls as opposed to public panels. However, *N.H.* 35.37.116–7 deals with the *amoenissimam* walls of Spurius Taedius, proving that wall painting itself was not an issue for moral opprobrium. A list of domestic luxuries drawn up in Seneca *Ep.* 114.9 does not mention this medium at all.

18 The criticism of Vitr. *De Arch.* 7.5.3–4, is aimed at the fantastic elements of wall painting, those motifs that *nec sunt nec fieri possunt nec fuerunt.*

19 Virgil *Georg.* 2.136–76 reminds us that these rural landscapes did not function regardless of Rome but rather were a reflection of and support for civic life. For the political readings of Virgil's *Eclogues*, see Galinsky 1996 pp. 91–3.

20 Ling 1991 pp. 29–31 briefly discusses the debate. Beyen 1957's belief in the theatrical nature of painting is updated by Little 1971. In opposition, Schefold in Andreae & Kyrieleis 1975 pp. 53–9 and Lehmann 1953 see the paintings as representations of real, architectural elements.

21 Von Blanckenhagen & Alexander 1990 pp. 10–27. Sacro-idyllic painting as a genre is discussed in Ling 1977 and Leach 1980.

22 Galinsky 1996 pp. 189–91 goes as far as to recognise this room as Augustus's "Syracusum."

23 The Egyptianising frieze of the House of Livia is mentioned in Ling 1991 p. 142. The Nilotic mosaic from Praeneste is published in Meyboom 1995.

24 The pyramid was built by the Porta Ostiense, where it still stands. See Steinby 1993– vol. IV pp. 278–9.

25 Local sculptures did, in fact, portray Augustus in the guise of pharaoh. See Strocka in Stucky & Jucker 1980 pp. 177–80.

26 See Amm. Mar. 16.10. The increasing emphasis on the ceremonial of imperial protocol is investigated by MacCormack 1981.

27 Pliny *Pan.* 49.4–5 provides an example of Trajan's apparent normality. Wallace-Hadrill 1982 shows how Pliny himself refutes his own examples by continually referring to the emperor as *domine*, despite his *recusatio* of that title p. 36.

28 The Domus Tiberiana is published by Krause 1985. See also Steinby 1993– vol. II pp. 189–99. For Caligula's efforts, see Van Deman 1924. See also Patterson 1992 and Royo 1999 pp. 209–301.

29 Perrin in Lévy 1987 p. 363.

30 Suet. *Calig.* 23–4.

31 Pliny *N.H.* 36.24.111.

32 Suet. *Calig.* 22.2 and Dio 59.28.5.

33 Josephus 19.1.11.71; Suet. *Calig.* 22.4.

34 Cima & La Rocca 1986 pp. 24–7 record how these estates gradually fell into imperial hands.

35 Royo 1999 pp. 136–44.

36 Wiseman 1987 p. 411. This is the culmination of a process by which Laurence 1993 p. 85 saw the emperor welding himself into the landscape, and hence ritual and myth, of Rome.

37 Suet. *Calig.* 4.19. Consider, too, Caligula's pleasure boats which recall the great ship of Ptolemy Philopater, recorded in Athen. 5.204e–206c and discussed in Barrett 1989 p. 200.

38 Suet. *Nero* 34–5.

39 Tacitus *Ann.*15.39.1. Suet. *Nero* 31.1. Steinby 1993– vol. II pp. 199–202.

40 Suet. *Nero* 39.2. Nero's perceived responsibility for the fire is recorded at 38.1–2. Morford 1968 pp. 160–1 and Warden 1981 assess the extent and nature of the area ascribed to the Domus Aurea in the past.

41 Tamm 1963 pp. 107ff. See Martial *De Spec.* 2.1–4 and Suet. *Nero* 39.2.

42 Suet. *Nero* 31.1–2 and Tacitus *Ann.* 15.42. Pliny *N.H.* 33.16.54 preferred to see the house as ringing the city. For descriptions of the Domus, see Böethius 1960 pp. 94–128. Excavation advances are recorded in Van Essen 1954, Sanguinetti 1957, Zander 1958, and, more recently, Fabbrini 1982 and 1986 and Ball 1994 pp. 183ff.

43 L'Orange 1953. The idea is refined to a programme of *apotheosis* in Ward-Perkins 1956. Hemsoll 1990 integrates this approach with the other prevailing views of the Domus Aurea. Böethius 1946 refutes L'Orange as does Perrin in Lévy 1987 pp. 359–75. Strabo 17.1.8–9 and Pliny *N.H.* 5.11.62 describe the palace at Alexandria.

44 Lehmann 1953 pp. 82–131.

45 Pliny *N.H.* 35.37.120. Dacos 1968 pp. 222ff. attempts to assess how much of the surviving painting can be ascribed to his hand.

46 Peters & Meyboom 1982 pp. 39–59 deal with these theatrical schemes.

47 Elsner in Elsner & Masters 1994.

48 Neropolis is discussed in Griffin 1984 p. 131 from Suet. *Nero* 55.

49 The role of theatricality in the Principate is examined by Bartsch 1994. Pages 1–35 deal with Nero and his descent into fiction/theatre. Edwards in Elsner & Masters 1994 p. 90 recognises this showing up of Roman ritual as theatre (e.g., Suet. *Nero* 25) as disgraceful in the eyes of the elite who prefer to disguise theatricality and so preserve authority.

50 For a discussion of the Architectural Revolution, see Sear 1982 pp. 96ff. MacDonald 1965 pp. 20–46 is a great exponent of this theory but is refuted in Hemsoll 1990 p. 18. Morford 1968 p. 178 sees the building rather as a result of a Neronian cultural revolution.

51 Mielsch 1987 p. 68.

52 Nero is branded *Graeculus* in Tacitus *Ann.* 14.45. See also *Ann.* 14.12 and Suet. *Nero* 51.

53 Vitellius attempted to outdo Nero himself, criticising the paltriness of the estate. Dio 44.4.1–2.

54 Dio 65.10.4. For excavations of these *horti* see Lehmann-Hartleben & Lindros 1935.

55 Martial *De Spec.* 2.5–12.

56 Various reconstructions appear in Giuliani 1977 and Finsen 1962. See also MacDonald 1965 pp. 53–4 and 64–5.

57 Finsen 1969 goes as far to suggest that this traditional arrangement made it unsuitable for Hadrian, presumably necessitating the building of the Villa at Tivoli.

58 Royo 1999 pp. 303–68 believes that the Flavian project is an attempt to create an imperial sanctuary. For the coins, see pp. 347–54.

59 Statius *Silvae* 4.2.

60 Suet. *Domitian* 14–17.

61 Mielsch 1987 pp. 72–4. Pages 149ff. discuss the political implications of the *villa* and its relation to Hadrian's Villa at Tivoli.

62 Boatwright 1987 p. 141 cites evidence for the conduct of official business here. For a full description, see Aurigemma 1961 and Giuliani 1975, updated by De Franceschini 1991. The latest discussion is that of MacDonald & Pinto 1995.

63 Boatwright 1987 pp. 118–9 and 152 deals with the alterations of the Palatine. The
   Hadrianic projects in these *horti* are described in Boatwright 1987 p. 155 and
   Lehmann-Hartleben & Lindros 1935 pp. 207–16.

64 S.H.A. *Had.* 6.6 & 19.2. Other Augustan restorations in Hadrianic religion are
   recorded in Beaujeu 1955 pp. 125–7.

65 S.H.A. *Had.* 19.10. The whole list 19.9–11, of which this forms a part, includes
   other restorations of Augustan monuments including the Saepta, Forum
   Augustum, and the Baths of Agrippa. See Boatwright 1987 pp. 33ff.

66 Pais 1979. Toynbee 1934 pp. 1–143 looks at the images of Rome and the provinces
   during Hadrian's reign.

67 Thornton 1975 pp. 433–4 and 443–5.

68 This is Raeder's 1983 catalogue.

69 The images of the Flavian emperors are catalogued in Daltrop 1966. The spread of
   imperial portraiture is considered by Stuart 1939. See also Price 1984 pp. 170–206.

70 The portraits of Hadrian are gathered in Wegner 1956. Zanker 1995 pp. 198–266
   discusses this portrait innovation. Above all, he understands the phenomenon as
   another example of emperors using their position to bring private fantasies into the
   public sphere.

71 For mixed assessments of Hadrian, see Dio 69.23.2–3 and S.H.A. *Had.* 27.

72 Tiberius's absence from Rome was understood as the cause of the descent into
   chaos under the rule of Sejanus. Tacitus *Ann.* 4.40. Similarly, Tiberius could not
   possibly uphold *Romanitas* away from Rome, and his stay on Capri was presented
   as an ongoing orgy of vice – *Ann.* 4.66. Dio 69.7 and S.H.A. *Had.* 8.11, however,
   see Hadrian working with the Senate. His eventual withdrawal is associated with
   illness, but even then he is seen to attend to the problem of succession. S.H.A. *Had.*
   24.11.

73 S.H.A. *Had.* 26.5.

74 Salza Prina Ricotti 1973 and 1982.

75 Juvenal *Sat.*6. 82–4.

76 Strabo 17.1.17a.

77 Stewart 1984 provides a wider anthropological view of the impulse for collecting
   and miniaturising. She refers to such exhibits as allusions (pp. 54 & 136) rather
   than models of the originals, creating a personal world (p. 162) rather than
   duplication of the public world. However, the view of the Canopus as souvenir has
   a wide following. Raeder 1983 pp. 302–3 reviews the possibilities. MacDonald &
   Pinto 1995 p. 197 follow this view, seeing the themes of the Canopus sculptures as
   symptomatic of those of the *villa* as a whole, brought together as a collection
   geared to remembrance.

78 Raeder 1983 p. 300 uses the results of these excavations to try and play down the
   Egyptian elements of the Canopus. See Van Buren 1955 for publication of some of
   those more recent finds.

79 Dio 69.11 believes that Antinous was a sacrifice, S.H.A. *Had.* 14.5, that he was a
   suicide. Paus. 8.97 offers no explanation at all.

80 Meyer 1991 p.186.

81 Kähler 1975 pp. 35–44.

82 Sweet 1973. Raeder 1983 p. 302 records other followers of this idea. Hannestad
   1982 rejects the notion of the Canopus as Serapeum, concentrating entirely on the
   theme of Antinous. He wants to find the obelisk of Antinous here (the obelisk now
   stands on the Pincian Hill, and the ongoing debate of its origins are summarised in
   Derchain 1975). He is refuted in MacDonald & Pinto 1995 pp.108–16.

Boatwright 1987 p.148 points out that the Canopus was built before the tragedy and so cannot be understood as being purpose built.

83 Grenier 1989 pp. 935ff. reconstructs the sculptural content of the Serapeum.

84 Raeder's 1983 discussion of the Ares figure goes further in recognising his nonbelligerent stance pp. 307–9. At pp. 298–315, he sees the whole Canopus as a place of *otium*, celebrating the peace and prosperity of the imperial age.

85 The most comprehensive treatment of these grottoes is found in Lavagne 1988 pp. 513–626.

86 Iacopi 1963. Lavagne 1988 pp. 515–56. Sauron 1991 furnishes his own unique opinion. The views of Stewart 1977 that the Odyssean sculpture reflects the peculiar character of Tiberius are perhaps undermined by the grotto's inclusion in a wider imperial tradition and, of course, the uncertainty of Tiberius's ownership of the grotto.

87 Zevi & Andreae 1982. See also Lavagne 1988 pp. 573–9.

88 Lavagne 1970 and 1988 pp. 579–88. Zander 1958 pp. 54–61. The vault mosaic is described in Sear 1977 p. 92.

89 Balland 1967. Lavagne 1988 pp. 589–94.

90 Saflund 1972 p. 101 sees the Scylla group as a continuation of the sculptural themes of grottoes. Page 37 also notes that a head from the *villa* is a copy of that of the man holding the wineskin in the Sperlonga Polyphemus group, and Raeder 1983 p. 294 fits the Pasquino group copy into the grotto tradition, if not the Canopus. Lavagne 1988 pp. 603–16 links the whole Canopus complex into the tradition but finds that its man-made nature precludes it from actually being a grotto proper.

91 The fullest publication of the Antinous sculpture is found in Meyer 1991. For a description of the portrait type see pp. 231–5.

92 Again, it is not so much the divinisation of Antinous that is unusual but its public nature. A contemporary example of private divinisation is found in Herodes Atticus's memorials for his favourite pupils. See Meyer 1991 pp. 186 and 196. Beaujeu 1955 pp. 168–169 and 240–57 discusses the nature of the cult of Antinous.

93 Intellectually, the Second Sophistic provided the greatest challenge to Rome. See Anderson 1993. Gleason 1995 pp. 131–58 deals with the achievement of manhood, and hence social participation, through speech – a good metonym for the phenomenon of the Second Sophistic.

94 Diocletian's palace at Split would drive the internalisation of the *palatium* to its ultimate expression – a fortress. See Wilkes 1986.

CHAPTER 4

1 Tacitus *Ann.* 14.17; Pliny the Younger *Ep.* 6.16.

2 For an architectural history of Pompeii, see Richardson 1988 and Zanker 1998.

3 For this temple and its renovation, see Richardson 1988 pp. 281–5 and Zanker 1998 pp. 135–6.

4 See, for example, Nielsen 1994 pp. 164–70 on palaces. For the houses of Delos, see Trümper 1998.

5 A good example of the latter would be the House of Sallust. See Richardson 1988 pp. 108–11.

6 Dwyer 1991 argues for the continued popularity of the *atrium* type.

7 Zanker 1998 p. 74.

8 Richardson 1988 pp. 215–16.

9 Richardson 1988 pp. 194–8 and Zanker 1998 pp. 93–102.

10 Again, note Raper's misunderstanding of this phenomenon in Raper in Burnham & Kingsbury 1979.

11 Published in Michel 1990.

12 Spinazzola 1953 p. 151. Pages 127–252 give a report on the decoration of Pompeian façades.

13 Spinazzola 1953 p. 189ff.

14 Richardson 1988 pp. 111–15.

15 Zanker 1998 pp. 40ff.

16 Vitr. *De Arch.* 6.5.2. Those who have used the axial view as their focus of their understanding of circulation around the Pompeian house include Wallace-Hadrill 1994, Bergmann 1994, Bek 1980, Clarke 1991, Drerup 1959, and Jung 1984.

17 Drerup 1959 p. 159 specifically sees the function of the vestibule to be to show off the house from a distance. Jung 1984 p. 75 also settles for this starting point.

18 Homer *Od.* 23.181–204.

19 For the black-and-white figural mosaics of Pompeii, see Clarke 1979. For the preponderence of vestibule mosaics, see pp. 9–11.

20 Mau 1899 p. 16.

21 For a short description of the House of Paquius Proculus, see de Vos & de Vos 1982 pp. 111–12.

22 Clarke 1979 p. 8.

23 Jung 1984 pp. 76 and 78ff. Grahame in Laurence & Wallace-Hadrill 1997 p. 163 notes this effect in the view through the House of the Faun.

24 Jung 1984 p. 83 suggests that the *tablinum* is lost in order to ensure an even source of light to the *atrium* and, hence, the view from the threshold.

25 de Vos & de Vos 1982 p. 130–1.

26 For the Houses of the Fountains, see de Vos & de Vos 1982 pp. 184–6.

27 Jashemski 1993 pp. 135–7.

28 See Moormann 1993 pp. 72–9 and Jashemski 1993 p. 343.

29 Bek 1983 proposes a chronological shift in *triclinium* views whereby the guests first enjoy increasingly extravagent views before they themselves become the viewed. Jung 1984 p. 98 uses the *triclinium* as another example of a privileged viewpoint.

30 For reports of the house in general, see briefly de Vos & de Vos 1982 pp. 138–41 and more fully Spinazzola 1953 pp. 367–434.

31 House of Pansa – Spinazzola 1953 pp. 297–314.

32 Jung 1984 p. 104 asks whether the real picture bestows an air of reality onto the painted or whether their interchangeability implies that they are not to be distinguished between. Jung is here almost at a point of acknowledging fantasy, but declines to make this more explicit.

33 Pliny *Ep.* 5.6.13.

34 Vitr. *De Arch.* 6.2.2.

35 Elsner 1995 p. 86.

36 Bek 1985 p. 140.

37 Parker-Pearson & Richards 1994 p. 2.

38 Lawrence 1987. Bourdieu in Douglas 1973.

39 Clarke 1991 uses wall painting as a guide to the use of the room, Grahame in Laurence & Wallace-Hadrill 1997 uses a method invented by Hillier and Hanson

to plot the levels of access to each room of the house, and Wallace-Hadrill 1994 pp. 17–37 combines both decor and access levels to assess the relative publicness of each room (note criticism of this model by Grahame pp. 136ff). These models are summarised by Ellis 2000 pp. 166–70.

40 Vitr. *De Arch.* 6.7.1–4.

41 Wallace-Hadrill 1994 pp. 3–61 discusses his views on the expression of status in the decor of Pompeian houses.

42 For a discussion of the relationship between slaves and slaveowners see Bradley 1984. On the physical place of slaves in the house see George in Laurence & Wallace-Hadrill 1997.

43 Andersson 1990.

44 Jansen in Bon & Jones 1997.

45 Nepos *Vitae* praef.6–7. Wallace-Hadrill in Kleiner & Matheson 1996 is of the opinion that, in denying the woman a specific space in the house, she becomes invisible. For him, only the *paterfamilias* benefits from the decor of the *domus*.

46 Nevett in Parker-Pearson & Richards 1994.

47 Allison 1993 pp. 4ff. Berry in Laurence & Wallace-Hadrill 1997 pp. 183–95.

48 Leach in Bon & Jones 1997 pp. 50–72. Riggsby 1997 considers literary evidence for the versatility of this room type.

49 Laurence 1994 pp. 122–32 discusses the "temporal logic of space." Lawrence 1987 p. 126 confirms that this is a multicultural phenomenon.

50 For the House of the Silver Wedding, see Richardson 1988 pp. 155–9. For the House of the Labyrinth, see Strocka 1991. The *oecus* is discussed pp. 44–8.

51 For the House of the Menander, see Maiuri 1933, Ling 1983, and Ling 1997. For the conscious integration of *atrium* and *tablinum*, see Clarke 1991 p. 171. The House of the Gilded Cupids is published in Seiler 1992.

52 For the House of the Centenary, see Richardson 1988 pp. 126–7.

53 For a brief guide to the House of the Fruit Orchard, see Richardson 1988 pp. 225–6.

54 de Vos & de Vos 1982 p. 114.

55 Laidlaw 1985 gives an extensive account of First Style decoration in Pompeii. Bruno 1969 p. 306 contends that the first monumental example of this style would be from the end of the fourth century B.C. inside the Hieron at Samothrace.

56 Richardson 1988 p. 107.

57 Richardson 1988 pp. 108–11.

58 De Franciscis in Andreae & Kyrieleis 1975 p. 13 and De Franciscis 1975 pp. 8ff.

59 de Vos & de Vos 1982 pp. 223–4. For the painting, see Ling 1991 p. 158.

60 Wallace-Hadrill 1994 p. 17 believes that all four styles give the house a public feel.

61 Van Buren 1938.

62 Published in Peters 1993. For these paintings see Clarke 1991 pp. 147–51.

63 Mau 1899 pp. 315–34. For the paintings, see Archer 1990 and Wirth 1983.

64 Lehmann 1953.

65 Dickmann in Laurence & Wallace-Hadrill 1997 p. 136 takes this distinction to its limit, proposing that the Greek peristyle was never integrated into the plan of the *domus*.

66 Elsner 1995 pp. 59–67. For the critical reviews, see Kellum 1996 pp. 805–7 (esp. p. 806) and Clarke 1996 pp. 375–80 (esp. pp. 376–7). See, too, George 1998.

67 Grimal 1969 pp. 104ff.

68 The House of the Tragic Poet is published in Mau 1899 pp. 307–14.
69 Lawrence 1987 pp. 162–73.

CHAPTER 5

1 Vitr. *De Arch*.7.5.1–4. See Elsner 1995 pp.51–8. Mau's system first appeared in Overbeck & Mau 1884 pp. 520–31.
2 Archer 1990 p. 123 agrees that "there is a strong measure of finality" about late Fourth Style in Pompeii. For post-Pompeian wall painting, see Clarke 1991 pp. 266–362 and Ling 1991 pp.175–97.
3 Barbet 1985 p. 182 plots the more predominant models. The Fourth Style-painted *alae* of the House of the Vettii provide a good example for such debate because they were painted before earthquake damage affected the room and have clear affinities to the Third Style. Archer 1990 accommodates them by choosing to believe in a number of different Fourth Styles that co-exist (p. 121). Schefold 1957 pp. 152–3, desperate to conserve the chronology, proposes that the paintings were damaged in a second, lesser earthquake.
4 Tybout 2001, however, vehemently defends the more traditional approach.
5 For the Boscotrecase paintings, see Von Blanckenhagen & Alexander 1990 pp. 28ff. The House of the Priest Amandus is described in de Vos & de Vos 1982 pp. 113–4. For the paintings, see Maiuri 1938 pp. 5–12.
6 Lehmann 1953 pp. 82–131.
7 Even Drerup 1959, whose work was seminal in analysing the reality of the domestic view, agrees that such Second Style vistas recreate reality.
8 Vitr. *De Arch*. 7.5.3–4. Ling 1991 pp. 52–5.
9 Trimalchio and Petronius have recently been investigated in Bodel 1994, Bryson 1990 pp. 48–55, Slater 1990, Walsh 1970 pp. 67–140, and Whitehead 1993.
10 Tacitus *Ann*. 16.18–19.
11 Tanner 1979 pp. 52–7 discusses the *Satyrica* specifically as transgression.
12 de Vos & de Vos 1982 pp. 167–74 and Mau 1899 pp. 315–34 give a report on the house. Clarke 1991 p. 208 talks of the "freedmen brothers" and their "nouveau-riche mentality."
13 Pet. *Sat*. 71. This is taken up in Whitehead 1993.
14 Pet. *Sat*. 29. For further discussion see Bodel 1994 and Dumont 1990 pp. 959–81.
15 Pet. *Sat*. 33. & Pet. *Sat*. 36. The significance of fantasy food is discussed in Tanner 1979 p. 55.
16 Contrast the singular *aedis* (or *aedes*) as temple (e.g., Livy. 2.21) and the plural *aedes* as house (e.g., Livy 2.7.11). For the link between *lararium* and Temple of Vesta, see Ferguson 1980 p. 61.
17 Pet. *Sat*. 77.
18 Pet. *Sat*. 60.
19 Pet. *Sat*. 32.
20 Pet. *Sat*. 30. Wiseman 1987 p. 394 suggests that the mounting of the *fasces* as a ship's prow may emulate the *atrium* of Pompey, decorated with trophies of his naval victories. Pliny *N.H*. 35.6.
21 Pet. *Sat*. 44.
22 Pet. *Sat*. 29.
23 The aspirations given expression on the tomb of Trimalchio would seem to bear many affinities with those on real freedman tomb reliefs. See Whitehead 1993.
24 Pet. *Sat*. 42.

25 Pet. *Sat.* 29.

26 Slater 1990 p. 79.

27 Pet. *Sat.*74. See Slater 1990 p. 79.

28 Pet. *Sat.* 29. See Slater 1990 p. 57. For a discussion of the image and its Pompeian counterparts, see Veyne 1963.

29 Pet. *Sat.* 72.

30 Pliny *N.H.* 36.7.48–8.50. Coarelli 1983 studies precisely this aspect of republican homes. For example, the Villa of Lucullus on the Pincian Hill imitated the Praeneste Sanctuary of Fortuna (pp. 201ff).

31 Pet. *Sat.* 77. The lack of architectural detail is proven by the difficulties experienced in re-creating the layout in Bagnani 1954.

32 Pet. *Sat.* 52, 29 & 69.

33 Clarke 1979 p. 10.

34 Clarke 1991 pp. 224–7.

35 Knights 1994 concentrates specifically on the *lararium* as the mediation between living and dead but also considers more general incursions such as the presence of the gods.

36 Maiuri 1938 p. 15.

37 de Vos & de Vos 1982 p. 141. For this painting, see Jashemski 1993 pp. 330–1.

38 Clarke 1991 pp. 98–105. Amongst a huge bibliography, see Henderson in Elsner 1996, Bevenuto 1994, and Fierz-David 1988. Ling 1991 p. 229 offers more information.

39 Spinazzola 1953 pp. 382ff.

40 Maiuri 1933 pp. 89ff.

41 Maiuri 1933 pp. 127–39.

42 Seiler 1992 pp. 37–49.

43 Maiuri 1933 pp. 121–58 describes the bathsuite. This mosaic is discussed on p. 146. See also Clarke 1979 p. 13.

44 Maiuri 1933 pp. 144–5. Clarke 1979 p. 14.

45 A wider discussion of black, apotropaic figures can be found in Clarke in Kampen 1996 pp. 184–98. Dunbabin 1989 discusses the perceived need for apotropaic images in the bathing context.

46 Maiuri 1933 p.57 ff.; de Vos & de Vos 1982 p. 112.

47 Maiuri 1938 pp. 326–7 and Jashemski 1993 pp. 38–41.

48 Clarke 1991 pp. 143–6. de Vos 1980 catalogues the use of Egyptian motifs in early imperial domestic settings.

49 Maiuri 1933 pp.121–58 and 74ff.

50 Michel 1980 pp. 393ff.

51 Jashemski 1979 and 1993.

52 Jashemski 1993 pp. 317–22; Michel 1980 pp. 391ff.

53 The best discussion of *horti* can be found in Purcell 1987. For the Prima Porta paintings, see Gabriel 1955.

54 Grimal 1969 is full of information on the status and function of gardens in Rome. Pages 41–61, which trace the traditions of gardens in Rome, are particularly enlightening on the religious and mythical aura of the garden.

55 Jashemski 1993 pp. 38–41.

56 de Vos & de Vos 1982 pp. 112–13 briefly describe the House of Fabius or Amandus. For the paintings, see Maiuri 1938 pp. 2–3.

57 Jashemski 1993 p. 84. Michel 1980 p. 400 rather sees these paintings as an expression of the pleasures of life.

58 Michel 1980 p. 387.

59 Jashemski 1993 pp. 317–22.

60 Michel 1980 p.391 ff.

61 Those who consider that garden paintings are extensions of real space include Ling 1991 p. 152 and Gabriel 1955 p. 6.

62 The garden sculpture of the House of Marcus Lucretius is discussed in Dwyer 1982 pp. 39–48. For sculpture in the garden of the House of the Silver Wedding, see Jashemski 1993 p. 113.

63 Seiler 1992 pp. 40 and 46; Jashemski 1993 p. 340.

64 Spinazzola 1953 pp. 395–413. Clarke 1991 pp. 198–201.

65 These panels are examined separately in de Vos 1980 pp. 15–21.

66 See Michel 1980 pp. 399 and 382.

67 Dwyer 1982 p. 47.

68 Jashemski 1993 pp. 153–5; Seiler 1992 pp. 117–21. The function and meaning of the sculpture is assessed in Seiler 1992 pp. 131ff. See also Jashemski 1993 pp. 159–64.

69 Michel 1990, including a description of the *viridarium* pp. 52–60. See also Jashemski 1993 pp. 36–7 and 315.

70 Peters 1993 pp. 340–9 and Jashemski 1993 p. 116; Maiuri 1933 p. 74ff. and Jashemski 1993 pp. 323–4.

71 Michel 1980 p. 397 notes this of the animals in the painting in the *xystus* of the House of Romulus and Remus (VII.vii.10) and attributes it to the wish to evoke a *paradeisos* setting.

72 Michel 1980 pp. 395–6 draws attention to parallels between these paintings and images found in public amphitheatres.

73 Jung 1984 p. 108. See Purcell in Cornell & Lomas 1995. Purcell in Shipley and Salmon 1996 reminds us of the role of villas in exploiting the landscape for profit.

74 Gabriel 1955 pp. 6–11; Michel 1980 pp. 378ff.

75 The view of Knights 1994 p. 140 that the peristyle shows respect for the natural order must be questioned.

76 Michel 1980 p. 378. Mielsch 1987 p. 117 sees this as the purpose of *villa* gardens also.

77 de Vos & de Vos 1982 p. 209 give a short description of the house. For a description of the painting, see Michel 1980 pp. 396–7 and Jashemski 1993 pp. 344–5.

78 Seiler 1992 pp. 37–49 publishes the peristyle.

79 Jung 1984 p. 100; Dwyer 1982 pp. 40–1.

80 Oliver 1987 pp. 153–70.

81 This is explicitly the opinion of Knights 1994 p. 116. For background to this theory, see Lawrence 1987 p. 26.

82 At the same time, the ill-defined nature of *Romanitas* allowed Rome to regulate her relationship with her colonies and provinces, able to embrace or distance them as the situation required. Attending the amphitheatre might make the Pompeians seem very Roman in their appreciation of the Italian ritual of gladiatorial combat, but their inability to control themselves as spectators, as in Tacitus's narration of the famous riot of 59 A.D. at *Ann.* 14.17, proved their inferior qualities.

CHAPTER 6

1 Balsdon, 1979 discusses Roman conceptions of their natural superiority.

2 See Thébert 1987 p. 343.

3 The most recent summary of the houses of Petra can be found in McKenzie 1990 pp. 105–8.

4 Brief surveys can be found in McKay 1975 and Ellis 2000.

5 Cicero *Ad. Q. Fr.* 1.1.27.

6 Caesar *De Bell. Gall.* 4.21.

7 Agricola circumnavigates the island at Tacitus *Agric.* 10. In a later speech, *Agric.* 33, he tells his troops that Britain can only be won when her terrain has been fully investigated.

8 Nicolet 1991 pp. 95–122 discusses Agrippa's map and its role in the wider imperial aims of the Principate.

9 The function of the *Res Gestae* in establishing the scope of the empire, is discussed by Nicolet 1991 pp. 15–28.

10 Ovid was supposedly exiled for offending Augustus. Williams 1994 pp. 3–49 argues that Ovid never was exiled and is simply writing generic poetry.

11 Contrast descriptions of Rome – *Trist.* 1.1.69–82 and 1.5.69–70 – with tales of Tomis – *Trist.* 1.1.126–7 and 5.2.63–4.

12 Ovid *Trist.* 5.10.5–10. For his understanding of spring see *Trist.* 3.12.13–28.

13 Ovid *Trist.* 1.3.89, 1.7.38, and 1.8.14. Williams 1994 pp. 12–13 discusses this funerary imagery.

14 Ovid *Trist.* 5.5.29–30.

15 Apuleius *Apol.* 88.2–3.

16 Apuleius *Apol.* 58.4–32.

17 Sidonius *Ep.* 4.8.1. For a reference to the crowded house of Cicero, see Plut. *Cicero* 8.3.

18 Sidonius *Ep.* 4.25.2.

19 Sidonius *Ep.* 8.4.1.

20 Sidonius *Ep.* 2.2. Percival 1997 pp. 279–292 discusses the literary conventions adopted by Sidonius Apollinaris.

21 Varro *De Re Rust.* 1.2.10, 1.13.7, 3.4.2–3, and 3.17.9.

22 A brief guide to the city can be found in Almagro 1957. Keay 1988 pp. 131–6 discusses the *atrium* houses of this and other Spanish colonies.

23 For a brief guide to Vasio, see Goudineau & de Kisch 1984. For some more background on the site, see Rivet 1988 pp. 286–90. Full publication can be found in Sautel 1929 and 1942.

24 Sautel 1942 vol. 1 pp. 134ff records the first finds from and his initial impressions of this house.

25 This was the aim of further excavations carried out by Goudineau 1979.

26 The houses of Glanum are published in Rolland 1946. Rivet 1988 gives a brief history of the city in its local geographical context pp. 196–200. Woolf 1998 pp. 106–41 discusses the urbanisation of Gaul and its part in the process of Romanisation.

27 Sautel 1929 vol. 1 p. 212.

28 Goudineau 1979 pp. 228–30. Sautel 1929 vol. 1 pp. 299ff.

29 Goudineau 1979 pp. 230ff. Sautel 1942 vol. 1 pp. 91ff.

30 Goudineau 1979 p. 228.

31 Bellet 1992 p. 21.

32 Sautel 1942 vol. 1 pp. 125ff.

33 Bellet 1992 pp. 40–50.

34 Woolf 1991 p. 30 advocates the importance of local elites in the process of acculturation. They will only adopt elements of other cultures, which can fulfil some need in their own.

35 Sautel 1929 vol. 1 p. 210.

36 The so-called winged corridor house type is discussed by Rivet 1969 pp. 53–9 and Smith in Todd 1978. I have here referred to this type as the row house, following Smith 1997 pp. 6–9.

37 Ward-Perkins 1938 p. 342 identified a round house under the foundations of the Roman *villa* at Lockleys.

38 For example, the pre-Roman stone, oval houses of Chysauster in Cornwall seem to have been used until the fourth century. See De La Bedoyère 1991 p. 141. For the pervasity of round houses, see Hingley in Mattingley 1997 pp. 81–102 esp. pp. 93ff.

39 Wheeler & Wheeler 1936 and Frere 1983. See also Branigan 1973 pp. 17–32.

40 Toynbee 1964 pp. 29ff discusses this phenomenon. See also Wheeler & Wheeler 1936 p. 6 and 226.

41 See King in Blagg & Millett 1990. The complexities of understanding syncretism as an expression of acculturation are discussed by Webster in Mattingley 1997.

42 For a general introduction to the cult, see Vermaseren 1977. For the Ostia site, see Calza 1946 pp. 183–205 esp. pp. 187–90. The Verulamium site is discussed by Wheeler & Wheeler 1936 pp. 113–20.

43 Beard in Thomas & Humphrey 1994 provides some ideas about how this peripheral cult may have fitted into the centre at Rome.

44 Tacitus, *Agric.* 21.

45 Frere 1983 pp. 244–65.

46 Ins 4 is published in Wheeler & Wheeler 1936 pp. 96–108.

47 Neal 1974 pp. 8–13.

48 Wheeler & Wheeler 1936 p. 85.

49 Wheeler & Wheeler 1936 pp. 86–9.

50 Frere 1983 pp. 237–41.

51 Scott 2000 comes to a similar conclusion in dealing with later British mosaics.

52 For the spread of Roman painting techniques around the empire, see Ling 1991 pp. 168–74. For British paintings, see Davey & Ling 1982.

53 Woolf 1994 pp. 15–16.

54 As Mattingley in Mattingley 1997 observes, the adoption of familiar symbols can often mask "hidden transepts."

55 Smith 1997. His ideas are refuted by Ellis 2000 p. 180.

56 Boxmoor is published by Neal 1976 pp. 53–110. See Smith 1997 p. 50.

57 In fact, such notions of Romanisation as a process of adding a "pure" Roman to a local, barbaric culture are now redundant. Modern theories of acculturation within the Roman empire have begun to accommodate difference and variety in the experience of being Roman. The best discussion of the new thinking can be found in the excellent papers of Mattingley 1997.

58 Wheeler & Wheeler 1936 pp. 93–6.

59 Frere 1983 pp. 161–76.

60 Smith 1997 pp. 172–98 notes this transformation but ascribes it only to the *villas* of late Antiquity.

61 Frere devotes his 1972 volume to this shop *insula*. For the decoration, see pp. 115–7. The social implications of the spread of luxuries is discussed as part of Wallace-Hadrill's statistical analysis of incidences of luxury in Pompeii 1994 pp. 143–74.

62 Painter 1977.

63 Tacitus *Agric.* 21.

64 Tacitus *Agric.* 4. O'Gorman 1994 builds on this idea in her work on Tacitean barbarians, seeing their presentation as being deliberately employed to explore *Romanitas* and the moral state of Rome.

65 See, for instance, Edwards 1999 p. 104.

66 See Yacoub 1996. The themes of African mosaics are discussed by Dunbabin 1978.

67 The most important discussion is Thébert 1987. However, see also Février 1990 pp. 49–71.

68 For a guide to Volubilis, see Thouvenot 1949.

69 The new quarter is fully published by Etienne 1960. The older houses are discussed at length by Jodin 1987. For the Maison de l'Ephebe, see Jodin 1987 pp. 140–1.

70 See, for example, Thébert 1987 p. 332. The Maison aux Travaux d'Hercule is published in Etienne 1960 pp. 30–4.

71 Etienne 1960 pp. 75–7 & 77–9.

72 Etienne 1960 pp. 50–4.

73 Etienne 1960 pp. 34–8 & pp. 44–6.

74 Etienne 1960 pp. 46–48.

75 For the Maison au Bacchus de Marbre, see Etienne 1960 pp. 54–6.

76 Etienne 1960 pp. 86–8.

77 Etienne 1960 pp. 68–70.

78 See Lancel et al. in Pedley 1980.

79 For the hellenisation of Carthaginian homes during the second century B.C., see Lancel 1995 pp. 134–92 and Pedley 1980 pp. 13–23.

80 For a brief explanation of Cato's involvement with Utica, see Lézine 1970 pp. 29–31.

81 Sidonius *Carm.* 7. 6–7, 501–3.

82 Woolf 1994 p. 136.

CHAPTER 7

1 For Greek influences on Italy, see Boardman 1994 pp. 225–91.

2 Discussions of the process of acculturation between East and West can be found in Jones 1963. See also Woolf 1994 and Alcock 1997.

3 Vitr. *De Arch.* 6.7.1–4.

4 Nevett 1999 pp.154–5.

5 This distinction survived until late Antiquity. See Amm. Mar. 31.2.16–18.

6 Nielsen 1994 pp. 164–70.

7 Vitr. *De Arch.* 6.7.5.

8 Millett in Alcock 1997 briefly discusses the artificial nature of dividing the empire into East and West.

9 Gawlikowski in Alcock 1997 and Tate in Alcock 1997.

10 See, for example, Schmidt-Colinet in Alcock 1997.

11 Hopkins 1979 and Rostovtzeff 1938.

12 Browning 1980. The most recent summary of the houses can be found in McKenzie 1990 pp. 105–8.

13 Diodorus Siculus 19.94.2–3.

14 Bejor 1999 explores the fashion for colonnaded streets in the East.

15 See Alston in Laurence & Wallace-Hadrill 1997.

16 An extensive history of the city is given by Downey 1961.

17 The Seleucid empire's appropriation of Hellenistic art is recorded in Smith 1991 pp. 223–8.

18 Downey 1961 pp. 97–103.

19 Amm. Mar. 22.9–14, 25.10, and 29.1–2. Liebeschuetz 1972 discusses how city and imperial administration intersected in this period.

20 Plutarch *Cato the Younger* 13.

21 Julian *Misop.* passim; John Chrys. *Hom. ad Pop. Ant.* 2.16–18, 15.11, 18.13, and 19.2.

22 The houses of Antioch are published in Levi 1947 and Stillwell 1961.

23 Stillwell 1961 pp. 45–48.

24 Joyce 1979 pp. 253–63 and Dunbabin 1999 pp.5–268 look at regional developments within mosaic craftsmanship.

25 For a description of the mosaics of the House of the Triumph of Dionysus, see Levi 1947 pp. 91–104.

26 Levi 1947 pp. 36–40.

27 The wide-reaching powers of Dionysus in both Greece and Italy are discussed in Carpenter & Faraone 1993. Kondoleon 1995 pp. 231–269 traces the spread of the iconography across the empire.

28 The association of Hellenistic kings with Dionysus is probably most famously verified by the processions of the Ptolemies in Alexandria. See Athen. 5.201.

29 See Levi 1947 pp. 211–14 and pp.16–21, respectively.

30 Levi 1947 pp. 109–10.

31 Levi 1947 pp. 326–37.

32 Levi 1947 pp. 204–11.

33 See Meeks & Wilken 1978 on how these groups interacted.

34 Smith in Lane 1996. Elsner in Alcock 1997 discusses the eastern iconography of the goddess.

35 Strabo *Geog.* 14.1.21; *IE* 26.1–6. See Rogers 1991 p. 99.

36 The results of excavation in Ephesus can be found in Wiplinger & Wlach 1996 and Hueber 1997.

37 Rogers 1991 discusses how successive parts of Ephesian history were brought together by religious ritual. See pp. 80–126 for the procession of statues. He concludes that the procession was a way of asserting the city's links with Artemis and Greece over her Roman heritage.

38 Foss 1979 p. 23.

39 Amm. Mar. 29.1.

40 Van Bremen 1996 pp. 156–70.

41 Nevett 1999 pp. 107–16.

42 The architectural history of Hanghaus 1 is published in Lang-Auinger 1996. The mosaic and painted decoration of Hanghaus 2, houses 1–5 is published in Jobst 1977 and Strocka 1977, respectively. The series *Forschungen in Ephesos* is yet to publish the full architectural report of Hanghaus 2.

43 Rogers 1991 pp. 80–126.

44 For the decoration of House 2.1, see Jobst 1977 pp. 38–54 and Strocka 1977 pp. 43–69.

45 For the decoration of Hanghaus 2.2, see Jobst 1977 pp. 55–95 and Strocka 1977 pp. 69–91.

46 The *domus* is published in Lang-Auinger 1996 pp. 92–101.

47 For the decoration of House 2.5, see Jobst 1977 pp. 107–11 and Strocka 1977 pp. 115–37.

48 The decoration of House 2.3 is published in Jobst 1977 pp. 96–106 and Strocka 1977 pp. 115–37.

49 1.3 is published in Lang-Auinger 1996 pp. 151–74.

50 Thébert 1987 p. 334. See Ellis 1988 and also Ellis in Gazda 1991.

51 Ellis 1988 sees such subdivision as an empire-wide phenomenon during late Antiquity.

52 Pliny *N.H.* 36.7.48–8.50 and 36.24.109 offers some examples of such behaviour in Rome.

53 Dunbabin 1999 p. 225.

54 See, for example, Erdemgil 1987 p. 59.

55 Clarke 1991 p. 219.

56 These finds are all briefly described in Erdemgil 1987 pp. 54–63.

57 Strocka 1977 p. 94 dates the painting of the niche to the early fifth century.

58 Erdemgil 1987 p. 60.

59 Elsner in Alcock 1997 specifically understands the Ephesian Artemis as an icon of eastern superiority over the west, a symbol of resistance to Roman rule pp. 184–91.

60 Ovid *Met.* 1.548ff.

61 Foss 1979 explores the changes overtaking Ephesus from late Antiquity onward. Pages 46–95 chart the architectural features of the city during late Antiquity.

62 Lang-Auinger 1996 pp.145–7.

63 Foss 1979 pp. 60–1.

64 Scott in Laurence & Wallace-Hadrill 1997 suggests that carefully chosen images were used to impress guests but also as a symbolic language confined to the elite as a sign of status.

65 See Reisch 1932 p. 77.

66 John Chrys. *Hom. ad Pop. Ant.* 17.9.

67 John Chrys. *Hom. ad Pop. Ant.* 3.3, 14.16, and 17.10.

68 *Codex Theod.* 15.1.39.

69 Bejor 1999 pp.106–10 sees this change as a widespread and long-lived phenomenon. Many colonnaded streets became souks under Arab inhabitation.

70 Libanius *Or.* 1.108, 1.183, 1.246; John Chrys. *Hom. ad Pop. Ant.* 14.15.

71 Reisch 1932 pp. 77–8. Fasolo 1956. Foss 1979 p. 52.

72 Palladius, *Dialogus* 13.

73 *Acta Conciliorum Oecumenicorum* 1.i.v.14.

74 *Acta Conciliorum Oecumicorum* 1.i.i.118. Both of these stories are retold by Foss 1979 pp. 38–9.

75 Amm. Mar. 14.7 tells of the burning of the house of Eubulus. Libanius *Or.*1.1 records a similar attack on the house of Candidus.

76 Foss 1979 p. 51. Miltner 1958 pp.115–18 but note review by Müller-Wiener 1960.

77 Carandini 1982 pp.194–230.

78 Aurigemma 1961 pp.154–62, De Franceschini 1991 pp. 463–77. A more in-depth study can be found in Hansen 1960.

79 Wilson 1983 pp.75–85 cites the similarities between these *villas* and Piazza Armerina. The full reports can be found in Ghislanzoni 1962 and Fouet 1978.

80 Lavin 1963.

81 Levi 1947 pp. 359–63.

82 Ellis 1988 is strongly of the opinion that an imperial super-elite emerged during late Antiquity who finally rendered some elements of private space wholly public. It is worth noting, however, that the sources he draws on are reusing old *topoi* concerning houses as much as they are commenting on the contemporary situation. Olympiodoros *Histories* Frg 41, for instance, is certainly not the first to

suggest that elite homes are like cities, and Sidonius is not innovative in depicting the dinner party parasite.

83 Libanius *Or.*1.119 & 1.3.
84 Aelius Aristides *Or.* 26.
85 Aelius Aristides *Or.* 26.102.
86 Contrast Amm. Mar. 16.10 with 14.6 and 28.4.
87 Swain 1996 pp.27–42.
88 Gleason 1995 pp.3–20.

EPILOGUE

1 Douglas 1966 p. 162 quoted in Parker-Pearson & Richards 1994 p. 26.

Bibliography

Alcock, S. ed. *The Early Roman Empire in the East* (Oxford) 1997

Alexander, M. & Ennaifer, M. *Corpus des Mosaïques de Tunisie* fasc.1–3 (Tunis) 1973, 1974

Allen, W. "Cicero's House and Libertas" *TAPhA* 75 1944 pp.1–9

Allison, P. "How Do We Identify the Use of Space in Roman Housing?" in Moorman 1993 pp. 1–8

Almagro, M. *Merida* (Madrid) 1957

Alston, R. "Houses and Households in Roman Egypt" in Laurence & Wallace-Hadrill 1997 pp. 23–39

Anderson, G. *The Second Sophistic: A Cultural Phenomenon in the Roman Empire* (London) 1993

Anderson, J. *Hunting in the Ancient World* (Berkeley, Calif.) 1985

Andersson, E. "Fountains and the Roman Dwelling. Casa del Torello in Pompei" *JDAI* 105 1990 pp. 207–36

Andreae, B. & Kyrieleis, H. ed. *Neue Forschungen in Pompeji* (Recklinghausen) 1975

Archer, W. "The Paintings in the Alae of the Casa dei Vettii and a Definition of the Fourth Pompeian Style" *AJA* 94 1990 pp. 95–123

Aurigemma, S. *Villa Adriana* (Rome) 1961

Bagnani, G. "The House of Trimalchio" *AJPh* 75 1954 pp. 16–39

Ball, L. "A Reappraisal of Nero's Domus Aurea" in La Follette, L. et al. *Rome Papers: The Baths of Trajan Decius etc.* JRS Supp. Ser. 11 (Ann Arbor, Mich.) 1994 pp. 183–229

Balland, A. "Une transposition de la grotte de Tibère à Sperlonga" *MEFRA* 79 1967 pp. 421–502

Balsdon, J. *Life and Leisure in Ancient Rome* (London) 1969

Balsdon, J. *Romans and Aliens* (London) 1979

Barbet, A. *La peinture murale romaine: les styles décoratifs pompéiens* (Paris) 1985

Barrett, A. *Caligula: The Corruption of Power* (London) 1989

Bartmann, E. "Sculptural Collecting and Display" in Gazda 1991

Bartsch, S. *Actors in the Audience – Theatricality and Doublespeak from Nero to Hadrian* (Cambridge, Mass.) 1994

Beagon, M. *Roman Nature: The Thoughts of Pliny the Elder* (Oxford) 1992

Beard, M. "The Roman and the Foreign: The Cult of the Great Mother in Imperial Rome" in N. Thomas & C. Humphrey eds. *Shamanism, History and the State* (Ann Arbor, Mich.) 1994 pp. 164–90

Beaujeu, J. *La religion romaine a l'apogée de l'Empire. Vol.1 La politique religieuse des Antonins* (Paris) 1955

Bejor, G. *Vie Colonnate. Paesaggi Urbani del Mondo Antico* RdA Supp. 22 (Rome) 1999

Bek, L. *Towards Paradise on Earth: Modern Space Conception in Architecture: A Creation of Renaissance Humanism* ARID Supp. 9 (Rome) 1980

"Questiones Conviviales: The Idea of the Triclinium and the Staging of Convivial Ceremony from Rome to Byzantium" *ARID* 12 1983 pp. 81–108

"Venusta Species: A Hellenistic Rhetorical Concept as the Aesthetic Principle in Roman Townscape" *ARID* 14 1985 pp. 139–48

Bell, C. *Ritual Theory, Ritual Practice* (New York) 1992

Bellet, M-É. *Recherches Archéologique Récentes à Vaison-la-Romaine et aux environs* (Avignon) 1992

Belting, H. *Likeness and Presence: A History of the Image Before the Era of Art* (Chicago) 1994

Benvenuto, B. *The Rites of Psychoanalysis or The Villa of Mysteries* (Cambridge) 1994

Bergmann, B. "Roman House as Memory Theatre: House of the Tragic Poet" *Art Bulletin* 76 1994 pp. 223–56

Berry, J. "Household Artefacts: Towards a Re-interpretation of Roman Domestic Space" in Laurence & Wallace-Hadrill 1997 pp. 183–95

Beyen, H. "The Wall Decoration of the Cubiculum of the Villa of P. Fannius Synistor near Boscoreale in its Relation to Ancient Stage Painting" *Mnemosyne* Ser. 4 10 1957 pp.147–53

Bieber, M. *Ancient Copies – Contributions to the History of Greek and Roman Art* (New York) 1977

Blagg, T. & Millett, M. ed. *The Early Roman Empire in the West* (Oxford) 1990

Bloch, M. *Ritual, History and Power: Selected Papers in Anthropology* (London) 1989

Boardman, J. *The Diffusion of Classical Art in Antiquity* (London) 1994

Boatwright, M. *Hadrian and the City of Rome* (Princeton, N.J.) 1987

Bodel, J. "Trimalchio's Underworld" in Tatum, J. ed. *The Search For the Ancient Novel* (Baltimore) 1994 pp. 237–59

Böethius, A. "Nero's Golden House" *Eranos* 44 1946 pp. 442–59
The Golden House of Nero (Ann Arbor, Mich.) 1960
& Ward-Perkins, J. *Etruscan and Roman Architecture* (Harmondsworth) 1970

Bon, S. & Jones. R., eds. *Sequence and Space in Pompeii* (Oxford) 1997

Boschung, D. *Die Bildnisse des Augustus* Das römische Herrscherbild 1.2 (Berlin) 1993

Bourdieu, P. "The Berber House or the World Reversed" in M. Douglas ed. *Rules and Meanings* (Harmondsworth) 1973 pp. 98–110

Bradley, K. *Slaves and Masters in the Roman Empire* (New York) 1984

Branigan, K. *Town and Country: The Architecture of Verulamium and the Roman Chilterns* (Bourne End) 1973

Browning, I. *Petra* (London) 1980

Bruno, V. "Antecedents of the Pompeian First Style" *AJA* 73 1969 pp. 305–17

Bryson, N. *Looking at the Overlooked* (London) 1990

Calza, G. "Il Santuario della Magna Mater a Ostia" *Mem.Pont.Acc.Rom.* 6 1946 pp. 181–205

Carandini, A. *Filosofiana, la villa di Piazza Armerina* (Palermo) 1982

Carettoni, G., ed. *La Pianta Marmorea di Roma Antica* (Rome) 1960

Das Haus des Augustus auf dem Palatin (Mainz) 1983

Carpenter, T. & Faraone, C. *Masks of Dionysus* (Ithaca, N.Y.) 1993

Carter, E., Donald, J. & Squires, J. eds. *Space and Place: Theories of Identity and Location* (London) 1993

Castrén, P. *Ordo Populusque Pompeianus: Polity and Society in Roman Pompeii* (Rome) 1975

Cima, M. & La Rocca, E. *Le tranquille dimore degli Dei – la Residenza Imperiale degli Horti Lamiani* (Venice) 1986

Clarke, J. *Roman Black & White Figural Mosaics* (New York) 1979

"The Early Third Style at the Villa of Oplontis" *RM* 94 1987 pp. 267–94

The Houses of Roman Italy 100BC–AD250: Ritual, Space and Decoration (Berkeley) 1991

"Hypersexual Black Men in Augustan Baths: Ideal Somatotypes and Apotropaic Magic" in Kampen 1996 pp. 184–98

"Deconstructing Roman Texts, Viewers and Art" *JRA* 9 1996 pp. 375–80

Clarke, M. *Rhetoric at Rome: A Historical Survey* rev. ed. D. Berry (London) 1996

Coarelli, F. "Architettura sacra e architettura privata nella tarda republica" in *Architecture et société* Collection de l'Ecole française de Rome 66 1983 pp. 191–217

Cornell, T. & Lomas, K. eds. *Urban Society in Roman Italy* (London) 1995

Dacos, N. "Fabullus et l'autre peintre de la Domus Aurea" *Dialoghi di Archaeologia* 2 1968 pp. 210–26

Daltrop, G. *Die Flavier* Das römische Herrscherbild 2.1 (Berlin) 1966

Davey, N. & Ling, R. *Wall Painting in Roman Britain* Britannia Monograph Ser. 3 (London) 1982

De Franceschini, M. *Villa Adriana: mosaici, pavimenti, edifici* (Rome) 1991

De Franciscis, A. *The Pompeian Wall Paintings in the Roman Villa of Oplontis* (Recklinghausen) 1975

"La villa romana di Oplontis" in Andreae & Kyrieleis 1975 pp. 9–17

De La Bedoyère, G. *The Buildings of Roman Britain* (London) 1991

Derchain, P. "A propos de l'obelisque d'Antinous" in J. Bingen, G. Cambier & G. Nachtergael eds. *Le Monde Grec. Hommages à C. Preaux* (Brussels) 1975 pp. 808–12

Dickmann, J-A. "The Peristyle and the Transformation of Domestic Space in Hellenistic Pompeii" in Laurence & Wallace-Hadrill 1997 pp. 121–36

Dixon, S. *The Roman Family* (Baltimore) 1992

Donley-Reid, L. "A Structuring Structure: The Swahili House" in Kent 1990 pp. 114–26

Douglas, M. *Purity and Danger: An Analysis of the Concepts of Pollution and Taboo* (London) 1966

Downey, G. *A History of Antioch in Syria from Seleucus to the Arab Conquest* (Princeton, N.J.) 1961

Douglas, M. & Isherwood, B. *The World of Goods: Towards an Anthropology of Consumption* (London) 1979

Drerup, H. "Bildraum und Realraum in der römischen Architektur" *RM* 66 1959 pp. 147–74

Dunbabin, K. *Mosaics of the Greek and Roman World* (Cambridge) 1999

The Mosaics of Roman North Africa: Studies in Iconography and Patronage (Oxford) 1978

"*Baiarum Grata Voluptas*: Pleasures and Dangers of the Baths" *PBSR* 57 1989 pp. 33–43

Dwyer, E. *Pompeian Domestic Sculpture: A Study of Five Pompeian Houses and Their Contents* (Rome) 1982

"Pompeian Atrium House in Theory and Practice" in Gazda 1991 pp. 25–48

Edwards, C. *The Politics of Immorality in Ancient Rome* (Cambridge) 1993

"Beware of Imitations: Theatre and the Subversion of Imperial Identity" in Elsner & Masters 1994

ed. *Roman Presences* (Cambridge) 1999 p. 104

Ellis, S. "The End of the Roman House" *AJA* 92 1988 pp. 565–76

"Power, Architecture and Decor: How the Late Roman Aristocrat Appeared to His Guests" in Gazda 1991 pp. 117–34

Roman Housing (London) 2000

Elsner, J. "Constructing Decadence. The Representation of Nero as Imperial Builder" in Elsner & Masters 1994 pp. 112–27

Art and the Roman Viewer: The Transformation of Art from the Pagan World to Christianity (Cambridge) 1995

ed. *Art and Text in Roman Culture* (Cambridge) 1996

"The Origins of the Icon: Pilgrimage, Religion and Visual Culture in the Roman East as 'Resistance' to the Centre" in Alcock 1997 pp. 178–99

J. & Masters, J. eds. *Reflections on Nero* (London) 1994

Erdemgil, S. et al. *The Terrace Houses in Ephesus* (Istanbul) 1987

Erim, K. *Aphrodisias: City of Venus* (London) 1986

Etienne, R. *Le quartier nord-est de Volubilis* (Paris) 1960

Fabbrini, L. "Domus Aurea: il piano superiore del quartiere orientale" *Mem.Pont. Acc.Arch.* 14 1982 pp. 5–24

Fabbrini, L. "I corpi edilizi che condizionarono l'attuazione del projetto del Palazzo Esquilino di Nerone" *Rend.Pont.Acc.Arch.* 58 1986 pp. 129–79

Fasolo, F. "La Basilica del concilio di Efeso" *Palladio* 6 1956 pp. 1–30

Favro, D. *The Urban Image of Augustan Rome* (Cambridge) 1996

Ferguson, J. *Greek and Roman Religion – A Sourcebook* (Park Ridge, N.J.) 1980

Février, P-A. *Approches du Maghreb Romain* vol. 2 (Aix-en-Provence) 1990

Fierz-David, L. *Women's Dionysiac Initiation: The Villa of the Mysteries in Pompeii* (Dallas, Tex.) 1988

Finsen, H. *Domus Flavia sur le Palatin; Aula Regia–Basilica ARID* Supp. 2 1962

La Résidence de Domitien sur le Palatin ARID Supp. 5 1969

Flower, H. *Ancestor Masks and Aristocratic Power in Roman Culture* (Oxford) 1996

Foss, C. *Ephesus after Antiquity: A Late Antique, Byzantine and Turkish City* (Cambridge) 1979

Foss, P. "Watchful Lares: Roman Household Organization and the Rituals of Cooking and Eating" in Laurence & Wallace-Hadrill 1997 pp. 196–218

Fouet, G. "La villa gallo-romaine de Valentine (Haute Gauronne). Aperçu préliminaire" *Revue des Comminges* 91 1978 pp. 145–57

Frere, S. *Verulamium Excavations vol. 1* (London) 1972

Verulamium Excavations vol. 2 (London) 1983

Frézouls, E. "Les Julio-Claudiens et la *Palatium*" in Lévy 1987 pp. 445–62

Gawlikowski, M. "The Syrian Desert under the Romans" in Alcock 1997 pp. 37–54

Gabriel, M. *Livia's Garden Room at Prima Porta* (New York) 1955

Galinsky, K. *Augustan Culture: An Interpretative Introduction* (Princeton, N.J.) 1996

Gazda, E. ed. *Roman Art in the Private Sphere* (Ann Arbor, Mich.) 1991

Geertz, C. *The Interpretation of Cultures: Selected Essays* (New York) 1973

George, M. "Servus and Domus: The Slave in the Roman House" in Laurence & Wallace-Hadrill 1997 pp. 15–24

George, M. "Elements of the Peristyle in Campanian Atria" *JRA* 11 1998 pp. 82–100

Ghislanzoni, E. *La villa romana in Desenzano* (Milan) 1962

Giuliani, C. "Il lato nord ouest della Piazza D'Oro" in *Ricerche sull'Architettura di Villa Adriana* Quaderni dell'Istituto di Topografia Antica della Université di Roma 8 (Rome) 1975 pp. 3–53

   "Domus Flavia: una nuova lettura" *RM*, Abteilung 84 1977 pp. 91–106

Gleason, M. *Making Men – Sophists and Self-Presentation in Ancient Greece* (Princeton, N.J.) 1995

Gold, B. *Literacy and Patronage in Ancient Rome* (Austin, Tex.) 1982

Gordon, A. *Illustrated Introduction to Latin Epigraphy* (Berkeley, Calif.) 1983

Goudineau, C. *Les Fouilles du Maison au Dauphin* (Paris) 1979
   & de Kisch, Y. *Vaison la Romaine* (Vaison) 1984

Grahame, M. "Public and Private in the Roman House: the Spatial Order of the Casa del Fauno" in Laurence & Wallace-Hadrill 1997 pp. 137–64

Grenier, J-C. "La décoration statuaire du 'Serapeum' du 'Canope' de la Villa Adriana" *MEFRA* 101 1989 pp. 925–1019

Griffin, J. "The Fourth *Georgic*, Virgil and Rome" in I. McAuslan & P. Walcot eds. *Virgil* (Oxford) 1990

Griffin, M. *Nero: The End of a Dynasty* (London) 1984

Grimal, P. *Les jardins romains à la fin de la République et aux premiers siècles de l'Empire* (Paris) 1969

Gruen, E. *Culture and Identity in Republican Rome* (London) 1992

Hales, S. "At Home with Cicero" *G&R* 47 2000 pp. 44–55

Hannestad, N. "Uber das Grabmal des Antinoos" *ARID* 11 1982 pp. 69–108

Hansen, E. *La Piazza d'Oro e la sua Cupola ARID* Supp. 1 1960

Hemsoll, D. "The Architecture of Nero's Golden House" in M. Henig ed. *Architecture and Architectural Sculpture in the Roman Empire* (Oxford) 1990 pp. 10–33

Henderson, J. "Footnote: Representation in the Villa of the Mysteries" in Elsner 1996 pp. 235–76

Hingley, R. "Domestic Organisation and Gender Relations in Iron Age and Romano-British Households" in R. Samson ed. *The Social Archaeology of Houses* (Edinburgh) 1990 pp. 125–48

   "Resistance and Domination: Social Change in Roman Britain" in Mattingley 1997 pp. 81–102

Hobsbawm, E. & Ranger, T. eds. *The Invention of Tradition* (Cambridge) 1983

Hope, V. "A Roof over the Dead: Communal Tombs and Family Structure" in Laurence & Wallace-Hadrill 1997 pp. 69–88

Hopkins, K. *Conquerors and Slaves* (Cambridge) 1978

Hopkins, C. *The Discovery of Dura Europas* (New Haven, Conn.) 1979

Hueber, F. *Ephesos, Gebaute Gesehiechte* (Mainz) 1997

Iacopi, G. *L'antro di Tiberio a Sperlonga* (Rome) 1963

Isager, J. *Pliny on Art and Society: The Elder Pliny's Chapters on the History of Art* (London) 1991

Jameson, M. "Domestic Space in the Greek City" in Kent 1990 pp. 92–113

Jansen, G. "Private Toilets at Pompeii: Appearance and Operation" in Bon & Jones 1997 pp. 121–34

Jashemski, W. *The Gardens of Pompeii* (New Rochelle, N.Y.) 1979

Jashemski, W. *The Gardens of Pompeii v. 2 Appendices* (New Rochelle, N.Y.) 1993

Jobst, W. *Römischen Mosaiken aus Ephesos 1. Die Hanghäuser des Embolos*. FiE 8/2 (Vienna) 1977

Jodin, A. *Volubilis Regna Iubae* (Paris) 1987

Jones, A. H. M. "The Greeks under the Romans" *DOP* 17b 1963 pp. 3–19

Joyce, H. "Form, Function and Technique in the Pavements of Delos and Pompeii" *AJA* 83 1979 pp. 253–63

Jung, F. "Gebaute Bilder" *Antike Kunst* 27 1984 pp. 71–122

Kähler, H. "Zur Herkunft des Antinousobelisken" *AAAH* 6 1975 pp. 35–44

Kajanto, I. *The Latin Cognomina* (Helsinki) 1965

Kampen, N. ed. *Sexuality in Ancient Art* (Cambridge) 1996

Keaveney, A. *Lucullus: A Life* (London) 1992

Keay, S. *Roman Spain* (London) 1988

Kellum, B. Review of Elsner 1995 *AJA* 100 1996 pp. 805–7

Kent, S. *Domestic Architecture and the Use of Space: An Interdisciplinary Cross-Cultural Study* (Cambridge) 1990

King, A. "The Emergence of Romano-Celtic Religion" in Blagg & Millett 1990 pp. 220–38

Kleiner, D. *Roman Sculpture* (New Haven, Conn.) 1992

Knights, C. "The Spatiality of the Roman Domestic Setting: An Interpretation of Symbolic Content" in Parker-Pearson & Richards 1994 pp. 113–46

Kondoleon, C. *Domestic and Divine: Roman Mosaics in the House of Dionysos* (Ithaca, N.Y.) 1995

Krause, C. *Domus Tiberiana: nuove ricerche* (Zurich) 1985

Laidlaw, A. *The First Style in Pompeii: Painting and Architecture* (Rome) 1985

Lancel, S., Robine, G. & Thiulker, J-P. "Town Planning and Domestic Architecture of the Early Second Century BC on the Byrsa, Carthage" in Pedley 1980 pp. 13–23

Lancel, S. *Carthage: A History* (Oxford) 1995

Lang-Auinger, C. *Hanghaus 1 in Ephesos: Die Baubefund* FiE 8/3 (Vienna) 1996

Laurence, R. "Emperors, Nature & the City" *Accordia Research Papers* 4 1993 pp. 79–87

Laurence, R. *Roman Pompeii: Space and Society* (London) 1994

Laurence, R. "Space and Text" in Laurence & Wallace-Hadrill 1997 pp. 7–14
  & Wallace-Hadrill, A. eds. *Domestic Space in the Roman World: Pompeii and Beyond* JRA Supp. Ser. 22 (Portsmouth) 1997

Lavagne, H. "Le nymphée au Polyphème de la Domus Aurea" *MEFRA* 82 1970 pp. 673–722
  Operosa Antra (Rome) 1988

Lavin, I. "The Hunting Mosaics of Antioch and their Sources" *DOP* 17 1963 pp. 179–286

Lawrence, R. *Houses, Dwellings and Homes: Design Theory, Research and Practice* (Chichester) 1987

Leach, E. "Sacral-idyllic Landscape Painting & the Poems of Tibullus's First Book" *Latomus* 39 1980 pp. 47–69
  The Rhetoric of Space (Princeton, N.J.) 1988
  "Occus on Ibycus: Investigating the Vocabulary of the Roman House" in Bon & Jones 1997 pp. 50–72

Leach, L. "The Politics of Self-Representation – Pliny's Letters and Roman Portrait Sculpture" *Classical Antiquity* 90 1990 pp. 14–39

Lehmann, P. *Roman Wall Paintings from Boscoreale in the Metropolitan Museum of Art* (Cambridge, Mass.) 1953

Lehmann-Hartleben, K. & Lindros, J. "Il Palazzo degli Orti Sallustiani" *Opuscula Archaeologia* 1 1935 pp. 196–227

Levi, D. *Antioch Mosaic Pavements* 2 vols. (Princeton, N.J.) 1947

Lévy, E. ed. *Le système palatial en Orient, en Grèce et à Rome* (Leiden) 1987

Lézine, A. *Utique* (Tunis) 1970

Liebeschuetz, J. H. W. G. *Antioch and Imperial Administration in the Later Roman Empire* (Oxford) 1972

Ling, R. "Studius & the Beginnings of Roman Landscape Painting" *JRS* 67 1977 pp. 1–16

   "The Insula of the Menander at Pompeii: An Interim Report" *AntJ* 63 1983 pp. 34–57

   "The Architecture of Pompeii" *JRA* 4 1991 pp. 248–56

   Roman Painting (Cambridge) 1991

   The Insula of the House of the Menander at Pompeii vol. 1 – The Structure (Oxford) 1997

Little, A. *Roman Perspective Painting & the Ancient Stage* (Kennebunk) 1971

L'Orange, H. *Studies in the Iconography of Cosmic Kingship in the Ancient World* (Oslo) 1953

MacCormack, S. *Art and Ceremony in Late Antiquity* (Berkeley, Calif.) 1981

MacDonald, W. *The Architecture of the Roman Empire vol. 1* (New Haven, Conn.) 1965

MacDonald, W. & Pinto, J. *Hadrian's Villa and its Legacy* (New Haven, Conn.) 1995

MacDougall, E. ed. *Ancient Roman Villa Gardens* (Washington, D.C.) 1987

McKay, A. *Houses, Villas and Palaces in the Roman World* (London) 1975

   Vitruvius: Architect and Engineer (London) 1978

McKenzie, J. *The Architecture of Petra* (Oxford) 1990

   La Casa del Menandro e il suo tesoro di argentaria 2 vols. (Rome) 1933

   Le pitture delle Case di M. Fabius Amandio del Sacerdos Amandus e di P. Cornelius Teges Monumenti della pittura antica scoperti in Italia, sec. 3, Pompei fasc. 2 (Rome) 1938

Marrou, H. *A History of Education in Antiquity* (Madison, Wis.) 1956

Mattingley, D. "Dialogues of Power and Experience in the Roman Empire" in Mattingley 1997 pp. 7–26

Mattingley, D. ed. *Dialogues in Roman Imperialism* JRA Supp. 23 (Portsmouth) 1997

Mattingly, H. "The Roman 'Virtues'" *HThR* 30 1937 pp. 103 ff.

Mau, A. *Die Geschichte der dekorativen Wandmalerei in Pompeji* (Liepzig) 1882

Mau, A. *Pompeii: Its Life and Art* (New York) 1899

Mazzoleni, D. "The City and the Imaginary" in Carter, Donald & Squires 1993 pp. 285–301

Meeks, W. & Wilken, R. *Jews and Christians in Antioch* (Ann Arbor, Mich.) 1978

Meyboom, P. *The Nile Mosaic of Palestrina* (Leiden) 1995

Meyer, H. *Antinoos* (Munich) 1991

Michel, D. "Pompejanische Gartenmalerei" in Cahn, H. & Simon, E. ed. *Taenia: Festschrift für Roland Hampe* (Mainz) 1980 pp. 373–404

Michel, D. *Casa dei Cei Häuser der Pompeji Band 3* (Munich) 1990

Mielsch, H. *Die römische Villa: Architektur und Lebensform* (Munich) 1987

Miles, D. *Forbidden Pleasures* (PhD Thesis – London) 1987

   "A View from the West in Alcock 1997 pp. 200–2

Miltner, F. *Ephesos. Stadt der Artemis und des Johannes* (Vienna) 1958 pp. 115–18

Mitchell, T. *Cicero, the Senior Statesman* (New Haven, Conn.) 1991

Moorman, E. ed. *Functional & Spatial Analysis of Wall Painting* BABesch Supp. 3 (Leiden) 1993

Morford, M. "The Distortion of the Domus Aurea Tradition" *Eranos* 66 1968 pp. 158–79

Müller-Wiener Review of Miltner 1958 *Gnomon* 32 1960 pp. 722–5

Nappo, S. "Urban Transformation at Pompeii in the Late Third Century and Early Second Century BC" in Laurence & Wallace-Hadrill 1997 pp. 91–120

Neal, D. *The Excavation of the Roman Villa in Gadebridge Park, Hemel Hempstead 1963–8* (London) 1974

"Northchurch, Boxmoor and Hemel Hempstead Station" *Herts.Arch.* 4 1976 pp. 53–110

Neudecker, R. *Die Skulpturen-Ausstattung römischen Villen in Italien* (Mainz) 1988

Nevett, L. "Separation or Seclusion? Towards an Archaeological Approach to Investigating Women in the Greek Household in the Fifth to Third Century BC" in Parker-Pearson & Richards 1994 pp. 98–112

Houses and Society in the Ancient Greek World (Cambridge) 1999

Nicolet, C. *Space, Geography and Politics in the Early Empire* (Ann Arbor, Mich.) 1991

Nielsen, I. *Hellenistic Palaces: Tradition and Renewal* (Aarhus) 1994

O'Gorman, E. "No Place Like Home: Identity and Difference in the Germania of Tacitus" *Ramus* 23 1994 pp. 135–54

Oliver, P. *Dwellings: The House across the World* (Oxford) 1987

Overbeck, J. & Mau, A. *Pompeji in Seinen Gebäuden, Alterhümern and Kuntswerken* (Leipzig) 1884

Packer, J. "Middle and Lower Class Housing in Pompeii and Herculaneum: A Preliminary Study" in Andreae & Kyrieleis 1975 pp. 133–46

Painter, K. *Mildenhall Treasure: Roman Silver from East Anglia* (London) 1977

Pais, A. *Il Podium del Tempio di Divo Adriano* (Rome) 1979

Parker-Pearson, M. & Richards, C. eds. *Architecture and Order: Approaches to Social Space* (London) 1994

Patterson, J. "The City of Rome: From Republic to Empire" *JRS* 82 1992 pp. 186–215

Pedley, J. ed. *New Light on Ancient Carthage* (Ann Arbor, Mich.) 1980

Percival, J. *The Roman Villa: An Historical Introduction* (London) 1976

"Desperately Seeking Sidonius: The Realities of Life in Fifth Century Gaul" *Latomus* 56 1997 pp. 279–92

Perrin, Y. "La Domus Aurea et l'idéologie Néronienne" in Lévy 1987 pp. 359–91

Peters, W. *La Casa di Marcus Lucretius Fronto a Pompei e le sue pitture* (Amsterdam) 1993

Peters, W. & Meyboom, P. "The Roots of Provincial Roman Painting: Results of Current Research in Nero's Domus Aurea" in Liversidge, J. ed. *Roman Provincial Wall Painting of the Western Empire* BAR Int. Ser. 140 (Oxford) 1982 pp. 39–59

Pollini, J. "The Findspot of the Statue of Augustus from Prima Porta" *Bull.Comm.* 1987 pp. 103–8

Price, S. *Rituals and Power* (Cambridge) 1984

Purcell, N. "Town in Country and Country in Town" in MacDougall 1987 pp. 187–203

"The Roman Villa and the Landscape of Production" in Cornell & Lomas 1995 pp. 151–80

"Rome and the Management of Water, Environment, Culture and Power" in J. Shipley & J. Salmon eds. *Human Landscapes in Classical Antiquity Environment and Culture* (London) 1996 pp. 180–212

Raeder, J. *Die statuarische Austattung der Villa Hadriana bei Tivoli* (Frankfurt) 1983

Rapaport, A. "Systems of Activities and Systems of Settings" in Kent 1990 pp. 9–20

Raper, R. "Pompeii: Planning and Social Implications" in B. Burnham & J. Kingsbury eds. *Space, Hierarchy and Society: Interdisciplinary Studies in Social Area Analysis* BAR Int. Ser. 59 (Oxford) 1979 pp. 137–48

Rawson, E. *Cicero: A Portrait* (London) 1975 (new ed. 1994)

Reisch, E. *Die Marienkirche*. FiE IV/I (Vienna) 1932

Rich, J. & Wallace-Hadrill, A. eds. *City and Country in the Ancient World* (London) 1991

Richardson, L. *A New Topographical Dictionary of Ancient Rome* (Baltimore) 1992
Pompeii: An Architectural History (Baltimore) 1988

Riggsby, A. M. "Public and Private in Roman Culture: The Case of the Cubiculum" *JRA* 10 1997 pp. 36–56

Rivet, A. *The Roman Villa in Britain* (London) 1969
Gallia Narbonensis (London) 1988

Robinson, O. *Ancient Rome: City Planning and Administration* (London) 1992

Rogers, G. *The Sacred Identity of Ephesos* (London) 1991

Rolland, H. *Fouilles de Glanum* (Paris) 1946

Rostovtzeff, M. *Dura Europas and its Art* (Oxford) 1938

Rowland, I. D. & Howe, T. N. *Vitruvius: Ten Books on Architecture* (Cambridge) 1999

Royo, M. *Domus Imperatoriae. Topographie, Formation et Imaginaire des palais impériaux du Palatin* (Rome) 1999

Rykwert, J. *The Idea of a Town* (Cambridge, Mass.) 1988

Sablayrolles, R. Éspace urbain et propoganda politique: l'organization du centre de Rome par Auguste (Res Gestae 19 à 21)" *Pallas* 28 1981 pp. 59–77

Saflund, G. *The Polyphemus and Scylla Groups at Sperlonga* (Stockholm) 1972

Saller, R. "*Familia, Domus* and the Roman Conception of the Family" *Phoenix* 38 1984 pp. 336–55

Salza Prina Ricotti, E. "Criptoportici e gallerie sotteranee di Villa Adriana nella loro tipologia e nelle loro funzioni" in *Les cryptoportiques dans l'architecture romaine* Collection de l'Ecole Française de Rome 14 1973 pp. 219–59
"Villa Adriana nei suoi limiti e nella sua funzionalità" *Mem.Pont.Acc.Arch.* 14 1982 pp. 25–55

Sanguinetti, F. "Lavori recenti nella Domus Aurea" *Palladio* 7 1957 pp. 126–7

Sauron, G. "De Buthrote à Sperlonga: à propos d'une étude récente sur le thème de la grotte dans les décors romains" *RA* 1991 pp. 3–42

Sautel, J. *Vaison dans l'Antiquité* 3 vols. (Paris) 1929
Vaison dans l'Antiquité Suppl. 3 vols. (Paris) 1942

Schefold, K. "Zur Chronologie der Dekorationen im Haus der Vettier" *RM* 64 1957 pp. 149–53

Schmidt-Colinet, A. "Aspects of 'Romanization': The Tomb Architecture at Palmyra and its Decoration" in Alcock 1997 pp. 157–77

Scott, S. "The Power of Images in the Late Roman House" in Laurence & Wallace-Hadrill 1997 pp. 53–67
Art & Society in Fourth Century Britain: Villa Mosaics in Context (Oxford) 2000

Sear, F. *Roman Wall & Vault Mosaics* RM, Ergnzungsheft 23 (Heidelberg) 1977
Roman Architecture (London) 1982

Seiler, F. *Casa degli Amorini Dorati* Häuser der Pompeji Band 5 (Munich) 1992

Shatzman, I. *Senatorial Wealth and Roman Politics* (Brussels) 1975

Slater, N. *Reading Petronius* (Baltimore) 1990

Slater, W. ed. *Dining in a Classical Context* (Ann Arbor, Mich.) 1991

Smith, J. *Roman Villas: A Study in Social Structure* (London) 1997
"Villas as a Key to Social Structure" in Todd 1978 pp. 149–86

Smith, J. O. "The High Priests of the Temple of Artemis at Ephesus" in E. Lane ed. *Cybele, Attis and Related Cults: Essays in Memory of M. J. Vermaseren* (New York) 1996 pp. 323–35

Smith, R. *Hellenistic Sculpture* (London) 1991

Spinazzola, V. *Pompei alla luce degli scavi nuovi di Via dell'Abbondanza* (Rome) 1953

Steinby, E. M. *Lexicon Topigraphicum Urbis Romae* (Rome) 1993–

Stewart, A. "To Entertain an Emperor: Sperlonga, Laokoon and Tiberius at the Dinner Table" *JRS* 67 1977 pp. 76–90

Stewart, S. *On Longing* (Baltimore) 1984

Stillwell, R. "Houses of Antioch" *Dumbarton Oaks Papers* 15 1961 pp. 45–57

Strocka, V. *Die Wandmalerei der Hanghäuser in Ephesos.* FiE 8/1 (Vienna) 1977
    Casa del Labirintho Häuser in Pompeji Band 4 (Munich) 1991

Strocka, V. "Augusta als Pharao" in R. Stucky & I. Jucker eds. *Eikones: Studien zum Griechischen und Römanischen Bildnis* (Berlin) 1980 pp. 177–80

Stuart, M. "How Were Imperial Portraits Distributed Throughout the Roman Empire?" *AJA* 43 1939 pp. 601–17

Swain, S. *Hellenism and Empire* (Oxford) 1996

Sweet, C. "The Dedication of the Canopus at Hadrian's Villa" *AJA* 77 1973 p. 229

Tamm, B. *Auditorium and Palatium* (Stockholm) 1963

Tanner, T. *Adultery in the Novel. Contract and Transgression* (Baltimore) 1979

Tate, G. "The Syrian Countryside During the Roman Era" in Alcock 1997 pp. 55–71

Thébert, Y. "Private Life & Domestic Architecture in Roman Africa" in Veyne, P. ed. *A History of Private Life vol. 1: From Pagan Rome to Byzantium* (Cambridge, Mass.) 1987 pp. 313–410

Thornton, K. "Hadrian & his Reign" *ANRW* II.2 (Berlin) 1975 pp. 432–76

Thouvenot. R. *Volubilis* (Paris) 1949

Todd, M. ed. *Studies in the Romano-British Villa* (Leicester) 1978

Toynbee, J. *The Hadrianic Style: A Chapter in the History of Greek Art* (Cambridge) 1934
    Art in Britain under the Romans (Oxford) 1964

Toynbee, J. *Death and Burial in the Roman World* (London) 1971

Trümper, M. *Wohnen in Delos: eine baugeschichtliche Untersuchung zum Wandel der Wohnkulture in hellenistischer Zeit* (Rahden) 1998

Turner, B. *The Body and Society: Explorations in Social Therapy* (Oxford) 1984

Tybout, R. A. "Roman Wall-Painting and its Social Significance" *JRA* 14 2001 pp. 33–55

Van Bremen, R. *The Limits of Participation: Women & Civic Life in the Greek East in the Hellenistic and Roman Periods* (Amsterdam) 1996

Van Buren, A. "Pinacothecae with Especial Reference to Pompeii" *MAAR* 15 1938
    "Recent Finds at Hadrian's Villa" *AJA* 59 1955 pp. 215–17

Van Deman, E. "The House of Caligula" *AJA* 28 1924 pp. 368–98

Van Essen, C. "La topographie de la Domus Aurea Neronis" *Mededelingen der Koninklyke Nederlandse Akademie van Wetenschappen* 17 1954 pp. 291–308

Vasaly, A. *Representations: Images of the World in Ciceronian Oratory* (Berkeley, Calif.) 1993

Vermaseren, M. *Cybele and Attis; The Myth and the Cult* (London) 1977

Veyne, P. "Cave Canem" *MEFRA* 75 1963 pp. 59–66

Viarre, J. "Palatium palais" *Revue de Philologie* Ser. 3 35 1961 pp. 241–8

Von Blanckenhagen, P. & Alexander, C. *The Augustan Villa at Boscotrecase* (Mainz) 1990

de Vos, A. & M. de Vos *Pompei Ercolano Stabia* (Rome) 1982

de Vos, M. *L'egittomania in pitture e mosaici romano-campani della prima età imperiale* (Leiden) 1980

Walbank, F. "The Scipionic Legend" *PCPhS* 193 1967 pp. 54–69

Wallace-Hadrill, A. "Civilis Princeps: Between Citizen and King" *JRS* 72 1982 pp. 32–48
 ed. *Patronage in Ancient Society* (New York) 1989a
"Rome's Cultural Revolution" *JRS* 79 1989b pp. 157–64
"Pliny the Elder and Man's Unnatural History" *G&R* 37 1990 pp. 80–96
"Elites and Trade in the Roman Town" in Rich & Wallace-Hadrill 1991 pp. 241–72
Houses and Society in Pompeii and Herculaneum (Princeton, N.J.) 1994
"Engendering the Roman House" in D. Kleiner & S. Matheson eds. *I Claudia: Women in Ancient Rome* (New Haven, Conn.) 1996 pp. 104–5
"Rethinking the Roman Atrium House" in Laurence & Wallace-Hadrill 1997 pp. 219–40

Walsh, P. *The Roman Novel* (Cambridge) 1970

Ward-Perkins, J. "The Roman Villa at Lockleys, Welwyn" *AntJ* 18 1938 pp. 339–78

Ward-Perkins, J. "Nero's Golden House" *Antiquity* 30 1956 pp. 209–19

Warden, P. "The Domus Aurea Reconsidered" *JSAH* 40 1981 pp. 271–8

Webster, J. "A Negotiated Syncretism: Readings on the Development of Romano-Celtic Religion" in Mattingley 1997 pp. 165–84

Wegner, M. *Hadrian* Das römische Herrscherbild 2.3 (Berlin) 1956

Wheeler, R & Wheeler, T. *Verulamium: A Belgic and two Roman Cities* (Oxford) 1936

Whitehead, J. "The Cena Trimalchionis and Biographical Tradition in Roman Middle Class Art" in Holliday, P. ed. *Narrative and Event in Ancient Art* (Cambridge) 1993 pp. 299–325

Whitehorn, J. "The Ambitious Builder" *AUMLA* 31 1969 pp. 28–39

Wilkes, J. *Diocletian's Palace, Split: Residence of a Retired Roman Emperor* (Sheffield) 1986

Wilkinson, L. *The Georgics of Virgil* (Cambridge) 1969

Williams, G. *Banished Voices: Readings in Ovid's Exile Poetry* (Cambridge) 1994

Wilson, R. *Piazza Armerina* (London) 1983

Wiplinger, G. & Wlach, G. *Ephesus: 100 Years of Research* (Vienna) 1996

Wirth, T. "Zum Bildprogramm in der Casa dei Vettii" *RM* 90 1983 pp. 449–55

Wiseman, T. "Conspicui postes tectaque digna deo: The Public Image of Aristocratic and Imperial Houses in the Late Republic and Early Empire" in *L'Urbs: Espace urbain et histoire* Collection de l'Ecole française de Rome 98 1987 pp. 393–413

Wood, N. *Cicero's Social and Political Thought* (Berkeley, Calif.) 1988

Woodman, A. *Rhetoric in Classical Historiography: Four Studies* (London) 1988

Woolf, G. *Becoming Roman* (Cambridge) 1998
Cultural Changes in Central France under Roman Rule (Cambridge PhD Thesis) 1991
"Becoming Roman, Staying Greek" *PCPhS* 40 1994 pp. 116–43

Yates, F. *The Art of Memory* (London) 1966

Yacoub, M. *Le Musée du Bardo* (Tunis) 1996

Yavetz, Z. "The *Res Gestae* and Augustus's Public Image" in F. Millar & E. Segal eds. *Caesar Augustus: Seven Aspects* (Oxford) 1984 pp. 1–36

Zaccaria Ruggiu, A. *Spazio privato e spazio pubblico nella città Romana* (Rome) 1995

Zander, G. "La Domus Aurea: nuovi problemi archittectonici" *Boll.Cent.Stor.Arch.* 12 1958 pp. 47–64

Zanker, P. *The Power of Images in the Age of Augustus* (Ann Arbor, Mich.) 1988
The Mask of Socrates (Berkeley, Calif.) 1995
Pompeii: Public and Private Life (Mainz) 1998

Zevi, F. & Andreae, B. "Gli scavi sottomarini di Baia" *La Parola del Passato* 37 1982 pp. 114–56

Index

Printed in Great Britain
by Amazon.co.uk, Ltd.,
Marston Gate.